BELARUS

BELARUS

WHAT EVERYONE NEEDS TO KNOW®

DAVID R. MARPLES AND
VERONICA LAPUTSKA

OXFORD
UNIVERSITY PRESS

Oxford University Press is a department of the University of Oxford.
It furthers the University's objective of excellence in research, scholarship,
and education by publishing worldwide. Oxford is a registered trademark of
Oxford University Press in the UK and certain other countries.

"What Everyone Needs to Know®" is a registered trademark of Oxford University Press.

Published in the United States of America by Oxford University Press
198 Madison Avenue, New York, NY 10016, United States of America.

Library of Congress Cataloging-in-Publication Data

ISBN 978–0–19–777296–6 (pbk.)
ISBN 978–0–19–777295–9 (hbk.)

DOI: 10.1093/wentk/9780197772959.001.0001

Paperback printed by Marquis Book Printing, Canada
Hardback printed by Bridgeport National Bindery, Inc., United States of America

The manufacturer's authorized representative in the EU for product safety is
Oxford University Press España S.A. of Parque Empresarial San Fernando de Henares,
Avenida de Castilla, 2 – 28830 Madrid (www.oup.es/en or product.safety@oup.com).
OUP España S.A. also acts as importer into Spain of products made by the manufacturer.

CONTENTS

PREFACE BY VERONICA LAPUTSKA

When I was born in Minsk, the Soviet Union was already in decline. I have vivid memories of the rogue empire collapsing. First, glasses from street soda machines disappeared. In a post-COVID-19 world, it seems unbelievable that people used to drink from the same glass, dispensed from machines around our cities and towns. Every time a glass was washed in the machine through the touch of a special button, and then by pressing another, soda would pour into the glass. This was popular in summer. I remember this moment, understanding as a child that things were getting worse, enough that the adults were stealing.

Second, food cards appeared. Adults would spend hours in long queues to get anything they could. There was nothing, anywhere—empty shelves in smelly shops, this is what I remember. When the cards were abolished, I used to play with the remaining ones in our modest household with my dolls. Back then, I dreamed of becoming a salesperson when I grew up as I really wanted to press the buttons of the cashier machines. I was fascinated by that action and was sure those women were doing an important job (they were, and I learned later in life that they were very important and popular individuals). Third, I remember my grandparents coming from Kamchatka in the Russian Far East, where they were working then, and bringing red caviar in big jars and my parents stuffing me with it, as there was little food in Minsk. I was so puzzled why I had to eat it and was protesting and testing my parents' patience.

Then I remember the beginning of the 1990s and a lot of chaos with constant hyperinflation; Belarusian money became a toy for me and my friends once the new banknotes with more zeroes were introduced. I remember privatization and my father telling me why it was good. I remember the feeling of anticipation of good changes, a new era, the collapse of the Communist system, prospects of travel around the world and consuming the goods that had been inaccessible before and could only be seen in foreign films or journals. I think I ate my first banana back then. My father's friends would bring me Snickers and Kinder chocolate, and these were the most valued presents children could get. We cherished them so much. My adult family members would go to numerous anti-Communist and anti-Soviet demonstrations. I remember watching sessions of the Supreme Council of Belarus live on state TV with my parents, where post-Communists and democrats were fighting and arguing. It was unprecedented that regular people could see how new laws were adopted and an independent state was functioning in front of everyone's eyes. I was glued to the screen.

I passed a range of entry exams (it was the requirement for best grammar schools then) and was accepted to a Belarusian grammar school. All our classes were in Belarusian, and we started to learn English immediately. Russian would be taught as a foreign language starting from the second year. We were divided into two groups to ensure the quality of learning as the language was foreign, just like English.

I remember while watching US president Bill Clinton's visit to Minsk in January 1994 with my parents on TV in our first studio apartment how people were shaking Clinton's hand at Victory Square and how I was so jealous. I wanted to be physically there badly, after my parents had told me how important that event was for the young state. I remember July 1994 when together with my grandmother (who had been a teenage

Ostarbeiter or *Zwangsarbeiter* during the war in Germany and had to hide this fact from the authorities until the 1990s, as I learned later she would likely have been sent to a labor camp) we went to vote during the first presidential election in Belarus in a distant village 110 miles from Minsk. We bumped into an agriculturalist who asked my grandmother politely whom she was going to vote for. She replied: "For Pazniak, my sons told me to do so and I will!" He was surprised: "What?! You should vote for Lukashenka, he is 'our man'!"

Then everything started to change. Referendums of 1995 and 1996 changed the structure of the main branches of power in Belarus, and Russian became a state language and ultimately pushed out Belarusian. The main aim of foreign policy was declared to be integration with Russia. I remember how teachers at my Belarusian grammar school grew sadder day after day. They felt that the renaissance of the Belarusian language was over. Again. But they could still openly talk to us about that. Yet. I remember how the white-red-white flag from the Supreme Council building was taken down and torn into pieces and how I hated those men in photos, shown on TV cheerfully laughing and putting their signatures on the flag I loved so much. Many adults I knew would go to Minsk city center and organize strikes at their workplaces. I remember recognizing their figures and faces on Russian First Channel (ORT) and NTV (then independent channels) as the state Belarusian TV was already aligned with the Lukashenka government and didn't show any of that.

In 1999, the next presidential election was supposed to take place, but Lukashenka's referendum of 1996 prolonged his term until 2001. Simultaneously, together with the Russian president Boris Yeltsin, he announced the establishment of the Union State of Belarus and Russia. Tens of thousands of people protested, many fighting with the militia and overturning cars. People outside Belarus likely do not remember this and label Belarusians as "softies," but the Internet is full of footage from those times. Suddenly, Lukashenka's political opponents unexpectedly died or disappeared. Forever. Everyone was terrified they might disappear forever, too. A larger terror began. People's fear was growing.

I want to share a bit about my family history, though not because my family story is unique. Quite the opposite, the hardships we went through in the twentieth century were very typical for many people originating from Belarus. My mother's family was repressed in 1939 when after the "re-unification of Belarus," as it is called in Belarusian history, the Polish family of my great-grandfather lost many acres of forest near Hrodna and it was nationalized by the Soviet authorities. Luckily, none of my family members was sent to Siberia. We do not know for sure, but according to our family version of events, it is possible that they bribed the Soviet soldiers. Neither of my great-grandfathers from the maternal side of my family survived the war. No one from that part of the family ever dared to research any deeper what had happened, as almost all of the ancestors had received higher education and obtained decent jobs in Soviet Belarus. They did not speak about politics.

The father of my paternal grandmother was arrested in 1932 in his village in central Belarus and was sent to the north of Russia. Their family was quite "well-off" compared to its peers, as they had several cows, pigs, hens, and bees, as well as some gold which later saved some family members from the GULAG after the war, as the village was occupied by the Nazis which could be seen to mean they "collaborated." Being a "kulak" in Soviet terms, but just a hard-working man trying to feed his six children, my great-grandfather was not willing to enter a collective farm and openly criticized Stalin at one of the village meetings. He came back only when the Second World War broke out, was quickly conscripted, and never returned. Neither my great-grandmother, nor my grandmother, who was a teenage slave worker (the Nazi term was *Ostarbeiter*) in Germany together with her older sister, ever found out where he died. My great-grandfather was rehabilitated during Khrushchev's thaw. After my grandmother's death, approximately ten years ago, when Russia uploaded the war archives to the Internet, I learned that my great-grandfather had received two medals for his bravery and was killed near Warsaw. I also saw multiple letters of my great-grandmother searching for her husband. The Soviet bureaucracy was unable to reply to a woman bringing up six children on her own after the war, or they simply did not want to.

I went to my first demonstration, a march commemorating the Chernobyl catastrophe, with my female classmates in 2001. We never told our parents. I knew back then that I would do my best to keep telling the truth about Belarus and what was happening there. Even after I left the country to continue my studies in 2009, having been harassed by the Belarusian KGB shortly before because of my Polish origin, I promised to myself I would continue. Though a resident in Poland, I kept returning to Belarus for work and research projects until 2020, when my previous work engagements and writings would make me a target for an arrest. In July 2024, together with my colleagues, prominent experts, researchers, and journalists, I was sentenced to ten years of imprisonment by the Belarusian regime. In October 2024, Lukashenka's regime put all twenty of us on their list of extremists and terrorists.

Back in spring 2009, while working on my thesis at the Belarusian National Library in Minsk, I came across Prof. David R. Marples's book *Belarus: A Denationalized Nation* and I became paralyzed. Everything written there was so true but felt very bitter. I read most of the book that day and later connected with David via Facebook and felt so honored he had accepted me, just a regular girl from Belarus. After a brutal crackdown of protests in the aftermath of the December 19, 2010, elections, while I was doing my master's degree in Warsaw, I started chatting with David on Facebook about what could be done to bring more attention to Belarus. This is how our friendship and collaboration started.

Writing this book with my outstanding and now long-term research partner, mentor, and friend David was a huge blessing, but also my personal confession and a form of therapy. I could never have done it without his knowledge, devotion, support, and compassion. I will be forever grateful to David for this. We started to work on this project separately in 2017, then went together to Belarus in 2019, when we both could still go there and hardly expected such an outcome, to be honest. I intended to put here on paper everything I have ever learned from my incredible school history teachers and university professors in Minsk, Vilnius, and Warsaw, what I read and witnessed myself, and what my smart and wise friends told me about Belarus's history.

When doing the research, conducting the interviews, and writing, I cried many times as I was reliving the fates of people who had suffered tortures, injustice, and died in post-1994 Belarus, and especially while writing about the 2020 events. Digital revolution made all the brutal video, audio files, and photos so naturalistic and engraved them in my memory. Like many Belarusians, I still have nightmares about those days, even though I wasn't in Belarus physically at that time. But mostly I am so proud of all those who have been devoting their lives and careers to the people of Belarus, by paying such high costs. I want to dedicate this book to all those who fought and keep fighting for a free and democratic Belarus and opposing repressive regimes there, including my great-grandparents and grandparents who are no longer with us.

Veronica (Veranika) Laputska
Warsaw, Poland
May 2025

PREFACE BY DAVID R. MARPLES

For years after declaring independence in 1991, Belarus remained a little-known republic in the West, despite its important geostrategic position between Poland and Russia, and as a conduit for Russian energy supplies to central Europe. In the late Soviet period, it was best known as a victim of the 1986 nuclear accident at Chernobyl, Ukraine, which covered its territory in dangerous radionuclides of cesium, strontium, and iodine. It was also known for its role and occupation during the German-Soviet War of 1941–1945, which the Soviet leadership termed the "Great Patriotic War," marked by monuments and historic sites throughout the country.

In February 2022, Russian forces attacked Ukraine from Belarusian territory in a failed attempt to occupy Kyiv and replace the Ukrainian government. Belarus was and has remained Russia's main ally in its ruthless invasion of Ukraine without thus far committing its own forces to the war. Less than two years earlier, the Belarusian leadership faced unprecedented mass demonstrations that lasted for months after Lukashenka declared himself the victor in the 2020 presidential election, despite reports from a number of polling stations that he had been defeated by challenger Sviatlana Tsikhanouskaya, a thirty-eight-year old housewife and former English teacher.

Earlier in the campaign, Tsikhanouskaya's husband Siarhei and another very popular candidate, Viktar Babaryka, were arrested and barred from taking part. A third candidate, Valery Tsapkala, a former ambassador to the United States and Mexico, and founder of the Hi-Tech Park, fled abroad to avoid arrest. Lukashenka managed to stay in power through mass repressions, including arrests, imprisonment, and torture of his opponents and those supporting change.

In this book, we seek to explain the background to these tumultuous events, looking at how Belarus, a republic of 10.19 million people (1991), entered the independence period after the collapse of the Soviet Union and elected Lukashenka, its first and only president, in 1994. Henceforth, it slid perilously into a dictatorship, which used state-controlled referendums to end the constitutional power sharing between president, parliament, and the Constitutional Court.

In turn, the regime curbed the independent media and arrested and harassed its opponents. It followed a pro-Russian path, forming an identity based largely on its Soviet legacy of victory in the Second World War. Elections became violent affairs, in which those opposing Lukashenka were arrested and served lengthy prison terms, and which Lukashenka won with the backing of Russia.

At the time of writing, not long after the largely unrecognized 2025 presidential elections in Belarus, there are no extant opposition political parties in Belarus, as the authorities have dissolved them all. No opposition candidates could take part and the elections have become a ritual. The slightest manifestation of protest is met with ruthless repression, arrests, and lengthy prison sentences. My coauthor of this book, Veronica (Veranika) Laputska, is herself sentenced to ten years of imprisonment if she returns to her homeland, and she has been branded a "terrorist" for opposing the Lukashenka regime.

Yet there were periods when EU leaders held out some hope that Belarus might follow a different path, even under Lukashenka. In 2009, Belarus joined the Eastern Partnership Project. Trade with the European Union rose exponentially. Several political prisoners were released, and the 2010 presidential elections allowed more freedom for opposition candidates to launch their programs. But protests after the announcement of election results once again ended in violence, as security forces attacked and bludgeoned a large crowd in Independence Square, with seven of nine candidates imprisoned at the end of the voting day. Still, some hoped for a dialogue with the regime.

Though a Russia-Belarus Union was initiated in April 1996, and formalized in 1999, little progress was made before Vladimir Putin became president of Russia in 2000. After the March 2014 Russian annexation of Crimea and attempts to take over the Donbas, the Union began to take on a more definite form. But there were acute tensions between the two leaders over energy issues and trade, as well as on a personal level. In 2014 and 2015, Belarus served as a mediator when an armistice was declared between Russian and Ukrainian forces in the Donbas in what were termed the "Minsk Accords." That they took place in Minsk was a propaganda triumph for Belarusian president Aliaksandr Lukashenka (Alexander Lukashenko from Russian) though he was only a bystander in decision-making.

Only after the 2020 presidential elections did Lukashenka finally bow to Moscow and abandon what had been hitherto a multi-vector foreign policy. The question today is whether Belarus can survive as an independent state, or be swallowed up by Russia, or reduced to a puppet regime. Can the sort of democratic wave we witnessed in 2020 lead to a different path, as part of the European community? Or will the repressive waves continue? How long must Belarusians continue to live under harsh authoritarian rule and violations of human rights that see people arrested merely for liking a Facebook post or logging on to foreign news agencies?

In this book, we explain Belarus to outsiders, tracing its development, history, and formation of modern identity. We look at its place in contemporary Europe and its relations with Russia, Ukraine, China, and other states; and we argue that the image of Belarus as a Soviet theme park or offshoot of Putin's Russian World is far-fetched and misguided.

As authors, we come from very different worlds, but each of us found our path to the study of Belarus. Veronica's Preface provides an illuminating and poignant account of her own background. I began my academic career with the study of Soviet Ukraine, the focus of my PhD, and published my first two books on the Chernobyl disaster in that republic, in 1986 and 1988. In the spring of 1991, I attended a conference on Chernobyl in Kyiv and then flew to Washington, DC, the next day to attend another gathering. At the reception to that function in a large facility, I encountered a group of Belarusians, including the champion figure skater Olga Korbut. I struck up a conversation with one of the attendees, Iouri Pankratz, who worked for the independent charitable association Children of Chernobyl. He asked why my studies only looked at Ukraine and not Belarus. He also invited me to attend a conference to be held the following spring in Minsk.

This invitation began my association with Belarus. It was immediately apparent to me that Minsk presented quite a different world to Kyiv in 1992. The conference was held in the Yubileinaya Hotel and foreigners were still a rarity—in Ukraine there were thousands of visitors from North America and western Europe by the late 1980s. I was given the warmest of welcomes and housed with a local family of two language teachers employed at what is today the Minsk Linguistic University and their two young sons. The itinerary was preplanned so that my days were mapped out ahead of time.

Belarus had no president in 1992. The Belarusian Popular Front was campaigning to gather signatures to force a new election to the Supreme Soviet, whose members had been elected in 1990, during the Soviet period. The legislature was, however, dominated by Communists, though its chair, Stanislau Shushkevich, whom we foreign delegates met during the conference period, was a scientist and not from the *nomenklatura* (the ruling elite). A main memory from that meeting was of

Ivonka Survilla, future president-in-exile of the Belarusian National Republic, unimpressed with Shushkevich's opening comments, which were in Russian, bellowing, "Have you forgotten your native language, Dr. Shushkevich?" He quickly switched to Belarusian.

I returned later the same year, and twice more in 1993. It was unexplored ground, it seemed, as far as Western scholars were concerned. And compared to Ukraine, it seemed singularly self-effacing, lacking the sort of nationalistic expression in cities like Lviv and Kyiv. There followed a deep exploration of the country, the historic sites, museums, art galleries, castles, and lakes, and also its people, both in the cities and rural communities. The two people with whom I talked most and who provided most insights into political and cultural life in Belarus have sadly both passed away: Hienadz Hrushavy (Gennady Grushevoy) (1950–2014), one of the founders of the Belarusian Popular Front, a professor of philosophy, and leader of the Charitable Fund called For the Children of Chernobyl; and Lyuba Pervushina (1960–2021), a professor at the Minsk Linguistic University who studied American literature and was an accomplished violinist, who died of COVID-19 after being forced to continue teaching, unvaccinated, at the height of the pandemic in September 2021. After 1992, Belarus became a priority for me, and I expanded my list of contacts and embarked on several research projects.

But I also immersed myself in local life: the markets, the banya, the cafés and restaurants, discussions late into the night about politics with some Minsk residents, soccer on Sundays with members of the opposition in Čaliuskincaŭ Park of Culture and Recreation; I visited collective farms, traveled widely, by train and bus, ate lunch in villages in the zone contaminated by the Chernobyl disaster, had altercations at the border on several occasions, all of which ended amicably, visited historic sites and monuments, gathered in Minsk for New Year's celebrations, stayed in hotels, private apartments, with families; in short, I felt almost part of local society and saw Minsk in particular as a second home.

In 2012, my visits were suddenly curtailed by a failure to acquire a visa, something I had not anticipated. I was writing about the republic frequently for an American weekly online journal, but that had not seemed to affect my earlier visits. There were reports that the authorities had created a "blacklist" of foreign scholars who were no longer welcome. My ban was voided in 2017, when it was possible to enter the country without a visa and stay for five days. The following year, the time was extended to thirty days, and once again I could carry out a regular research trip. Sadly, my last visit was in 2019, as described by Veronica, when we spent time at various Stalinist mass execution sites and at the Trascianiec death camp to the east of the city. The following year, the COVID-19 pandemic precluded a visit, and the repercussions of the 2020 protests and mass arrests exacerbated the problem. But I anticipate a return before long.

And despite the current dilemmas, there are reasons to believe that the people have not lost their spirits and desire for change, and that the hopes engendered by the 2020–2021 protests may eventually be fulfilled.

David R. Marples
Edmonton, Alberta, Canada
May 2025

ACKNOWLEDGMENTS

This book is based on knowledge of and experience in Belarus culled over three decades of study, research, and participation in urban life, mainly in Minsk but with excursions by bus, train, and car, to most areas of the country.

My indebtedness to people has accumulated over time, but I would like to express my thanks to those who have helped me along the way. Some of the people, sadly, are no longer living, some moved abroad after the 2020 uprising or earlier, and I would like to mention particularly Henadz Hrushavy and Uladzimir Padhol, who was originally my research assistant but is today a professor at the University of Rennes in France.

More recently, I have benefited from conversations with several emerging Belarusian scholars and friends who provided unique insights into the social and political conditions in the country, including Tatsiana Kulakevich, Katsiaryna Lozka, Hanna Asipovich, Alesya Rudnik, Olga Belakova, Yulia Mankevich, Ales Lahviniec, and others too numerous to mention.

Special thanks to my original host in Minsk, the late Lyuba Pervushina, a professor at Minsk State Linguistic University, and to Yulia Shymko, my assistant in the late 1990s, and now a Professor at the Audencia Business School in Nantes, France.

I would also like to thank my students at the University of Alberta who have contributed to this project, particularly my recently graduated MA student Rachel Schwartz, 2019 PhD student Ernest Gyidel, and two former PhD students whose theses were very helpful in writing my sections on Belarus between 1914 and the early 1930s—both resulted in positively reviewed books—Per Anders Rudling and Lizaveta Kasmach. I also benefited from the research of other scholars, too many to be named here, but I will single out University of London's Andrew Wilson and University of Exeter's Nelly Bekus. Both always have something original and profound to say.

On behalf of Veronica and myself, I express appreciation to our editor Hannah Doyle, who has guided this project from the outset with patience, thoughtful advice, and wisdom; and to Zara Cannon-Mohammed for her help with editing and design. We also are so grateful to Viyaleta Sauchyts for her brilliant photography and her generosity in allowing us to use one of her 2020 photographs for the cover design.

Most of all, I would like to thank my family, two sons and two daughters, and especially my wife Aya Fujiwara, herself a scholar and researcher at the University of Alberta.

D.R.M.

As this book accumulated my many experiences and encounters, endless conversations and very passionate discussions at time, I would like to thank a number of people whom I've met on my personal and academic journey, who contributed to my knowledge and my opinions, and also supported me all the way through.

First, I would like to thank my Belarusian friends, mentors, and individuals who awakened so many positive qualities in me and my dedication to the study of Belarus and understanding why it is crucially important to do so: Daša Slabčanka, Veranika Mazurkevich, Aleś Łahviniec, Franak Viačorka, Maryna Kavaleuskaya, Tatsiana Zarembiuk, Aleś Zarembiuk, Alex A., Siarhei K., Laksiej Lavončyk, Viktoria Khakimava,

Yuliya Labanava, Ivonka Survilla, Prof. Zina Gimpelevich, Alena Kudzko, Sveti Hai, Dr. Larissa Doroshenko, Aleś Alachnovich, Hanna Liubakova, Dr. Tatsiana Chulitskaya, Vlad Kobets, Alina Koushyk, Pavel Belavus (imprisoned in Belarus), Hanna Sous, Dzmitry Hurnevich, Dr. Anton Saifullayeu, Prof. Roza Turarbekova, Prof. Pavel Tereshkovich, Andrei Kutsila, Zmitser Papko (Vinsent), Felix Lipski, Volha Dashuk, Victor Asliuk, Lena K.S., Alex Shlyk, Yury Melnichek, and Veranika Lindarenka my many wonderful friends whom I cannot name fearing their personal safety. For the same reason I also cannot mention the names of many brilliant university professors and teachers who still live in Belarus and have taught me so much.

I want to express my deepest gratitude to my Polish friends, colleagues, and mentors, who have taught me so much and accepted me so cordially in my new home: my alma mater, the Center for East European Studies of the University of Warsaw and Director Jan Malicki and the Center's professors, including Prof. Kazimierz Wóycicki and the late Prof. Jerzy Targalski, as well as Prof. Urszula Jarecka, Prof. Annamaria Orla-Bukowska, Dr. Łukasz Adamski, Dr. Ernest Wyciszkiewicz, Prof. Przemysław Żurawski vel Grajewski, Paulina Siegień, Joanna Spyra, Michał Węglarz, Andreas Martin Speiser, Agnieszka Ostrowska, Tomasz Bładyniec, Jakub Górnicki, Wojtek Przybylski, and Jarek Domański.

I am eternally grateful to my dear Ukrainian friends and colleagues who keep inspiring me with their bravery and internal light and who have always been supportive of democratic Belarus: Prof. Anatolii Kruhlashov, Myroslava Gongadze, Dr. Olena Babakova, Daryna Onyshko, Yulia Reshitko, Prof. Yeuhen Fedchenko, Dr. Olga Yurkova, Liubov Tsybulska, Marta Sakhnevych, and late Bohdan Solchanyk (killed on February 20, 2014, in Kyiv, among the Heavenly Hundred).

I cannot thank enough my friends and mentors who made my stay at the United States Holocaust Memorial Museum, at the Tel-Aviv University, at the YIVO in New York, and at the Lviv Center for Urban Studies, where I was researching on the Holocaust in Belarus and learning Yiddish, so pleasant, thought-provoking, and enlightening: Emma Lacey-Bordeaux, Stefan Turkheimer, Dr. Vadim Altskan, Liudmila Gordon, Lea Kalisch, Rabbi Tobias Divack Moss, Valentina Fedchenko, Yuliya Oreshina, Daria Starikashkina, Prof. Jeffrey Kopstein, Prof. Justin Cammy, Prof. Rebecca Margolis, Anne and Jonathan Dubitzky, Dr. Peter Mentzel, Dr. Elisabeth Anthony, Prof. David Frey, Peter Pomerantsev, and Ani Chkhikvadze.

Last but not the least, I want to thank wholeheartedly my dear friends and colleagues from various countries: Monika Bičkauskaitė-Aleliūnė, Dr. Julijana Andriejauskienė, and Dr. Justina Smalkyte from Lithuania; Victoria Donu, Stela Roman, and Artur Gurau from Moldova; Lucie Creighton, Pavel Havliček, Jakub Lewandowski, and Michal Madl from Czechia; Rast'o Kužel, Ivan Godarsky, Tomas Bella, *Zomri* group, and Peter Jančarik from Slovakia; Dr. Jörg Forbrig from Germany; and Dr. Edit Zgut-Przybylska from Hungary. No number of pages are enough to mention the many other amazing people I had the honor to meet and be inspired by.

And, of course, I cannot express enough gratitude to my dear parents and family. I love you forever.

V.L.

1

WHY BELARUS?

For years after declaring independence in 1991, Belarus remained a little-known republic in the West, despite its important geostrategic position between Poland and Russia, and as a conduit for Russian energy supplies to central Europe. In the late Soviet period, it was best known as a victim of the 1986 nuclear accident at Chernobyl, Ukraine, which covered its territory in dangerous radionuclides of cesium, strontium, and iodine.

In February 2022, Russian forces attacked Ukraine from Belarusian territory in a failed attempt to occupy Kyiv and replace the Ukrainian government. Belarus was and has remained Russia's main ally in its ruthless invasion of Ukraine without thus far committing its own forces to the war. Less than two years earlier, the Belarusian leadership had faced unprecedented mass demonstrations that lasted for months after Lukashenka declared himself the victor in the 2020 presidential election, despite reports from a number of polling stations that he had been defeated by challenger Sviatlana Tsikhanouskaya, a thirty-eight-year-old housewife and former English teacher.

Earlier in the campaign, Tsikhanouskaya's husband, the well-known vlogger Siarhei Tsikhanouski, and another very popular candidate, former chair of the BelarusGazpromBank Viktar Babaryka, were arrested and barred from taking part as presidential candidates. A third candidate, Valery Tsapkala, a former ambassador to the United States and Mexico and the founder of the Belarusian Park of High Technologies (Hi-Tech Park), fled to Russia to avoid arrest. Two—Babaryka and Tsapkala—were important establishment figures, a clear sign of disaffection for the president in high circles. The third, Tsikhanouski, was a populist, who traveled around the country gathering interviews for his YouTube channel, which had about 2 million followers. He represented the grassroots of society rather than its leadership. Lukashenka, backed by his security forces, managed to stay in power through mass repressions, including arrests, imprisonment, and torture of his opponents and those supporting change.

In this book, we seek to explain the background of these tumultuous events, looking at how Belarus, a republic of 10.19 million people in 1991, entered the independence period after the collapse of the Soviet Union and elected Lukashenka, its first and only president, in 1994. Henceforth, it slid gradually into a dictatorship, which used state-controlled referendums to end the constitutional power sharing between president, parliament, and the Constitutional Court. In turn, the regime curbed the independent media and arrested and harassed its opponents. It followed a pro-Russian path for the most part, forming an identity based largely on its Soviet legacy of victory in the Second World War. Elections became violent affairs, in which those opposing Lukashenka faced harassment, were arrested and served lengthy prison terms, and which Lukashenka won with the backing of Russia.

The newly elected president relied on referendums held in 1995 and 1996 to strengthen his power and change the direction of the country. Through them, he reduced the parliament from its original 260 seats to 110 and filled it with his own supporters. He changed the national flag and symbols back to those of the Soviet era, lacking only the hammer and sickle. He moved the country's Independence Day from July 26, marking the declaration of state sovereignty of 1990, to July 3, to commemorate the liberation of Minsk from the Nazis in 1944.

He asserted presidential power over both the Constitutional Court and the newly founded upper chamber of parliament called the Council of the Republic. And through a third referendum in 2004, he removed the limitations on the number of times one could run for president.

Shortly after the 1994 election, Lukashenka removed editors of major newspapers that criticized his policies, while keeping around him a close circle of followers who were prepared to endorse all his ideas. The move away from democracy coincided with a refusal to embark on the sort of shock therapy that had transformed the economies of neighbors Poland and Russia. The government subsidized state companies and limited the sale of land. Indeed, the latter policy was one of the referendum questions in 1996, with the president advocating a no vote.

Yet there were periods when EU leaders held out some hope that Belarus might follow a different path, even under Lukashenka. In 2009, Belarus joined the Eastern Partnership Project, an initiative of Poland and Sweden, and involving those countries located between Russia and the EU: Armenia, Azerbaijan, Georgia, Moldova, Ukraine, and Belarus. Trade with the European Union rose exponentially. A few political prisoners were released, and the 2010 presidential elections allowed more freedom for opposition candidates to launch their programs. But protests after the announcement of election results once again ended in violence, as security forces attacked and bludgeoned a large crowd in Independence Square, with seven of nine candidates imprisoned at the end of the voting day, two of whom were badly beaten, and over 700 people arrested. Still, some hoped for a dialogue with the regime.

Though a Russia-Belarus Union was initiated in April 1996, and formalized in 1999, little progress was made toward making it a reality before Vladimir Putin became president of Russia in 2000, and even then, it took a few years before the Union was revived and developed. But after the Russian annexation of Crimea in March 2014 and attempts to take over the Donbas, the Union began to take on a more definite form. There were acute tensions between the two leaders over energy issues and trade, as well as on a personal level between Lukashenka and Putin, but the relationship survived out of necessity. In 2014 and 2015, Belarus served as a mediator when an armistice was declared between Russian and Ukrainian forces in the Donbas in what were termed the "Minsk Accords." Its host was Lukashenka, anxious to play a larger role on the world stage, although he would play little part in the discussions that followed.

Only after the 2020 presidential elections did Lukashenka finally bow to Moscow and abandon what had been hitherto a multi-vectored foreign policy divided between Russia and the European Union. The EU and Western states imposed sanctions on both countries, leaving the Belarusian leadership with few options. The question today is whether Belarus can survive as an independent state or be swallowed up by Russia and reduced to a puppet regime. Can the sort of democratic wave witnessed in 2020 lead to a different path, as part of the European community? Or will the repressive pattern continue? How long must Belarusians continue to live under harsh authoritarian rule and violations of human rights that see people arrested and given lengthy prison sentences merely for liking a Facebook page or logging on to foreign news agencies?

In this book, we explain Belarus to outsiders, tracing its development, history, and formation of modern identity. We look at its place in contemporary Europe and its relations with Russia, Ukraine, China, and other states; and we argue that while the image of Belarus as a Soviet theme park or offshoot of Putin's Russian World are far-fetched and misguided, it has constantly been restricted in its development, partly through its geographical location and dependence on Moscow, but also because it has become victim to the self-aggrandizement of Lukashenka's dictatorship. We argue, in other words, that today's Belarus is not a reflection of popular sentiment or mindset, but something that has been created through certain factors: the control over institutions and media by a single figure, manipulation and distortions of the past to justify contemporary circumstances, and the use of terror and violence to maintain control.

Why were the presidential elections of 2020 so different from previous ones?

After 1994, when Lukashenka won an election that was in line with international standards according to the most international observers, elections in Belarus followed a pattern that became increasingly predictable. The initial campaign would see candidates come forward and organize a campaign to gather 100,000 signatures. Lukashenka usually assured himself of the largest number by having signature forms at factories, for workers to sign as they left work. In some cases, the signatures were tied to the distribution of wages. Under the close supervision of the chair of the Election Commission, the close Lukashenka ally Lidziya Yarmoshyna, the signatures were closely inspected for their legality. Many candidates found their campaigns invalidated at an early stage and were disallowed from further participation in the election. In turn, the Election Committees were staffed overwhelmingly with supporters of the president, and thus very few seats were allocated to those who might support the opposition.

A second feature of past elections was the lack of influence of Belarusian political parties. The opposition parties tried to unify their effort in 2006 and selected a single candidate in Aliaksandr Milinkevich, a university professor from Hrodna. The choice was quite different from 2001, a delayed election, when the rival candidate to Lukashenka was the leader of the unofficial trade union and thus could expect support from workers. Milinkevich's campaign was undermined once the former Rector of Minsk State University, Aliaksandr Kazulin, entered the contest, and thus repeated the situation of 1994, when there were two democratic candidates running against Lukashenka and Vyachaslau Kebich.

Third, and perhaps critically, the results of elections were always decided in advance, with a healthy but highly unlikely margin of victory for the president. Opinion polls conducted by independent agencies ranked Lukashenka as the likely winner in the post-1994 elections, but always within the range of 30–50% (the lowest such ranking was 27%), with much smaller totals for his opponents (the highest ranking being around 10%, with the exception of 2001). The reason is that Belarusians, while they might be dissatisfied with certain aspects of life, credited the president for the relatively high living standards they were experiencing vis-à-vis their neighbors to the south and east, as well as maintaining a stable and peaceful society free from the wars in which Russia seemed to be constantly involved—Chechnya in 1994–1997 and 2000–2001, Georgia in 2008, and Ukraine after February 2014.

Fourth, the regime often resorted to violent tactics against public demonstrations, particularly those questioning the official results of the election. In 2006 and 2010, post-election rallies ended in violence in central Minsk. Riot police brutally dispersed a tent city in Kastryčnickaja Square in 2006 that had been in place for several days and acted even more ruthlessly in Independence Square in 2010. Such actions created an atmosphere of fear, intended to dissuade future such actions and confirming that the regime in Belarus was not about to be replaced. These events, particularly in 2010, left international observers from EU countries highly disillusioned with the prospects for any democratic changes in Belarus.

In 2020, however, circumstances had changed. First, the elections coincided with a worldwide pandemic, and just as Belarusians had begun to feel its effects. The government had struggled economically for several years, engaged in disputes over energy prices with Russia, but more important, it was still attempting to recover fully from the world recession of 2008–2009. The president's dismissal of COVID-19 as a hoax left many residents feeling abandoned. Some resorted to self-help operations, often at a municipal level. There was a general awareness that the Lukashenka regime was not about to help, and the numbers of sick and dying were rising rapidly.

What Lukashenka had termed his "social contract" with the population had seemingly been abandoned. Many Belarusians organized voluntary assistance for each other, and for doctors and hospitals. Many more organized homeschooling and working from home, on their own initiative without waiting for the introduction of such measures from the government. At this moment, many of Belarus's inhabitants, of all social backgrounds and age groups, realized that the state was largely failing to carry out its most important function—health security. And, most important, they understood they were capable of taking care of themselves, without the help of the government, by relying on grassroots initiatives and themselves.

Second, there were also new candidates who attracted national attention, who did not emerge from the old opposition and the various political parties. On the contrary, two were from the elite: Viktar Babaryka, former chair of the Belgazprombank, and Valery Tsapkala, a founder of the Hi-Tech Park and former Plenipotentiary Ambassador of Belarus to the United States and Mexico. Both had well-documented links to Russia, raising in the minds of the authorities a fear that they had Russian backing. Lukashenka's suspicion was obvious during the campaign when he ordered the arrest of thirty-two members of the Russian Wagner Division who were evidently on their way to Africa.

Third, a whole new generation of educated, financially independent, well-traveled, and emancipated people was now living in Belarus. Thanks to the Hi-Tech Park (as the Belarusian Park of High Technologies was called by Belarusians) and many other start-ups that emerged in Belarus, the IT sector was booming. Tens of thousands of people knew from their real experience about democracy and economic freedom because of their work and travel and thanks to widespread

Internet penetration. They did not trust any state propaganda and were striving to attain European values and standards of living.

Lastly, 2020 saw the first election in which social media played an important, and even critical role in the emerging campaign of the rivals. By contrast, the regime approached the election largely in the same way as on previous occasions, but perhaps even more nonchalantly, buoyed by the 2015 campaign and the following parliamentary elections that saw the removal of all potential opposition from the parliament.

Who were the initial candidates and what happened to them?

Many of the initially running candidates were members of the political forces, well known to Belarusians for their oppositional stance against the incumbent or new leaders of such parties and associations. Thus, Yury Hubarevich was the leader of the Movement for Freedom, led by oppositional candidate Aliaksandr Milinkevich. Hanna Kanapatskaya was a member of the United Civic Party (UCP) and one of the only two oppositional candidates elected to the House of Representatives of the Belarusian Parliament in 2016, and a much more vocal one than her colleague Alena Anisim, head of the Belarusian Language Society and also a potential presidential candidate, who ultimately decided against running. Mikalai Kazlou was at the time head of the United Civil Party, which had been a significant opposition political party with several prominent members fighting against Lukashenka for decades, like UCP's former chairman Anatol Liabedzka.

Volha Kavalkova was one of the informal leaders of the unregistered Belarusian Christian Democratic Party. Siarhei Cherachan was chairman of the Belarusian Social-Democratic Hramada party, headed previously by the first leader of independent Belarus, Stanislau Shushkevich; he was also head of the Supreme Council, the predecessor of the Belarusian two-chamber Parliament, and an enemy of Lukashenka since the early 1990s. Aliaksandr Tabolich was a rock musician in a band that opposed the government, as well as a tattoo master. Uladzimir Niapomniashchykh was a civil activist from Homiel, who was also critical of the government and leaning toward opposition political forces. Andrei Dzmitryieu was one of the leaders of Tell the Truth association, whose other leader Tatsiana Karatkevich ran in the presidential election of 2015, one of the most peaceful ones since 1994 but largely ineffectual in terms of the opposition's impact.

Natallia Kisel and farmer Yury Hantsevich were not known to the wider public and had no previous political or activist backgrounds. Aleh Haidukevich was the leader of the pro-government Liberal Democratic Party and son of the party's previous leader, Siarhei Haidukevich, who had run in several previous elections as an alternative candidate to Lukashenka but was known for being pro-government.

The most prominent candidates who had no experience in previous political campaigns, and who attracted unprecedented attention, were Siarhei Tsikhanouski, Valery Tsapkala, and Viktar Babaryka. Siarhei Tsikhanouski, a founder of the YouTube channel "A Country for Living," ironically meaning Belarus, had managed to travel to many small Belarusian towns and cities to speak about local corruption, unemployment, and the overall ineffectiveness of the Belarusian state system. People knew him, and his channel became very popular. Previously Siarhei had spent several years in Moscow, where he worked in the video-making industry. His opponents accused him of ties with Russia, commented on his strange past, and discovered that on his social media posts from 2014 and 2015, Siarhei had claimed that Crimea belonged to Russia—a position not even accepted by the Belarusian authorities at that time. Nevertheless, thousands of people were keen to add their signatures for Siarhei's candidacy until he was arrested on May 6, 2020, for allegedly protesting the Union with Russia. At that moment, Tsikhanouski was sentenced to fifteen days of arrest, which thus caused him to miss the day of the registration of his initiative group by one day. His wife, Sviatlana (discussed in detail below), registered her candidacy as a replacement for him, which changed the modern history of Belarus.

Valery Tsapkala, was a former diplomat, part of Lukashenka's nomenklatura and original 1994 campaign team, and a founder of the Belarusian Park of High Technologies. He managed to attract many potential voters due to his impressive biography and recent successes of the Hi-Tech Park and the rapid growth of the IT sector in Belarus, although he had stepped down as director several years earlier in 2017. Tsapkala was also targeted by some oppositionists for being a former ally of Lukashenka. However, he built his pre-election slogans on his alleged disagreement with Lukashenka, who had dismissed him from the Hi-Tech Park directorship. His wife, Veranika, was a leading manager of Microsoft in Belarus and was often seen in public with Valery. They appeared to be a successful power couple, well-educated, had experienced living abroad, spoke foreign languages, and were raising twin boys together.

Viktar Babaryka was well known as the head of a successful institution, Belgazprombank, which was a branch of one of the largest banks in Russia—Gazprombank—affiliated with Gazprom, the monopolist gas industry in Russia. In addition, however, Babaryka was known to many citizens of Belarus and the city of Minsk in particular because of his charitable cultural activities. He founded OK16 venue, which hosted many important cultural events, including a large annual Teatro festival and regular concerts, exhibitions, and performances. He had initiated "ART-Belarus," with many paintings of artists born in Belarus that had been returned to the country, including the famous *Eva* by Chaim Soutine, an expressionist painter of Jewish origin born in Smilavičy, Belarus, in 1893, who had emigrated to Paris, France, at the age of twenty. Babaryka's wife had died in an accident in August 2017, and he had not remarried. His two children were young and successful, which contributed to his image of a good person and effective manager. Babaryka's son Eduard was running a successful crowdfunding platform Ulej at the time of the 2020 election.

On May 20, 2020, the Central Election Commission of Belarus registered candidates of fifteen initiative groups who announced their intention to run in the presidential election. They represented the following candidates: Aleh Haidukevich, Yury Hantsevich, Yury Hubarevich, Natallia Kisel, Aliaksandr Tabolich, Sviatlana Tsikhanouskaya (running instead of her husband Siarhei who became the head of her election headquarters once he was released from his first arrest), Valery Tsapkala, Viktar Babaryka, Uladzimir Niapomniashchykh, Hanna Kanapatskaya, Volha Kavalkova, Mikalai Kazlou, Aliaksandr Lukashenka, Andrei Dzmitryieu, and Siarhei Cherachan.

At this stage all those proposing to run in the presidential election (not candidates for the election yet; this is a peculiarity of the Belarusian election legislation) must collect 100,000 signatures from their potential supporters. Potential candidates started to travel around the country collecting signatures. Despite the pandemic, Belarusians became extremely engaged, and lines to put a signature under candidates, especially Babaryka, Tsikhanouski, and Tsapkala, were very long. This fact shocked the Belarusian authorities, who had not expected this much interest, and made them realize that the population had become bold enough to show their political preferences and interest in new candidates.

In June 2020, Lukashenka admitted that he had ordered the arrest of Siarhei Tsikhanouski, which ultimately led to the lengthy 19.5-year prison term he received on February 23, 2023. Tsikhanouski was detained in Hrodna on May 29, 2020, after a provocation when a woman approached him and tried to get closer, at which point two policemen appeared out of nowhere and a minute later one of them was lying on the ground claiming that Tsikhanouski had pushed him.

Another prospective candidate, Viktar Babaryka, whose campaign had gathered by far the most signatures, was arrested together with his son Eduard on June 18, 2020, following criminal charges to Viktar and Eduard for alleged economic crimes. Not only was equipment from Babaryka's office removed, but also paintings of world-famous artists from Belarus he had managed to collect for their ART-Belarus project. *Eva* by Soutine was among them and became the symbol of resistance and women's post-election protests. Viktar was later sentenced to fourteen years of imprisonment under charges of money laundering and receipt of a bribe. Eduard Babaryka was imprisoned for eight years on similar charges.

The third ambitious opponent of Lukashenka, Valery Tsapkala, fled to Russia with his children in July 2020 fearing repression, and leaving behind his wife Veranika, who would later play an important role in 2020 events inside the country. Subsequently, Valery and Veranika and their twin boys were based in Latvia until 2021, when they moved to Greece. At the time of writing they were living in Albania and developing a new business there.

Following the arrests of Babaryka and Tsikhanouski as well as Tsapkala's departure from the country, many independent candidates withdrew from the campaign or claimed they hadn't collected enough signatures. Others were refused the right to be registered. On July 14, 2020, Sviatlana Tsikhanouskaya was registered as a candidate for presidency. Her four opponents were Hanna Kanapatskaya, Andrei Dzmitryieu, Siarhei Cherachan, and Aliaksandr Lukashenka.

What were the main features of Tsikhanouskaya's campaign?

On July 19, 2020, three women representing Tsikhanouski—his wife and presidential candidate Sviatlana, the wife of Valery Tsapkala Veranika, and Maryia Kalesnikava, who headed Babaryka's campaign—decided to unite the efforts and human resources of three election headquarters to continue the election campaign together. The "three graces," as they were nicknamed, traveled across the country and managed to activate even inhabitants of small towns in rural areas, who had not been overtly protesting the Belarusian regime, with the exception of the 2017 protests against the tax on the unemployed.

The fact that women led the campaign made it very special. As opposed to previous campaigns in which most candidates were males, the three women seemed very empathetic, shared personal sensitive stories about their families and childhood, and were easily approachable for people who were showing up for the rallies. They shook hands and hugged Tsikhanouskaya's potential voters, talked to them, and listened to their concerns.

Tsikhanouskaya was a perfect compromise for those who wanted to see more women in power and those who were more conservative. She kept repeating that she was running the campaign out of love for her husband who was imprisoned and she would rather "make cutlets at home" instead. But she was a woman, giving impressive speeches, and ready to fulfill her pre-election promises: to hold a new election with all interested candidates, including the imprisoned Tsikhanouski and Babaryka; to hold a referendum to return the Constitution of 1994; and limit presidential terms, which had subsequently been changed under Lukashenka's rule. Veranika was the quintessence of a successful top manager, mother, and wife, which attracted other hard-working mothers; while Maryia Kalesnikava, a professional musician, having lived abroad, developed a successful career, and speaking fluent English and German, was successful and single at the same time, and thus was liked by more emancipated women and many young people.

Another important and beneficial feature for Sviatlana and her team was the now omnipresent social media and Internet penetration. All three women were using their Facebook and Instagram pages, writing regular and detailed entries, and holding livestreams from the rallies. This publicity gave an additional feeling of easily approachable politicians, which had not been the case before in Belarus. Belarusian and foreign media were following Tsikhanouskaya and her team everywhere and were also organizing livestreams, thus amplifying the reach to the electorate. Belarusians saw the scale of the campaign and became brave enough to join the rallies and more confident in their ability to change the country, as so many people in so many places were present at the rallies.

Tsikhanouskaya, Kalesnikava, and Tsapkala visited Minsk, Brest, Mahilioŭ, Hrodna, Barysau, Babrujsk, Homiel, Baranavičy, and other towns. In some of them, such as Pinsk, Stoŭbcy, Salihorsk, and Sluck, local authorities refused to host the trio, giving some ungrounded reasons or using the excuse of limiting gatherings due to the COVID-19 pandemic, which had been previously denounced by Lukashenka, who called it a "psychosis" and not a dangerous disease. On July 30, Tsikhanouskaya, Kalesnikava, and Tsapkala managed to gather 70,000 people for a rally, the first time since the 1990s that so many people had gathered for a public event. Fearing that even more people would come and openly criticize the regime, the authorities refused to let Tsikhanouskaya organize a further rally at Bangalore Square in Minsk and confused the rally's participants, many of whom went to a different location.

At the end of July, Tsikhanouskaya decided to relocate her children abroad, fearing for their safety. On August 8, 2020, now fearing for her own personal safety, Sviatlana decided not to spend the night at her apartment, following the detention of two people from her election headquarters.

Did Tsikhanouskaya win the 2020 election?

Because the 2020 campaign was so lively, many Belarusians took an active part in it. Numerous people of different ages and professional backgrounds joined the initiative groups of Babaryka, Tsapkala, and Tsikhanouski to collect the necessary 100,000 signatures for them around the country. When the three election headquarters unified under Sviatlana Tsikhanouskaya, they adopted the practice of wearing white bracelets made of rubber or any other materials, and asked their supporters to do the same, especially on election day. Thus, thousands of people all over the country as well as those voting abroad, supporting Sviatlana's candidacy, were able to recognize each other. The same policy was also adopted on August 9, 2020, when they were waiting in line to vote.

Many other individuals decided to become citizen observers. Belarusian authorities demonstrated their cynicism again when they claimed that due to the COVID-19 pandemic, most observers had to observe the voting process from a suitable distance outside the polling stations, including the early voting, used previously by the regime to manipulate the results. Social media and conventional media were sharing absurd photos of observers watching the voting process outside schools and kindergartens using binoculars, standing behind fences surrounding the polling stations, or watching from outside windows.

Notably, this was the first election since 2001 in which the authorities postponed their invitation to the OSCE ODIHR (Office for Democratic Institutions and Human Rights of the Organization for Security and Cooperation in Europe) to observe the voting. The ODIHR had been the only reliable international institution that would consistently criticize the regime for discrepancies during elections and serve as an authority for the Belarusian state to address and admit certain shortcomings. This time, the authorities issued an invitation so late that the ODIHR officially refused to organize an election observation mission. One can speculate that the Belarusian regime was afraid of an independent institution watching all the violations, arrests, and later violence happening before and after election day. Without the presence of the ODIHR, Belarusians were left alone to observe irregularities of the elections. The mission of the Commonwealth of Independent States, which had never criticized Belarusian elections before, was not expected to behave differently this time.

During this election, Belarusians organized themselves into new election observation initiatives: Honest People and the Voice. Zubr (Bison, unrelated to the organization of the same name that operated in the early 2000s), which had been active since the 2018 local elections, also contributed to the collection of data on polling stations and members of election commissions. Two other important citizen observers' organizations with a long history of election observation in Belarus—Human Rights Defenders for Free Elections (HRDFE) and Right to Choose—were also active. However, in 2020, thanks to the involvement of IT experts, including cofounder of the Voice Pavel Liber, senior director of Belarusian IT giant EPAM, observation and registration of falsifications were made using mobile phones and special bots.

Independent Belarusian media attempted several times to hold exit surveys via their online platforms on social media channels to establish the probable outcome of the election. Some of them calculated only 3% support for Lukashenka, which certainly was not representative, as the survey only covered the Internet audience. Nevertheless, "Sasha 3%" became a nickname, an Internet meme, this time for Lukashenka, and irritated the authorities so much that they banned any further online surveys. The media came up with a creative solution and organized polls using euphemisms for the names of presidential candidates, and again Lukashenka still received minimal support.

Diasporas internationally also demonstrated extraordinary activity at this time. All the continents with Belarusian citizens held rallies and protests opposing the arrests of the presidential candidates and were determined to vote at Belarusian embassies and consulates around the world. Taking into consideration the fact that Belarusians abroad were predominantly against Lukashenka and had left their homeland in numerous cases for political reasons and fearing persecution, the embassies set up an obligatory registration in corresponding consulates to ensure the possibility to vote. Many Belarusians managed to do so before election day, but many more were unable to take part. On August 9, 2020, international media were showing thousands of Belarusians lining up in front of Belarusian embassies and consulates to vote. Many of them were wearing white bracelets to mark themselves as supporters of Tsikhanouskaya. The embassies and consulates, though, set up two more obstacles for people to vote: the first to vote were those who had registered at local consulates earlier, and only a few voters could be simultaneously present inside the diplomatic offices due to the COVID-19 pandemic. As a result, thousands of people living outside the country failed to cast their vote on election day.

On August 9, 2020, huge numbers wearing white bracelets started to queue to vote from the early morning in Belarus. Again, citing COVID-19 pandemic restrictions, election commissions tried to limit the number of voters that could be in the line at polling stations. The authorities had not expected such a high turnout. Tired of the lack of support with the start of the pandemic and numerous violations during the campaign when candidates were arrested and many journalists and activists were detained, Belarusians wanted to show their solidarity by turning up at the polling stations. Many of them were able to take photographs of their ballots and protocols and send them via the Voice platform, thus enabling an alternative counting process.

Closer to the end of the voting process, precinct election commissions started to place restrictions on voting, which caused many people to rebel. During election day, the commission members saw hundreds of people wearing white bracelets, thanks to social media. On August 9, the authorities blocked independent media websites and social media, but it became obvious how many people across the country were determined to vote for Sviatlana Tsikhanouskaya. When polling stations closed without enabling all the voters to cast their ballots, people spoke up and yelled at election commissioners demanding to be allowed to vote. In many places, militia were already waiting and trying to intimidate those who were arguing with the local election bodies.

When the final election protocols were placed outside polling stations, people continued to send data via the Voice platform and then could see that Tsikhanouskaya was ahead. That coincided with the voters' assessment of the huge number of those who were queuing for months before to put their signatures for alternative candidates, numerous participants of election rallies, people who showed up to vote on election day, and conversations people were having with each other and revealing that they intended to vote for Tsikhanouskaya.

The Voice and Zubr platforms started to publish the first results alongside proof of falsifications made at numerous polling stations. Data from photos of final protocols were hugely different from the data published by the Central Election Commission (CEC). Evaluation of 1,310 final protocols sent to the platforms out of an overall number of 5,767 demonstrated that around 80% of votes were cast for Sviatlana Tsikhanouskaya, which made it impossible for Lukashenka to obtain 80.1% of votes as claimed by the CEC. In their final report, the Voice, Zubr, and Honest People demonstrated the impossibility that the numbers pronounced by the authorities could be correct. Belarusians felt that their votes were stolen. In addition to pre-election repressions, years of apathy and discontent with the regime (especially among young and middle-aged generations) led to anger, which emboldened them to flood the streets in protest.

The various reports indicate that it was almost impossible for Lukashenka to have won the election either with 80% of the vote or a majority vote in the first round. Almost certainly, Tsikhanouskaya was leading at that point. But we do not have sufficient information to declare her the outright winner. While she was clearly winning in the city of Minsk, where Lukashenka's support was at its weakest even before 2020, we do not have full information from smaller towns and rural areas, which have been the mainstay of his support in earlier elections. Most likely, she was well ahead, but whether she had attained over 50% of the vote is hard to verify.

Why did mass protests begin after August 9, 2020?

The eruption of mass protests in Belarus after August 9, 2020, marked a pivotal moment in the country's recent history. These protests reflected a myriad of underlying factors. For over two decades, Aliaksandr Lukashenka had presided over Belarus, fostering an authoritarian regime characterized by restricted civil liberties, limited political competition, and a controlled media. The 2020 presidential election, however, proved to be a turning point, sparking widespread dissatisfaction, arising initially from the government's failure to respond to the COVID-19 crisis and earlier attempts to impose taxes on those unemployed for more than six months in a year (2017).

Past elections had also resulted in protests, most notably in 2006 when a tent city was set up in Kastryčnickaja Square and lasted for several days before being broken up by the authorities; and 2010, which had ended in brutal violence in Independence Square and the incarceration of seven out of nine presidential candidates. The electoral tradition indicated that the riot police would be on alert and prepared to respond in a similar fashion in 2020, particularly after witnessing the large crowds attending rallies for Sviatlana Tsikhanouskaya.

The opposition campaign, led by the three original electoral camps, but ultimately led by Tsikhanouskaya (as the candidate), Veranika Tsapkala, and Maryia Kalesnikava, accused Lukashenka of electoral fraud and demanded transparency. Tsikhanouskaya's original demands had been simple: freedom for political prisoners and the holding of new, democratic elections outside the control of government forces. Thus there was no indication that she intended to embark on a political career in the post-election period.

After August 9, however, there were widespread reports of vote rigging, intimidation at polling stations, and a lack of impartiality, all of which fueled discontent among the Belarusian electorate. The subsequent declaration of Lukashenka's victory with over 80% of the vote to a mere 10% for Tsikhanouskaya caused outrage and galvanized the populace to take to the streets. Various Belarusian embassies worldwide reported an electoral victory for Tsikhanouskaya in their localities, and in several Minsk precincts in which vote counts were reported, she was clearly well ahead.Though the actual results will always remain unclear, it is almost certain that the opposition candidate was ahead and may have won outright.

The sociopolitical climate in Belarus also played a significant role in the mass protests. Years of economic stagnation, rising inflation rates, and widespread corruption had gradually eroded the people's faith in the government. The younger generation, particularly, faced limited job opportunities, curtailing their aspirations for a prosperous future. Protesters demanded radical reforms and systemic change. Many were well traveled and could compare Belarus unfavorably with countries of the EU.

As the protests gained momentum, the Lukashenka regime responded with its traditional heavy-handed approach using means at his disposal: the KGB, the riot police, and the Ministry of Internal Affairs troops. Many of these individuals remained loyal to Lukashenka because they were afraid of retribution if he was removed from office. Reports of police brutality, arbitrary arrests, and suppression of dissent emerged. Images of peaceful demonstrators being violently dispersed dismayed the international community, further fueling support for the protestors' cause. The defense of civil liberties and human rights became central themes of the protests, as they embodied the people's desire for freedom and democracy.

For some time, the makeup of the protesters embraced most of the civil community: students, teachers, blue- and white-collar workers united in a common cause and on a scale hitherto unseen with tens of thousands in the streets. Many carried the white-red-white national flag, created initially for the first independent Belarusian state known as the Belarusian People's Republic (alternatively as the Belarusian National Republic or Belarusian Democratic Republic) that lasted for nine months between March and December 1918. The flag had been notably absent during Tsikhanouskaya's election campaign, but during the protests it became the main symbol of opposition to the resumed presidency of Lukashenka.

The regime responded with tactics of extreme violence on a scale not seen before. Belarusian election campaigns during the Lukashenka era had often ended with repressions. In 2010, a short but violent confrontation had occurred in Independence Square, and six of the nine presidential candidates spent the election night in prison, most badly bruised. A seventh, Uladzimir Niakliaieu, was brutally beaten before even reaching his fellow protesters and was taken to the hospital. The level of violence was taken to a different level in 2020 (see below). Nonetheless, 2020 was a turning point in the history of independent Belarus, a failed uprising but one that demonstrated a change in the mindset of the population, one that broke the bonds remaining between the president and his people in what has been termed a "social contract."

Why did women play such a prominent role in the protests?

During the 2020 election, women played a very special role for many reasons. Their importance grew gradually following a sequence of events, which elevated women to a different level. The widespread and rapid reactions were amplified by the Internet and social media. For the first time, this happened at the start of the official campaign in May. When Sviatlana Tsikhanouskaya registered her initiative group to collect the signatures and thousands of people started to form lines to leave their signatures for her all over Belarus, Lukashenka was taken by surprise. He tried to apply his usual misogynistic rhetoric trying to invalidate Sviatlana and condemned the whole idea of a female presidency, pointing out that the Belarusian constitution "is not written for a woman," as it is "too hard for a woman to bear the burden" of a presidential post. The Belarusian public reacted immediately. Many Belarusian women, including celebrities, denounced Lukashenka's statement, while numerous media supported their position and spread videos featuring many women who were opposing Lukashenka's speech.

For the second time, a female figure attracted attention, this time in the form of a heroine of a painting. It occurred after the arrest of Viktar Babaryka and his son Eduard. The Belgazprombank's art collection, the core of the ART Belarus project, became another "victim" of the criminal investigation against the father and the son. All the works of art were expropriated, including one of the most valuable ones in contemporary Belarus, the painting *Eva* by Chaim Soutine.

Immediately the Belarusian Internet came up with multiple collages depicting the painting's heroine Eva, who became the symbol of protesters in Belarus and the origin of the hashtag #evolution instead of "revolution." On newly emerged collages and memes, Eva was showing a middle finger, implicitly reflecting the attitude of the Belarusian people to the authorities, and thus Eva became the most popular picture to be printed on T-shirts, cups, or stickers. Later, with the spread of the female protest movement in Belarus, Eva's image was transformed multiple times. On some of them, Eva was dressed in white clothes and holding flowers, just like the Belarusian female protesters; on others the heroine was behind bars, like many peaceful protesters who had been punished for their political activities. Thousands of people inside the country and abroad started to reproduce images of Eva on a large scale, creating a new pop-art phenomenon.

The third milestone was marked after Tsikhanouskaya, Kalesnikava, and Tsapkala declared their intention to campaign together. Immediately (and as they later stated unintentionally) the three women invented their own logo: a heart, a fist, and a victory sign. These symbols became viral on the Internet and offline. Belarusians started to reproduce them during rallies, put them on T-shirts, and made other merchandise with them. Images of the three women were also reproduced on T-shirts and posters, and the trio itself became the symbol of resistance, something unprecedented in modern Belarus, where almost exclusively men were the bright political figures and fighters against injustice.

Subsequently, in August, Sviatlana Tsikhanouskaya, Maryia Kalesnikava, and Veranika Tsapkala faced a number of repressive measures and threats. Tsapkala joined her husband, who first fled to Russia one day before election day following persecution threats. Tsikhanouskaya was forced to leave the country for Lithuania two days after election day and during protests, on August 11, after a conversation at the Central Election Commission. At the CEC office she was also forced to make a humiliating video addressing her electorate. Later, Sviatlana admitted that she regretted her actions but said she had no choice as the authorities were threatening to harm her children and family.

A Coordination Council Presidium was established on August 14, 2020, for the transition of power, which included five women and three men. In addition to Tsikhanouskaya and Kalesnikava from the initial election women's trio, three remarkable women joined the presidium: Svetlana Alexievich, a Nobel laureate in literature and the author of the famous *The Unwomanly Face of War*; Volha Kavalkova, Belarusian Christian Democracy cochair, who was initially running in the presidential election and then joined Tsikhanouskaya's team; and Liliya Ulasava, an experienced and well-known lawyer and mediator. Soon, the Belarusian authorities invented a mechanism to impose repressions against the Presidium's women. First, they detained Volha Kavalkova. After imprisoning her for several days, they brought her to the border with Poland and forced her to leave Belarus. Later the Committee of State Control detained Liliya Ulasava.

Further repressions continued when Maryia Kalesnikava was abducted in Minsk city center on September 7, 2020. The next day, she was taken to the Belarusian-Ukrainian border with her colleagues Anton Radniankou and Ivan Krautsou. Unlike the accompanying men, Kalesnikava refused to go to Ukraine, tore up her passport, and had to be returned, still under arrest, to Belarusian territory. Afterward, she was charged with multiple offenses and received a prison term of eleven years. In 2022, Maryia fell ill and required an operation in a prison hospital. Subsequently, her health deteriorated. From February 2023, Kalesnikava's family had not received any correspondence from her and her condition was unknown until her father was allowed to visit her in November 2024. Lukashenka then proudly announced to the official media that this had happened, thanks to him. Her predicament made Maryia an extremely popular woman, and she was featured on protesters' posters, became the symbol of a new female Belarusian protest movement globally, and received multiple international awards for her resistance.

Later in September 2020, Svetlana Alexievich declared on social media that some unknown people were trying to break into her Minsk apartment. European diplomats and journalists immediately arrived at Alexievich's home to protect her from the intruders and remained there to guard her for several days. Previously, Alexievich had to provide evidence in the criminal case against her colleagues from the Coordination Council Presidium. Ultimately, Alexievich left Belarus and started to work on her new book describing the Belarusian protests.

Not only the famous trio and well-known women such as Alexievich became the driving force of the protests. Ordinary women made the Belarusian revolution very special as they drove it for many months. Already during the first most brutal days of the post-election crackdown on August 9–11, thousands of people were detained. When released, most people opined that the women had faced less violence in detention centers and prisons, but still were humiliated, beaten, and raped. Several hundred women self-organized a Telegram chat aiming to stop further brutality.

On August 12 and 13, 2020, Belarusian women across the country started to form "chains of solidarity." In white clothes and holding hands, they called upon the authorities to stop the violence and hear their voices. Simultaneously a group of women living abroad organized a flash mob on social media, speaking in different languages and calling to stop the violence under the hashtag #She4Belarus. They were also wearing, without prior agreement with women based in Belarus, white clothes. It was a subconscious move to wipe off all the blood and dirt people had witnessed during the brutal violence against the post-election protesters.

On August 14, when a mass demonstration happened in front of the House of Parliament in Minsk, military forces put down their shields in front of the female protesters who approached them. In response, the women started hugging and kissing the soldiers. This was later criticized by both men and women, who argued that all the violence and injustice imposed on post-election protesters should not be forgotten and forgiven. The aftermath of this event showed that indeed the authorities were not going to give up and were preparing more repressions. Nevertheless, the women showed their bravery by approaching the army and militia and talking to them, while having no means to protect themselves and being extremely vulnerable.

In September 2020, harsher repressions were imposed on the protesting women who hitherto had been safer compared to the men protesting earlier. Those women who joined student protests and solidarity chains after the abduction of Maryia Kalesnikava on September 7, 2020, were brutally beaten and detained. One woman lost her child as a result of the violence. The Belarusian state media cynically lied about her misfortune on TV, stating that she had aborted her pregnancy.

Also in September, Sviatlana Tsikhanouskaya, Volha Kavalkova, and Veranika Tsapkala reunited in Warsaw for an official meeting. When speaking to journalists, they praised the courage of their colleagues and friends, especially their "feisty girlfriend" Kalesnikava, who despite the risk of persecution at home opted for imprisonment instead of forced emigration. In several statements from abroad, the exiled Tsikhanouskaya condemned Belarusian police for beating women and girls and praised the women's courage.

"White protests" and female marches became a regular tradition happening in Belarus at least once a week on Saturdays. Belarusian women marched through cities and towns both at home and abroad, held hands, carried flowers and posters, and sang lullabies and the famous Belarusian folk song "*Kupalinka*" about the sad destiny of a village girl. Women became so involved that the most popular manicure in the summer and autumn of 2020 in Belarus in beauty salons was white and red, as it symbolized the colors of protest connected to the white-red-white flag. Many female Belarusians organized flash mobs and created videos for Belarusian and international audiences, becoming heroines of posters, paintings, theater performances, and documentaries in Belarus and abroad. Women would gather for "female" protests every Saturday and each would have a special name, continuing until the protest activities stopped.

Other famous Belarusian women outside politics took a stance fighting against the regime. Female solidarity reached an unprecedented level. Three Belarusian pop singers living and working in Russia—Rita Dakota, Anzhelika Agurbash, and Katya Iowa—wrote songs and published videos on YouTube condemning the brutality and violence used against the protesters and praising Belarusian women and men who resisted. Anzhelika Agurbash protested multiple times in front of the Belarusian embassy in Moscow until she was detained and threatened.

Prominent Belarusian singer Anna Sharkunova released several songs following the election and post-election events in Belarus, devoting them to protesters, to Raman Bandarenka who was beaten to death in November 2020 by close associates of Lukashenka, and to Belarusian political migrants and Belarusian women. The singer had to leave Belarus to avoid retribution. Belarusian actresses of the most successful and oldest Yanka Kupala Drama Theater in Minsk resigned their positions, along with the whole crew, and left Belarus. Abroad, they organized multiple performances and continued to criticize the regime. Marharyta Liauchuk, an opera singer, was a key figure in the protests of musicians and cultural workers and published many satirical songs on YouTube attacking Lukashenka and his closest supporters. Her joint project with musician Andrei Pavuk, "Red Greens," alluded to the colors of the official Belarusian flag with its title and openly satirized Lukashenka and his regime.

Belarusian female athletes, including Olympic gold medalist swimmer Aliaksandra Herasimenia and basketball players Alena Leuchanka and Katsiaryna Snytsina, became leaders of the Independent Belarusian Sports Solidarity Foundation, which united athletes who stood up against Lukashenka and the state in August 2020 by signing a petition condemning the regime. Later, they were joined by runner Krystsina Tsimanouskaya, who fled from the Tokyo Olympic Games to Poland to protest the pressure put on her by Belarusian coaches. Melitsina Staniuta, a renowned artistic gymnast, the recipient of multiple awards at world championships, and the great-granddaughter of prominent Belarusian theater actress Stefaniya Staniuta, was fired from state TV after she spoke up against the closure of the symbal.by store selling merchandise with Belarusian national symbols. She also signed a petition of Belarusian athletes condemning the post-election violence and falsifications and ultimately had to leave the country.

Another important symbol of Lukashenka's harassment of women protesters was Volha Hizhynkova, a former Miss Belarus, who was tortured for months in prison because of her photographs from the protests where she was holding a white-red-white flag. Lukashenka then made another cynical statement saying that he didn't fight with women. Remarkably, when the authorities organized a series of pro-government rallies, their participants were using a wordplay "a beloved [Belarus] cannot be given away," where "a woman" from the original expression was substituted with "Belarus," which has a female grammatical gender in the Belarusian and Russian languages. On the one hand, this expression was pointing out that he would not give away "his" Belarus to protesters or other politicians and showed his possessive attitude to a country he believed to be his own. On the other hand, this was again another misogynistic expression stressing that when a man loves a woman, he will not let her go, which is a limitation of freedom and is very much in line with the overall abusive rhetoric of the Belarusian leader.

These are just a handful of stories of many prominent women who stood up against the cruelty of the authorities and election results falsifications. Thousands went through the repressive machine and hundreds became political prisoners. This rapid emancipation cost many women their careers, health, and families, but the scale of women's involvement was unprecedented. Years later, Tsikhanouskaya's team was often criticized for not putting more women in charge of the Transition Cabinet. Despite that criticism, many women became more visible and outspoken after the 2020 revolution.

What was the role of social media in the opposition campaign to the incumbent president?

Since the start of the election campaign, all three major candidates—Tsikhanouski, Babaryka, and Tsapkala—made good use of their social media channels, unlike Lukashenka, who had never been especially interested in them, being from an older generation, and confident in his power and public support. He only started to develop his channels in late 2020, realizing their value in propaganda. Other alternative candidates, such as Hanna Kanapatskaya and Andrei Dzmitryieu, were also present on social media platforms and used them extensively.

After Tsikhanouskaya, Kalesnikava, and Tsapkala united their campaigns, they reinforced the usage of their social media pages to make it a centerpiece of their election campaign. The Voice, Honest People, and *Zubr* election observation groups followed suit. Many media, previously focused on lifestyle and beauty, began publishing political content on their Instagram, Facebook, YouTube, Twitter (now X), and Telegram channels, in addition to more serious media outlets. The young and educated population of Belarus was eagerly using social media to obtain the news, to watch the campaign, and also to communicate with each other about protests and coordinate protest activities.

The political revolution was achieved primarily thanks to Telegram, the platform owned by Russian IT mogul Pavel Durov, who had been residing for several years in Dubai, following the attempts of Russian authorities to put pressure on him and made him share the data. NEXTA, Belarus of the Brain, Tea with Raspberry Jam, My Country—Belarus, and many other channels had been growing since the beginning of 2020, when people wanted to obtain reliable information about the COVID-19 pandemic, but the official media were silent about it. Telegram enabled its users to send instantly documents, photos, and videos to the administrators of channels, who then would spread the information further to their multi-thousand audience after some fact-checking.

When the election campaign began, Telegram again was utilized to obtain timely information, to share details on ongoing repressions, to coordinate protest activities, and to communicate between Belarusians living in the country and abroad. In the light of blockage of many independent media websites and arrests of many journalists, Telegram channels became the leading information platform for Belarusians starting from August 9, 2020.

The authorities' response to the protesters, who took to the streets to demonstrate their disagreement with the official election results and the three days of violence during August 9–11, was to apply a total blackout in Belarus and cut people off from the Internet. Eventually, the Internet was returned to service, as the blackout had paralyzed the work of the beneficial IT sector. Allegedly, residents of the Belarusian IT Hi-Tech Park put pressure on the authorities to restore it. Thus, the public was able to see what had been published in Telegram and the scale of violence and brutality used by the riot police and the army. The transcripts terrified and shocked Belarusians so much that several hundred thousand people took part in a protest on August 16, 2020. This action launched a series of marches taking place every Sunday in all cities and towns of the country.

Every Sunday, the protest would have a special dedicated name and would be coordinated by NEXTA, Belarus of the Brain, and other channels, which specified the time and routes. Participants of the demonstrations would self-organize using the Telegram chats in their respective districts before marching to the city center of a relevant city or a town. Belarusians would come up with chats to unite people of the same profession or district of simply a group of friends.

Later in 2020, when protesters moved to the yards of residential areas and the police started to use violence in the city center, people started organizing "yard chats," coordinating gatherings of neighbors. Others would set up concerts, often with famous musicians, tea drinking, and picnicking with children. Later, IT activists created an interactive map dze.chat (which in Belarusian means "where is the chat?") online where people could add their neighborhood chats from Telegram and get together. When repressions entered a new and more intensive phase, most administrators of such chats were arrested and imprisoned, and the chats themselves were branded by the Belarusian KGB as "extremist media." As of 2024, only the chats of Belarusians living abroad remained on the online map.

Many such yards had their specific decorations in white and red colors or even murals, like the "Square of Changes" yard. That yard in the city center became famous once its inhabitants made a mural devoted to the "DJs of Changes"—two men who created an official hymn for the 2020 revolution song "Changes" by the late Viktor Tsoy, a famous Soviet rock musician. In the Soviet Union the song became a symbol of *perestroika*. In 2020, Tsikhanouskaya used this song during her campaigning. On August 6, when authorities banned Tsikhanouskaya's rally at the last moment, two sound engineers Kiryl Halanau and Ulad Sakalouski operating in the initial rally location put on the song "Changes" and stood still performing the "Victory" sign with their arms. A mural with this same scene was painted in the Square of Changes. The two men were immediately detained and arrested, but their deed became another symbol of the protests.

The police repeatedly destroyed the mural, but local inhabitants, among them artist and teacher Raman Bandarenka, kept repainting it. Using their Telegram chat, local inhabitants would inform each other about the concerts and events happening there as well as about the police arrivals. On November 11, when Bandarenka saw in the chat that the police had returned once again, he wrote there, "I'm coming out," which became a slogan of further protests. Later that night he was killed. Independent investigations and leaked conversations of people close to Lukashenka pointed to the involvement of Natallia Eysmant, Lukashenka's press officer, and athletes Dzmitry Shakuta and Dzmitry Balaba close to Lukashenka in the murder of Bandarenka.

Starting from May 2020 when the authorities detained Tsikhanouski, they marked the launch of anti-bloggers' and anti-influencers' campaign to quell the power of social media. Ihar Losik (editor of Belarus of the Brain), Eduard Palchys, and Uladzimir Tsyhanovich were tried together with Tsikhanouski and received lengthy terms of 13–16 years. Tsikhanouski and Losik were released following the Trump administration's negotiations in September 2025. Aliaksandr Ivulin, Aliaksandr Kabanau, Siarhei Piatrukhin, and Volha Takarchuk served 1–3-year prison terms and left the country. The case of the editors of NEXTA was investigated with the help of the detained Raman Pratasevich (see below). Stsiapan Putsila and Yan Rudzik received 20 and 19 years of imprisonment terms in absentia at the trials for their online activities. All bloggers' channels were declared to be "extremist," which implied legal consequences to all users who might comment or even react to their posts on social media. After a media outlet becomes "extremist," any online engagement with them can lead to criminal charges, according to Belarusian legislation.

The Belarusian authorities decided to eliminate completely any activities criticizing the government on social media. For a critique of the police or government on their social media pages or in private chats, Belarusians were receiving prison terms. This crackdown led to widespread self-censorship and fears and made most Belarusians who stayed in the country cover up their real views publicly.

How did Belarus achieve the growth of the IT sector and what role did IT play in the 2020 revolution and subsequently?

The Belarusian population was one of the most well-educated in Europe in the Soviet period. After the collapse of the Soviet Union, there was increasing demand for higher education, and the number of educational institutions, both public and private, issuing university degrees was growing. In the early 2000s, Belarusians became involved in the global trend of the growth of the IT sector. As many Belarusian citizens possessed a good educational background in mathematics or similar fields and spoke foreign languages, some Belarusians started to work for tech giants, such as Google, Microsoft, and eBay in Europe and the United States. Other Belarusians began working on their own IT projects in Belarus.

While working on the team of Aliaksandr Lukashenka and after his service as the ambassador of Belarus to the United States and Mexico (1997–2002), Valery Tsapkala came up with an idea to create a Hi-Tech Park in Belarus, which would have tax exemptions and other benefits to attract IT businesses to register and operate there. Subsequently Tsapkala became the Hi-Tech Park director, a post he held from 2005 to 2017. During these years the Park attained prosperity and popularity.

Most Belarusians had often struggled to develop businesses because of the country's unfavorable tax conditions and multiple checks—usually in the form of KGB audits—from many state bodies and state enterprises that dealt mainly with heavy industry. Thus, IT became a perfect solution for educated young prospective inhabitants of Belarus. Many would take special courses after graduating from the universities with degrees in a different field to start working in IT. Good salaries and low flat revenue taxes in Belarus made this field especially attractive. Gradually, Hi-Tech Park attracted globally known Belarusian companies such as Wargaming, Viber, itransition, maps.me, MSQRD, Flo, PandaDoc, EPAM, Apalon, and many more, contributing around 5.5% of Belarusian GDP in 2018. The Park attracted companies working on cryptocurrencies and block-chain start-ups development.

By 2020, it had around fifty resident enterprises exporting IT services to seventy countries and employing more than 61,000 people. The famous Belarusian YouTube blogger Vlad Bumaga (Vlad A4) also became a resident of the Hi Tech Park in 2020. US secretary of state Mike Pompeo also visited there in February 2020 during his official visit to Minsk. In addition, many more companies operated outside the Park, thus making the IT industry practically the top field in which to work among young, educated people.

Many of these people became the driving force of the 2020 protests in Belarus and also suffered because of the repressions. Not only did they physically attend the marches, demonstrations, and yard gatherings and put out flags and national symbols in the nice neighborhoods in which they could afford to live, thanks to their IT salaries, they also played an active role in the election headquarters of presidential candidates and election observation. Pavel Liber, the EPAM director, contributed to the creation of the Voice platform, which enabled Belarusians to register falsifications during the elections. Liber had to leave Belarus in the aftermath and created many more digital initiatives, including New Belarus—a project aiming to maintain contacts for all Belarusians living abroad, including access to doctors and psychologists, advertisement of Belarusian business, head hunting for Belarusian experts, and simply chatting with each other.

PandaDoc was another successful IT start-up, already operating between Minsk and Silicon Valley in 2020, which attracted a lot of attention during the 2020 campaign. In August 2020, Mikita Mikado announced the launch of the initiative Protect Belarus, which assisted those individuals from the law enforcement agencies who wanted to transfer to IT and opposed the violence. Mikita was able to cover expenses of their studies and sometimes their relocation. The Belarusian authorities responded with the arrest of four key employees of PandaDoc residing in Minsk, who were charged with alleged fraud. Three of them spent half a year in prison, while their project manager, Viktar Kuushynau, was confined for over a year. Mikado had to abandon an idea to help Belarusian security officers to enable the release of his team. His initiative was overtaken by another IT businessman, Yaraslau Likhacheuski, living in Europe for many years by then.

Another group important for Belarusian protests, Cyberpartisans, emerged from IT specialists denouncing the regime of Lukashenka in the wake of the 2020 protests. Cyberpartisans were behind many projects, including the Black Book of Belarus where they were able to share the names and personal data of all the members of special security forces, riot police, and police involved in brutal detentions, beatings, and tortures of protesters in 2020. There, they also leaked information about judges and prosecutors who sentenced innocent Belarusians to prison terms and fines for their civic activities. Several times the group hacked state institutions' websites, creating a panic in Belarus. Cyberpartisans contributed to many investigations carried out by independent journalists and ByPol, an organization of former law enforcement agency employees. In December 2022, Cyberpartisans began to cooperate with the Kastus Kalinouski battalion of Belarusians fighting for Ukraine in response to the Russian invasion of the latter country, where they provide cybersecurity and cyberintelligence.

How did the Lukashenka regime survive?

The elections saw a complete swing in Lukashenka's attitude toward Russia. At the start of the campaign, a group of Wagner PMC soldiers arrived in Minsk, as a stopover en route to a mission abroad, most likely in Africa. Lukashenka may have feared that the mercenaries intended to remove him from office, or saw an opportunity for some positive propaganda, and promptly had them all arrested by the KGB. Though they were eventually released and returned to Moscow, the incident reflects Lukashenka's uncertainty as to the Putin regime's support for his election campaign.

Two of the initial election candidates, Valery Tsapkala and Viktar Babaryka, had close ties with Russia, and it was no secret that Putin was frustrated by Lukashenka's unwillingness to take a more active part in Russian-led structures such as the CSTO and economic union. For over a decade, the two leaderships had wrangled over the price of Russian oil and gas, arbitrary restrictions on Belarusian dairy exports to Russia, and the more recent attempts by Putin to integrate the two countries more tightly in the Russia-Belarus Union. However, Putin has consistently recognized the validity of Belarus's controversial presidential elections, despite the inflated figures for the incumbent president and deeply flawed system. After the post-election protests, Lukashenka was obliged to turn to Putin for help, in the forms of a new loan and the guarantee of support for his leadership, by military backing if needed.

Though the two presidents had clashed repeatedly since 2005 on such questions as payments for oil and gas prices, Belarus's exports of dairy products, and Lukashenka's commitment to Russian-led organizations such as the Eurasian Economic Community, the CIS, and the Russian-Belarus Union, ultimately Russia was committed to the survival of the Minsk regime. In fact, the 2020 protests, from Russia's perspective (and likely that of Lukashenka), were Western-inspired and Western-funded, and followed the so-called color revolutions earlier in the century and the Maidan uprising in Ukraine in 2013–2014. Russia was interested in a deeper integration of Belarus within the "Russian World," and the two presidents had agreed in principle on a number of points for this purpose.

For Lukashenka, however, there were two prime questions: the first was his personal survival as leader of Belarus; and the second his freedom of maneuver and autonomy from Moscow. Despite the inherent contradictions, he was able to some extent to achieve both, at least in the short term.

A second factor was the loyalty of the elite: his cabinet, security forces, police, and army. Though there were some significant defections and resignations after the elections—particularly in the Foreign Ministry—most of those in the power structure remained supportive of Lukashenka and were prepared to take part in severe repressions to keep him in power. Even Foreign Minister Uladzimir Makei, the official in the leadership most oriented toward connection with the West, opted to support the regime (his son, also a member of the Foreign Ministry, resigned). They were aided by the peaceful nature of the mass protests, which remained disciplined and nonviolent, even in the face of batons and beatings. The protesters' most provocative actions were to identify the security forces by pulling down their masks. So the authorities resorted to violence safe in the knowledge that a civil war was unlikely.

A possible means of eliciting political change was a general strike, something that Tsikhanouskaya called for after she had moved abroad. A full comprehensive strike never began. However, since August 2020 sporadically groups of people at many large and small factories and plants all over Belarus. On August 17, 2020, after the first big Sunday march, Lukashenka visited the Minsk Wheel Tractor Plant, where a protest was underway. The workers were shouting "Leave!" and one of them even said out loud: "Officer, shoot yourself!" Lukashenka confronted him, arguing that the worker should man up, as there were many workers, and Lukashenka was the one standing against them (which was not true, as Lukashenka was surrounded by his security team). This was the climax of his confrontation with the workers. But they did not have the resolve to embark on a general strike when their careers constituted the only source of income to support their families. Many of them were threatened to lose their jobs and go to jail, while others received unexpected bonuses and calmed down. One year later, most initiators of the strikes had been put in jail or had left the country. In the same fashion, student protests were curtailed by the threat of expulsion from university programs. The faculties generally were even less willing to abandon the security of their positions in support of a strike. The few that did speak out were unceremoniously dismissed. Several resigned. But the majority stayed in place and admonished protesting students.

The regime also cracked down quickly on any alternative source of power. Tsikhanouskaya was forced to flee to Lithuania on the evening of August 11 after a meeting with security forces, fearing for the safety of her family. Others were arrested, and later received wildly inflated terms of imprisonment, often for ten years or more. Moreover, Tsikhanouskaya, who most likely won the election, had never promised any long-term leadership. Her goals were the release of political prisoners and the holding of new elections. At the time of the protests, she never formally announced herself as the victor, or even saw herself and role as that of a politician. Also, though widely popular, support in her homeland weakened gradually the longer she remained outside the country.

Another factor was opposition unity, which had always been difficult to maintain since Lukashenka became president. The most popular political leader in 2020 and beyond, Viktar Babaryka, was in prison facing a sentence of indeterminate length, as was his brilliant campaign manager Maryia Kalesnikava. Both were reportedly ill and kept in isolation. The number of political prisoners in prisons and camps around Belarus kept growing. By the early 2020s, the figure was over 1,500. The exiled leader and her supporters were successful in acquiring the support of European and North American governments, but they found it achingly difficult to retain influence in their homeland.

Even in their own circles there was dissension. One of the original candidates, Valery Tsapkala, quickly distanced himself from the Tsikhanouskaya leadership. His speeches became increasingly erratic and included fanciful schemes, such as trying to raise funds to remove Lukashenka. But there were two other relationships that—at least initially—failed to develop, which were crucial to the opposition campaign.

The first was cooperation between the Transitional Cabinet and the Kalinouski Regiment fighting as a unit of the Ukrainian army against the Russian invasion. The latter's rationale was that the defeat of the Russian army in Ukraine would lead to regime change in Moscow and Minsk. Its numbers were small, around 1,000 troops at most, but the Ukrainians sent the Brigade into the war's heat spots. In theory, the Regiment itself might overthrow Lukashenka, or it might combine with units of the Belarusian army, should the latter be sent into Ukraine. Its reputation among the opposition was high, but for some time it did not recognize Tsikhanouskaya as the legitimate leader of Belarus and contacts were limited. The troops' position was evident: they were doing the fighting and suffering losses, while the exiled opposition were being serenaded in different European capitals.

The second was the lack of links between the Shadow Cabinet and the Zelenskyy government in Kyiv. The Ukrainian government opted to keep open its links with the official Minsk regime, leaving its ambassador in place in the Belarusian capital. Arguably, it was an astute move, as the exiles could hardly help Ukraine's cause effectively, whereas Lukashenka repeatedly stated that there would be no invasion of Ukraine by the Belarusian army, despite his general support for the Russian cause. Mykhailo Podolyak, the advisor to the leader of Zelenskyy's office, commented on February 13, 2023, that Ukraine was not supporting the opposition because it had seen little evidence of anti-war activity among its members. In Germany, in mid-May 2023, Zelenskyy and Tsikhanouskaya did meet each other briefly and exchanged friendly greetings, but Ukraine was apparently disappointed that there was no longer any resistance inside the country to Lukashenka. At the time of the encounter, Lukashenka was ailing and unable to walk alongside Putin at the Victory Day parade (May 9, 2023) in Moscow.

Earlier in 2023, dissension within the opposition manifested themselves further, when Zianon Pazniak, founder and initial leader of the Belarusian Popular Front; Pavel Usau, head of the center for Political Analysis and Prognosis; and Dzmitry Shchyhelski, former Belarusian psychiatrist, visited the Kalinouski Regiment members in Bakhmut at the height of the conflict there between the Russian and Ukrainian armed forces. Usau, a political scientist from Mahilioŭ and a longtime resident in Warsaw, joined Pazniak's Free Belarus movement, as an alternative to the Transitional Cabinet. Pazniak, who has also revived his political activity, dismisses Tsikhanouskaya and her team as pro-Russian, an epithet he has also bestowed upon a number of political rivals in the opposition in the past. Free Belarus at this time was also working actively with the ByPol group of former Belarusian security officers based in Warsaw, although ByPol also coordinated its activities with the Tsikhanouskaya Transitional Cabinet.

Taken together, all these factors allowed Lukashenka to survive after the presidential elections of 2020, though the key ones were support from Putin and his Security Council in Moscow and the reluctance of the protesters to use violence in the weeks of protest after August 9 of that year. There was no discernible anti-Russian sentiment in Belarus either. The population, subjected to a barrage of propaganda supporting the Russian invasion of Ukraine, probably had a major impact. Notably, the Tsikhanouskaya election campaign had remained firmly neutral on alignment of Belarus with Russia or the European Union. The use of the white-red-white national flag and deeper identification with the traditional opposition—both political parties and individuals—came later, after the transitional cabinet was formed. By that time, the former longtime leader of the United Civil Party Anatol Liabedzka had been appointed a member of the shadow cabinet, and the movement could be associated with the opposition movement in place since the early 1990s.

What happened to Lukashenka's opponents after 2020?

As of writing, Sviatlana Tsikhanouskaya, Volha Kavalkova, and Veranika Tsapkala are still living abroad. Several members of the Presidium of the Coordination Council are detained. Its other member, Pavel Latushka, former minister of culture and ambassador of Belarus, resigned from his position as director of Yanka Kupala Drama Theater and left Belarus. Some time later he appeared in Warsaw with his former colleague, Uladzimir Astapenka, previously an experienced diplomat and ambassador to Argentina. Together they formed the National Anti-Crisis Management (NAM), which acquired status as the de facto center of power of Belarusian politicians in exile in Warsaw.

Upon her arrival in Vilnius, Sviatlana Tsikhanouskaya was quickly surrounded by both seasoned and more recent activists and experts. They shaped the Office of Sviatlana Tsikhanouskaya (OST), which started international lobbying for her recognition as Belarus's de facto president-elect. OST gradually expanded its activities to the legal assistance of Belarusian political migrants in the EU and the families of repressed activists in Belarus; and promotion and support of cultural, business, and educational activities of Belarusians living abroad. OST in Vilnius became the major center of political life of Belarusians living in Lithuania and across Europe.

Though NAM and OST cooperated, they often disagreed. Together they contributed to the establishment of the United Transition Cabinet in August 2022, which attracted Latushka, Aliaksandr Azarau (Head of ByPol), Valery Sakhashchyk (with security background), and Valery Kavaleuski (with diplomatic background).

According to Tsikhanouskaya, she established the United Transition Cabinet (UTC) at a time of national crisis. Her goal was to protect the interests and rights of citizens and ensure the move to democracy in Belarus. Five basic objectives were laid out. First, to protect and consolidate the sovereignty of the country and attain its "de-occupation"; second, to introduce measures to end the illegal leadership of Lukashenka and move the state from dictatorship to democracy through free and fair elections. The third goal was the restoration of constitutional law and order; the fourth was the release and rehabilitation of political prisoners; and lastly, to develop and carry out decisions to achieve democracy in Belarus.

In September 2022, two women joined the United Transitional Cabinet: Tatsiana Zaretskaya, responsible for economic and business matters, and Alina Koushyk, former TV anchor and journalist of Belsat TV, was responsible for national revival. Two months later, Zaretskaya left the UTC, citing threats to her friends, colleagues, and family members. However, Belarusian journalists had published an explosive investigation that revealed Zaretskaya overstated her success in business, citing the failure of the UTC to vet her credentials. The report was published by the largest independent portal *Zerkalo* (formerly tut.by), on November 3, 2022.

Zaretskaya's departure marked the beginning of multiple reshuffles, entrances, and exits within the UTC. In 2022, Volha Harbunova, former political prisoner, feminist, and founder of shelters for woman victims of domestic abuse, was appointed Representative for Social Issues in the UTC. The main role of this position was to organize help for political prisoners in Belarus as well as their relatives, and includes legal, humanitarian, psychological, and social assistance. A longer-term goal is to ensure that a future Belarus will develop as a social welfare state with effective laws safeguarding the rights of vulnerable people.

In 2023, ByPol was divided into ByPol and BelPol, following an internal scandal between the former security and police officers working in the organization. Basically they accused each other of working for the Belarusian security forces and internal intelligence as well as corruption. This was followed by a negative media campaign against Azarau in both Belarusian and Russian expert circles, who left ByPol and established BelPol.

As a result, Azarau was asked to leave the UTC. And in 2024, Sakhashchyk, Harbunova, and Kavaleuski departed. Sakhashchyk was replaced by Vadzim Kabanchuk from the Kastus Kalinouski Regiment, Kavaleuski by the aforementioned diplomat Uladzimir Astapenka. In August 2024, Margo Vorychava was nominated as Representative for Youth. In January 2025, Alina Koushyk departed to head a reformed Belsat TV in Warsaw.

UTC's seeming disorganization became a propaganda tool wielded by the state, and by those in competing opposition camps, including Zianon Pazniak, a longtime leader of the

Belarusian Popular Front, once the strongest anti-Soviet and later anti-Lukashenka force in Belarus. OST also created independent Belarusian embassies—de facto representative offices in Brussels and Prague.

Tsikhanouskaya remains the recognized leader of democratic Belarus and Belarusian opposition, and in Lithuania, even as a president-elect. In the years since her exile to Lithuania, she has managed to visit key countries of the democratic world and establish working relationships with the leaders of the United States, France, Germany, Poland, Lithuania, Latvia, Estonia, Czechia, Sweden, Canada, and the majority of EU countries, who met in Argentina and announced their intention to expand their advocacy work in the Global South.

Despite receiving numerous awards and establishing a foundation for Belarusian women leaders, Valery and Veranika Tsapkala were gradually ostracized because of their growing number of controversial statements and heated arguments, questionable activities, and repeated cooperation with discredited figures. Usually, these statements were directed against Tsikhanouskaya, maintaining that she was spending her time in meaningless European and US official meetings rather than being focused on removing Lukashenka. These attacks contain many misogynistic and chauvinistic remarks. For example, Valery Tsapkala has maintained that Tsikhanouskaya has no mandate to lead the opposition and "is only capable of frying cutlets"; and that in 2020, people were not voting for her but against Lukashenka. Also, his supporters have mocked the Belarusian language.

Such comments only two years after the flawed election suggest that there was much bitterness toward Tsikhanouskaya from those who had ambitions to take her place. Other examples of inflammatory and unwarranted critiques came from Pazniak and from a former presidential candidate now resident in the United Kingdom, Andrey Sannikau, who referred to Tsikhanouskaya as an "impostor." Valery Tsapkala has tried to bolster his own position by using his wealth: campaigning to gather funds to remove Lukashenka or to buy out political prisoners from the regime in Minsk. The most charitable explanation for such activity is that Tsapkala's own ambitions have superseded common sense and entered the realm of fantasy. He was rather the third most popular candidate among the main challengers at the start of the 2020 presidential campaign, after Babaryka and Tsikhanouski.

Viktar Babaryka's campaign headquarters remained active in Poland and Lithuania. In August 2020, they announced a new political party, Razam ("together" in Belarusian), following up on a recorded statement by Babaryka before his arrest. In spring 2021, its campaign committee, the Coordination Council, was formed, which included Ivan Krautsou and Tatsiana Khomich, sister of Maryia Kalesnikava. Khomich additionally acted as the main representative of Maryia Kalesnikava and her advocates abroad.

On May 27, 2024, many members of Babaryka's team were elected to the Coordination Council, the only elected body of the Belarusians operating abroad. Previously the Coordination Council members were appointed. This time the coalition of Latushka's team with the Movement for Freedom, a political association founded prior to the 2006 presidential election in Belarus, gathered most votes and won the elections. Notably, only 6,723 people voted in the 2024 Coordination Council elections, which Belarusian authorities had already discredited as an extremist formation. As Lukashenka announced the upcoming 2025 presidential election for January, the most pressing question of the legitimacy of Sviatlana Tsikhanouskaya and other oppositional leaders living abroad remained.

2

THE LAND AND ITS PEOPLE

What is Belarus's geographical location and what natural resources and industry does it possess?

Belarus is a landlocked state in central Europe, about one-third of which comprises forests. Its total area is 80,300 square miles, making it slightly smaller than the United Kingdom or about the size of the state of Kansas in the United States. It is also crossed by several major rivers, the longest of which are the Dniapro at over 1,200 miles, the Western Dzvina (612 miles), the Nioman (562 miles), the Prypiać (465 miles), the Sož (389 miles), and the Biarezina (337 miles). Altogether, there are about 21,000 rivers in the country and about 11,000 lakes. It is located on a flat plain with its highest point only 1,135 feet, namely Dzerzhinsky Hill in the Dziaržynsk district of Minsk region. In the northwest, it is crossed by the Belarusian Ridge, a series of rolling hills, while in the southwest, the Palesie region is a large territory of swamps and marshes extending into the northwestern region of Ukraine. The northern part is known as the Belarusian Lake District.

Forests are another notable feature of the Belarusian landscape. The largest forest is shared with Poland in the west and named Biełaviežskaja pušča (Białowieża in Polish) and remains from the much larger primeval forest that once existed at 350,000 acres. It is a UNESCO World Heritage site with a total area of over 1,100 square miles in the Brest and Hrodna regions of Belarus, and the Podlaskie Voivodeship of Poland. It is famous for its varieties of bison, and in the Soviet period its hunting lodges were used by Leonid Brezhnev and other leaders for weekends of shooting. The closest settlement to the forest, the town of Hajnówka, is partly Belarusian-speaking and is a center of Belarusian culture in Poland, and Belarusians comprise over a quarter of the population. The most common trees in Belarusian forests are pine (coniferous) and birch.

It shares its borders with Russia (770 miles) in the east; Ukraine (674 miles) to the south; Poland (248 miles) to the west; and Lithuania (422 miles) and Latvia (107.5 miles) to the north. Belarus is divided into six *voblasti* (provinces) of roughly equal size, each of which has a city of the same name: Minsk, Hrodna, Brest, Viciebsk, Mahilioŭ, and Homiel. Minsk, the capital, is the only city with an expanding population and currently the residence of over 2 million people, followed by Homiel (481,000), Mahilioŭ (380,000), Viciebsk (365,000), Hrodna (350,000), and Brest (340,000). The population reached a peak of 10.2 million in 1992 and has since fallen to about 9.1 million today, a ranking of ninety-seventh worldwide. It is heavily urban (77.8%), with only about 2 million people currently residing in the countryside, a dramatic reversal of the demographic makeup one century earlier.

Much of the industry developed in the postwar period under Soviet rule, such as machine tools, engineering, tractors, light industry, mining, services, and food products—particularly in the dairy industry. Belarus is a world leader in the production of butter and sunflower oil, and a major producer and exporter of potash. More recently, prior to 2020, Belarus developed into a leading center of information technology. In addition to its forests, the country has deposits of peat, small amounts of oil and gas, rock salt, dolomite, and limestone. Its mineral deposits include potassium salt, phosphorites, clay, and quartz sands.

In November 2020, the Astraviec nuclear power plant, a VVER reactor with a capacity of 1200 megawatts in Hrodna region close to the border with Lithuania, began to generate electricity. A second unit of identical size was connected to the grid in May 2023. The plant is both financed and operated by the Russian company *Atomstroyeksport* (Atom Construction Export). The reactors operating currently were built by AEM Technologies at the Atommash factory in Volgodonsk, Russia. There are plans being developed to construct a second station in Minsk. In the summer of 2023, Russia reportedly transferred some tactical nuclear weapons to Belarus, and one likely site of such weapons is Asipovičy, the location of nuclear-capable short-range missile launchers moved from Russia to Belarus in 2022. The receipt of such weapons contravenes Belarus's commitment to the non-nuclear proliferation treaty following its voluntary removal of nuclear weapons from its territory after it became independent in 1991. However, this clause was omitted from the new version of the Constitution adopted after the February 27, 2022, national referendum.

What is Belarus's demography and ethnic composition?

The Belarusian population has been consistently measured by census takers since 1926. In the Soviet period, there were further censuses in the years 1937 (withdrawn from circulation), 1939, 1959, 1970, 1979, and 1989. The Republic of Belarus has conducted censuses at ten-year intervals, hence in 1999, 2009, and 2019. There are some watersheds between these censuses that had an extreme impact on the population. They include the annexation of Western Belarus from Poland in September 1939 (the only Polish census in the interwar period was in 1931), the Nazi German invasion and occupation, the Holocaust that resulted in the elimination of the Jewish population, and the major nuclear disaster at Chernobyl just south of the border. More recently, the upheaval that followed the mass protests of 2020 resulted in large-scale migration both eastward and westward.

Several trends can be discerned. First, Belarusians make up over 80% of the population as designated by ethnicity. The figure was 80.6% in 1926, 82.9% in 1939 (pre-expansion), 81.1% in 1959, 77.9% in 1989, and in the independence period it has continued to rise to 84.9% by the 2019 census. Russians are the largest minority and reached a peak of 13.2% in 1989 before declining to 7.5%, partly through assimilation and partly through migration. The Jewish population made up 8.2% in 1926—more than the Russians—but by 1959 had fallen to 1.9%, and further migration during the postwar period saw it dwindle to 0.1% by 2019, or about 13,700 people. Other major minorities are border populations: Poles in the west and Ukrainians in the south, with small groups of Armenians and Tatars. Most of the Armenians moved to Belarus in the independence period between 2009 and 2019.

The population continued to rise in the postwar period from just over 8 million in 1959 to a peak of 10.15 million by 1989, and reaching a reported peak of 10.37 million in 1993. Thereafter Belarus has seen a slow but steady population decline, as the mortality rate exceeded the birth rate for the first time. Life expectancy had also begun to fall and by 1997 was roughly 5–8 years less than the European average for women, and 8–13 years less for men. Among the most notable causes for the alarming decline were circulatory and nervous disorders, cancer, and sexually transmitted diseases, with a notable rise in the 1990s of tuberculosis and thyroid gland cancers among children linked to the Chernobyl accident. The effects of alcoholism were likely the main cause of the low life expectancy among males, followed by smoking.

The population in 2024 was just over 9.1 million according to official sources. The figure may be overstated since one source has reported that the exodus after the 2020 protests has been between 500,000 and 600,000, or approximately 7% of the population. Henadz Karshunou, former director of the Institute of Sociology of the Belarusian Academy of Sciences, has estimated that about 120,000 Belarusians fleeing from the regime moved to Poland, 50,000 to Lithuania, 25,000 to other countries of the European Union, and 11,000 to Georgia. The number migrating to Russia is not known, but believed to be similar in total to that moving to Poland. In October 2024, during her visit to Warsaw, Sviatlana Tsikhanouskaya stated that around 250,000 Belarusians had moved to Europe since 2020.

A trend toward urbanization became noticeable in the postwar period of the Belarusian Soviet Socialist Republic (BSSR) and continues into the present, as the rural population declines. The proportion of urban population is 78.4%, whereas in 1960 it was 32% and in 1970 it was 43.4%. In 1960, for example, there were 34,442 Belarusian villages. Today the figure is 23,008 and falling. The villages have become havens for the elderly, as young people seek education and careers in the towns and cities. Mortality rates in the countryside are more than double those in urban areas. Farming accidents have long been a major cause of death and injuries. In turn, the population is aging, with over 15% over the age of sixty-five, though this trend is similar in most central and east European countries—Belarus's world ranking in this regard is forty-two (Japan in first place has over 28%).

The city of Minsk is a boom area and has been a focus of state investment. It is the only part of Belarus where the population is increasing. The city population in 2024 was 2.06 million, making up around 23% of the national total. Elsewhere all regions have a declining population. The next largest city, Homiel, has a population of 480,951, or more than four times less than Minsk. Given the central location of Minsk, it has become the focal point of the republic in every respect. If one includes Moscow and London in the list of European cities, then Minsk is currently the tenth largest city in Europe and comparable in population to Paris and Rome, despite the fact that France and Italy have roughly seven times more inhabitants than Belarus.

Who are the Belarusians and what is modern Belarusian national identity?

Belarusians are one of the three East Slavic peoples (the prefix "Bela" meaning "white"), the others being Russians and Ukrainians, who are much more numerous and better known. In Soviet historiography, the authorities perpetuated a theory that modern Russia originated from Kyivan Rus, a principality of the medieval period. Ukrainians argue, to the contrary, that Kyivan Rus was the origin of the Ukrainian state. No doubt, it is possible to date modern Belarusians from this state, particularly given the power of Polack in the tenth and eleventh centuries. The people we know today as Belarusians also spent 500 years in the Grand Duchy of Lithuania (GDL), which eventually amalgamated with the Polish state as the Polish-Lithuanian Commonwealth. In the GDL, the Slavic community was noted for its religious beliefs (Uniate or Greek Catholic) and the use of an early version of the Belarusian language in official circles.

The partitions of the Polish-Lithuanian Commonwealth in 1786, 1793, and 1795 saw Belarusian territories incorporated into the Russian Empire under a ruler, Catherine II, who had no tolerance for non-Russian cultures or languages. Belarusians fought in several campaigns alongside the Poles against the Russian Empire. Thus, the origins of the modern state of Belarus lie in a brief period beginning in the early twentieth century and continuing—with profound interruptions such as a world war, revolutions, and civil war—until the late 1920s. We will deal in more detail with these processes below. Suffice it to say here that the foundations of the language were laid and altered by the Soviet regime.

The role of Vladimir Lenin, a Marxist revolutionary and founder of the world's first Communist state is, oddly, pivotal. After the Soviet occupation of Belarusian lands at the end of the civil war period, Lenin saw the need to recognize non-Russian languages and cultures rather than to focus on doctrinaire Marxism or centralization of a Russian state. The establishment of the BSSR resulted in the most active period of Belarusian state building in the 1920s, concomitantly with the milder New Economic Policy replacing the earlier grain requisitions. In the BSSR, Jews and Russians predominated in the towns, with Belarusians in the countryside. But Belarus gained a National Academy of Sciences, and the language was taught in schools. Some analysts maintain that the version of the language used in this period, based on the standardized version by the Belarusian scholar Branislau Tarashkevich (1892–1938), is the purest form of the language, called "*tarashkevitsa*" after his last name. It continues to be used by the Belarusian diaspora and some Belarusian media and cultural initiatives.

The Stalin regime undid much of the work toward any development of a Belarusian national identity. It produced a modified version of the language in the early 1930s, and arrested, imprisoned, and often executed most Belarusian intellectual leaders, including Tarashkevich. Still, the Belarusians maintained their own statehood, albeit controlled from Moscow, despite the overwhelming prevalence of the Russian language and Soviet culture until the late 1980s. With the Gorbachev period bringing change and opportunities for political and cultural expression, the BSSR began to enjoy a revival of national aspirations. The formation of the Belarusian Popular Front was one such development.

Yet various factors continued to hinder the formation of a singular national identity. The first factor was Russification, promoted during the Soviet period, which was strengthened by the pervasive urbanization of the state. The BSSR was an industrial republic, linked to the Soviet center and doing reasonably well economically for much of the postwar period. In 1990, when the government in Minsk decreed that Belarusian should be the sole state language in Belarus, it aroused considerable opposition. It lasted only five years before Russian was elevated to the same status. The Popular Front's policies were considered extreme by some, and the party could not attract the support of most of the population.

Another problem was that the foundations of a national identity often depend on historical events—often myths or distortions—that are considered defining. In the Belarusian case, some seemed far-fetched and not exclusively linked to the titular nation, such as the 1514 Battle of Orša between the Grand Duchy of Lithuania and Moscow and the 1794 Kościuszko (Kastsiushka in Belarusian transcript) uprising. The 1863 Kalinouski uprising is more logical, as is the formation of the Belarusian People's Republic in 1918. Since the 1960s, however, the focus has been on the Great Patriotic War of 1941–1945, the role of the partisans in Belarus, and the victory over the Nazis. Lukashenka perceived the logic of using the war as his main identity marker for national statehood and continued and modified earlier Soviet focus.

The result is that Belarusians appear to have ambivalent identities, and a mixed approach to the Soviet period, which might have been considered otherwise as more destructive of the national character. The opposition protests of 2020 accused the regime of adopting tactics similar to those of the Nazis and evoked memories of the partisans in their resistance. Thus, one might say that Belarusians have been molded by events of the twentieth century that have permeated all sectors of society. A 2022 study conducted by the independent Belarusian sociologist Philip Bikanau divides contemporary Belarusians into five discernible groups: the conscious, the Soviet, the emerging, the indifferent, and the Russified. The opposite ends of the spectrum are the conscious—supporting Belarusian language and culture and a pro-European direction for the state—and the Russified—rejecting the national language and culture and backing a Russian direction.

On nationality issues, the five directions are reduced to three: the conscious, the Soviet and Russified, and the indifferent. Notably, the last category remains significant throughout Bikanau's survey. In terms of the components of the question of who can be considered a Belarusian, speaking the national language ranks the lowest, well behind "someone who considers himself/herself a Belarusian" and "someone raised in Belarusian culture who considers it his/her own." The key characteristics of the image of Belarusians are kind-hearted, good-natured, peaceful, responsive, honest, and calm.

Various surveys carried out in the pre-2020 period indicated similar responses. In terms of political support for various parties, there have never been the sort of clear-cut opinions one might expect in a long-term dictatorship. One reason is that the Lukashenka leadership has never supported political parties, not even if they are pro-government, regarding them as an unnecessary barrier to the natural relationship between the president and the people. By 2024, almost all had been dissolved. Belarusians are sympathetic to Russians and perhaps a majority believe they are correct to pursue the war in Ukraine. But few want to be part of a Russian state or the Russia-Belarus Union, and even fewer would be willing to fight in Ukraine for the Russian side.

The sociologist Andrei Vardamatski informed the authors in a 2022 interview that Belarusian views were largely formed by media and social media and thus influenced by the Russian cultural hegemony and its control of television. YouTube, which is less susceptible to state control but also an active tool of the state, is also highly influential. Along with state television and Russian television, it is the main media influence for Belarusians. As opposition parties have been eliminated, and opposition media curbed, residents have only the resort of social media such as Telegram's and YouTube's NEXTA channel to read alternative views. Both NEXTA and Belsat have been based outside Belarus, in Warsaw, Poland, although the Polish government has cut funding considerably for the latter.

Two major alternative sites for Belarusian news in Belarusian language are Belarusian Service of the Radio Liberty/Radio Free Europe (practically fully suspended in April 2025 under the Trump administration) and *Nasha Niva*. The former's

Svaboda site, based in Prague, provides considerable insights into events in Belarus, while the latter is a revival of the first Belarusian newspaper founded in 1906. It went through several phases after independence, but the online version, founded in 1997, has been a reliable source of news in the Belarusian language. Until 2017, it was edited by the translator and publicist Andrei Dynko, and after that date by Yahor Martsinovich, who had been a political prisoner in the aftermath of 2020 events and was recently released. Both outlets have carried the torch of accurate reporting in the Belarusian language for Belarusians inside and outside the country.

Another factor in defining national identity is the migration of key opposition figures outside the country, particularly young, well-educated people keen to change the Lukashenka dictatorship. Together with a purge of leading academics from major institutions, it constitutes a brain drain that adversely affects support for the "conscious" element of Belarusian society. Today, it has become a dangerous practice even to speak Belarusian in the streets of Minsk because it is identified with the opposition. The sector that Bikanau identifies as "indifferent" is growing, as priorities switch from politics and democracy to topics such as inflation and job security. In addition, the lengthy and growing absence of key opposition leaders from their homeland renders them inconsequential. Increasingly, they begin to quarrel among themselves, reflecting the difficulty of operating outside the country. The war in Ukraine, nonetheless, does continue to elicit concern because of the involvement of the Belarusian state and fear that it may become part of the Russian military campaigns.

Is it true that most Belarusians identify closely with Russian culture and language?

At various times in the past, Belarus has had opportunities to develop its own culture and language, but they have been limited because the territory that makes up the current state has been part of a foreign empire. This was the case in the Polish-Lithuanian Commonwealth, the Russian Empire, and the Soviet Union. All of them made their impact on Belarusian self-identification. The origins of the modern Belarusian language lie in the East Slavic principalities of the medieval period, and what has been termed Old East Slavic was the predominant language during the rise of the Grand Duchy of Lithuania. The Chancery Slavonic combined Old East Slavic and Church Slavonic. In the sixteenth century, as the Renaissance and Reformation swept Europe, the Belarusian scholar and printer Francysk Skaryna published a Belarusian version of the Bible, believed by many to be the first book to appear in the Belarusian language.

After the partitions of Poland in 1795, toward the end of the reign of Russian Empress Catherine II, Belarusian lands became part of the Russian Empire, with a ban on the usage of the native language following the 1830–1831 uprisings in Belarus, Poland, and Lithuania that lasted until 1905. After the revolution of this year, the Belarusian language experienced a revival, with books, newspapers, and periodicals appearing, as well as plays. After the First World War, as different forms of a Belarusian state emerged, Belarusian was the official language spoken in the republic, along with Russian, Polish, and Yiddish. Because of the demographic divide between nationalities, Belarusian was spoken mainly in the villages, whereas the other languages prevailed in urban centers. Nevertheless, the short-lived People's Republic of March 25, 1918, declared Belarusian to be the state language.

The 1920s saw significant progress in the period known as "Belarusization" after Lenin encouraged the cultural development of national republics in the period of the New Economic Policy. Even before the official launching of the new policy, there were some significant developments, including the founding of the Belarusian State University in 1921. In January 1922, the Institute of Belarusian Culture was founded, and it included some of Belarus's best-known scholars, writers, and poets. They included Yanka Kupala, Yakub Kolas, Yasep Losik, and Stsiapan Nekrashevich (Ściapan Niekraševič), the original chairman of the institute. One of its main tasks in 1922–1924 was to standardize the Belarusian language. It was also charged with developing libraries, museums, archives, and archeological expeditions.

Other measures of the period of Belarusization included the operation of the State Museum and Central Archives, and the publication of books in the Belarusian language. Public institutions, similarly, began to switch to the Belarusian language, and Aliaksandr Khatkevich led a commission to oversee the direction of national policy. The movement did much to reverse the harsh policies introduced from the time of Catherine II and also led to the inclusion of more Belarusians in Soviet institutions and the Communist Party. According to one source, 80% of civil servants were conversing in Belarusian by 1927.

On January 1, 1929, the Institute of Belarusian Culture was transformed into the Belarusian Academy of Sciences, under the leadership of Usevalad Ihnatouski, a historian and politician. Its vice president was Yakub Kolas, who had been named People's Poet of Belarus three years earlier. His original name was Kanstantsin Mitskevich and his poems, prose, plays, and other writings focused on the Belarusian peasantry and intelligentsia. A major contribution to Belarusization was also provided by migrants from the western regions of Belarus, and the reform extended to parts of the Smolensk region outside the border, which included significant enclaves of Belarusians.

Whatever progress was made with the development of the Belarusian language and culture fell into decline after Stalin consolidated his power in Moscow. Priority in education and careers was given to the Russian language, and attempts were made to modify the Belarusian language to bring it closer to Russian. In May 1929, the Central Committee of the Communist Party in Moscow sent a commission to the BSSR, which provided a critique of the changes to the republic a month later.

Linked to it was the discovery of a (fictitious) Union for the Liberation of Belarus in 1930–1931, which resulted in the arrests of 110 leading figures of Belarusian culture and science. A language reform in 1933 brought the Belarusian alphabet more in line with Russian. Belarusization had ended, to be replaced with repressions.

In the postwar years, Russification became the norm, and the number of Belarusian schools declined. Toward the end of the Soviet period, another revival occurred. In 1990, Belarusian was declared the state language of the republic. Similar events happened in other Soviet republics, but in the BSSR, knowledge of the native language was at a lower level. Moreover, the bulk of publications, scientific, and literary works were in Russian, and the prospects of starting anew made many institutions reluctant to make the switch to Belarusian. Further, most of the teachers lacked sufficient knowledge of the Belarusian language, even in Minsk.

Lukashenka took the drastic step in 1995 of including a referendum question on promoting Russian to a state language, of equal status with Belarusian. The question, placed first on the ballot, was "Do you agree with assigning the Russian language the status equal to that of the Belarusian language?" Over 4 million people voted in favor, 86.8% of the total, and just over 613,500 opposed. There followed widespread closure of Belarusian-language schools, and the Russian language soon intruded into television and radio programs. For some time, the Belarusian language became a symbol of the opposition. Lukashenka himself always gave his speeches in Russian. Political parties such as the Belarusian Popular Front and the Council for Belarusian Culture made the Belarusian language a priority, but they operated on the fringes of public life. By 2024, the former had been banned, and the latter declared an "extremist" organization.

It would be inaccurate, however, to say that Belarusians have adopted Russian culture and language as their own. Undoubtedly, most people speak Russian at home, and slightly less than 30% of the population describe themselves as fluent in Belarusian. Yet 51% maintain that Belarusian is their native language, and over 5 million people have a basic knowledge of it. One can note other distinctive trends. In the early twenty-first century, as relations between the Russian and Belarusian leadership deteriorated, Lukashenka adopted a form of "soft nationalism" that embraced to some degree the distinctiveness of the Belarusian language and even offered some speeches in the native tongue. The campaign was somewhat ritualistic, confined to billboards, advertisements, and television clips, but that is not to say it was ineffective. On public transport and shopping malls, announcements are still provided in Belarusian.

Two other factors enhanced the use of the Belarusian language, which some analysts maintained was limited to elderly villages in settlements that were quickly becoming depopulated. The first was social media and the Internet, where the use of Belarusian enabled some users to join distinctive platforms that permitted them to express views unacceptable to the traditional print media. Younger Belarusians took advantage of opportunities such as the usage of social media platforms of Instagram, *VKontakte* (VK), Facebook, X (Twitter), and others, which expanded rapidly. The government for some time was unable to monitor such activities closely. On some sites, the use of Russian was frowned upon. Belarusian writers, poets, musicians, artists, and actors also used the Belarusian language frequently, thus forming its attractive intellectual or even elite status.

The second was the 2020 uprising that followed the presidential elections of August 9. The development was gradual. During the campaign itself, most candidates were speaking in Russian, including Tsikhanouskaya and her team, and earlier the opposition candidates Viktar Babaryka and Valery Tsapkala. The switch to more native forms was strictly a result of the nationalization of the opposition campaign during the mass protests, but most social media communication was in

Belarusian, alongside the use of the banned national flag and symbols. The increase in usage coincided with the perception of the Russian leadership under Vladimir Putin as hostile once it opted to defend Lukashenka and keep him in power.

Such moves, in turn, moved Lukashenka away from the period of soft nationalism and back to his earlier embracing of Russia. In November 2022, the Minsk regime added the slogan "*Zhyve Belarus*" (Long live Belarus), a traditional greeting between Belarusians, to its list of banned "Nazi" slogans, maintaining that it originated from collaborators with the Nazis during the occupation of Belarus in 1941–1944. In fact, the slogan was coined by Yanka Kupala and used extensively by protesters in 2020. Based on the new ruling, those who use it in public now face prison sentences of up to four years.

Thus, as the 2025 election approached, the critical situation for the Belarusian language remained and the situation has been exacerbated by mass emigration or imprisonment of many of the protesters since 2020 and the bans on cultural institutions and the Belarusian Popular Front. There was at the time of writing no extant organization based in Belarus defending and promoting the Belarusian language, meaning that by default most of the population was using Russian as the language of communication.

Does Belarus have a significant diaspora and where is it located?

Historically, the Belarusian diaspora has been dispersed around the globe with the biggest centers in the United States, continental Europe and the UK, Israel, Russia, and Ukraine. In the 1920s, many inhabitants of Western Belarus also moved to Argentina and spread from there to some countries of South America.

In the 1990s–2000s, there were several waves of Belarusians—their number was never very large—who left Belarus for political reasons. Usually, those waves coincided with post-election repressions, which targeted not only professional politicians, but also active people who were tortured or repressed by the riot police after their participation in post-election demonstrations. Often prominent intellectuals, musicians, and writers became victims of persecution and relocated to other countries.

In this same period, the most famous emigrants were Belarusian writers Vasil Bykau, nominated for the Nobel Prize in literature, and Svetlana Alexievich, who won the Nobel Prize in literature in 2015. Bykau, who was also a cofounder of the Belarusian Popular Front and a strong opponent of Lukashenka and his regime, left for Finland in 1998 and then lived in the Czech Republic, Germany, and France before returning home when his health greatly deteriorated. Bykau died in 2003 in Belarus, and his funeral brought together numerous opponents of Lukashenka and became a political event.

Svetlana Alexievich spent many years in the early 2000s in France, Germany, and Italy before coming back to Belarus in 2013. She had been less critical of the government than many people expected her to be until 2020, when she became part of the Coordination Council Presidium set up by the exiled Tsikhanouskaya. Following her interrogation in the Prosecutor General's Office on September 24, 2020, she left Belarus for Europe shortly afterward. Her books were removed from the school programs in 2021.

Despite waves of political migration, which took place several times since the end of 1990s until 2020, most Belarusians were leaving Belarus for economic and professional reasons. The 2020 protests changed this dynamic. After 2020, tens of thousands of Belarusians left Belarus for political reasons, mainly to Poland, Ukraine, Georgia, and Lithuania. Many relocated their businesses, including many IT start-ups. In this same year, the Polish government initiated the Poland Business Harbour program, enabling thousands of IT experts and dozens of businesses to relocate to Poland and attracting many high-skilled individuals. The program was suspended in

2024 with the change of the Poland's ruling party. Many other IT businesses relocated to Lithuania, Latvia, Cyprus, and the United States. Belarusians managed to open their restaurants, bars, design showrooms, and art galleries. After the start of the full-scale Russian invasion of Ukraine (February 2022), most Belarusians and their businesses moved from there to Poland, thus adding several dozen thousands on to previously immigrated Belarusians.

Most European capitals had Belarusian cultural centers and organized language schools for children, with Warsaw and Vilnius becoming Belarusian meccas abroad. In Warsaw, the Free Belarus Museum, Belarusian Youth Hub, and Belarusian Solidarity Center opened in addition to the Belarusian House, operating since 2011, all uniting Belarusians for cultural, educational, and political activities. The Free Belarus Museum in Warsaw and the Belarusian House in Vilnius had a special mission to collect artifacts connected with the Belarusian uprising of 2020 and the individual protesters. Belarusians abroad started their sports clubs, running and exercising for triathlons together. Belarusian IT and start-up communities united in Warsaw and Vilnius over IMAGURU and Ū Hub organizations. Belarusian women and men launched social clubs and YouTube channels creating a platform to raise issues relevant to the specifically Belarusian female population, such as Women of a Difficult Behavior, Those who Left and who Stayed, Maximalno, and many others.

3

THE MAKING OF MODERN BELARUS

What do we know about the Polack Principality and its development?

The city of Polack (aka Polacak) is located on the Palata River where it meets the Dzvina River and derives its name from the former. Its history is linked with the principality of the same name, and it originated at least by AD 862 when it was founded by the Kryvichans, an East Slavic tribe whose earliest sojourn in the area began at least three centuries earlier. Some scholars believe its origins were much earlier, dating back to the period of the Vikings. Its early known history was framed by its turbulent relations with the principalities of Kyiv and Novgorod, and its territory comprised about 60% of the modern-day Belarusian state, including the future cities of Minsk, Brest, Viciebsk, and Orša. According to the Russian Primary Chronicle, our main source of knowledge about this period, Prince Rurik, the Novgorod ruler, donated the principality to one of his subordinates. The largest and most powerful state of this early medieval period was Kyiv, and the development of Polack and its territory was framed by its relationship with the Prince of Kyiv. The other great rival was Novgorod to the north. Thus Polack was caught between the two and the squabbles of the ruling dynasties. By 992, a Christian eparchy had been established in the city, though the first churches were founded in Druck and Turaŭ.

We know that Polack stood on a main trading route that linked this part of Europe to the old Thracian settlement of Byzantium, which later became known as Constantinople and today is Istanbul. The various stories about this period claim that a Scandinavian called Rahvalod arrived in Polack and ruled there until about 980. It was strategically well placed between Novgorod to the north and Kyiv to the south. The city is linked to the rise of the Kyivan prince Volodymyr, much revered today in both Ukraine and Russia as the founding father of the three East Slavic states Ukraine, Russia, and Belarus, although his connections to Ukraine are the most obvious since there was no Muscovite state in this period. Volodymyr was in Novgorod in 980 and enmeshed in a power struggle with his chief rival, Yaropolk, in Kyiv. He sought to form an alliance with Polack against his rival by marrying the daughter of Rahvalod, Rahneda. She dismissed him, however, and expressed her preference for Yaropolk, believing that Volodymyr was illegitimate.

In the words of the University of London's Andrew Wilson, and perhaps he was not intending to speak literally, Volodymyr "was certainly a bit of a bastard." He raped and abducted Rahneda, after killing her parents and their two sons. A few years later Volodymyr, famously, converted to Christianity, but prior to this act, he had five wives, of whom Rahneda was the fifth, despite her animosity to him. Her sentiments toward him did not dissipate and she evidently attempted to murder him while he was sleeping. Though Volodymyr survived, his marriage ended and he banished both Rahneda and their oldest son, Iziaslau, to Polack, after which she most likely became a nun. He also ordered a new city built for the mother and named after the son. The name was later modified to Zaslaŭje, which is today located near Minsk. Rahneda died in AD 1000 and her son a year later. Iziaslau's son, Brachyslau, became the prince of Polack and ruled for the next forty-three years. After his death, his son—Iziaslau's grandson—Usiaslau "the Bewitcher" ruled until 1101. During Usiaslau's rule, the prince supervised the construction of the St. Sophia Cathedral in Polack, which was built in the 1050s and remains its main landmark today.

Although Polack can be described as an important site in the medieval history of Belarusian lands, its importance gradually declined as other centers emerged, as well as impressive churches in towns like Turau and Druck. By the twelfth century, Polack's authority came under challenge from Minsk, Viciebsk, and Druck. A new enemy emerged in the shape of the Knights of the Sword, a German tribe intent on establishing Christian communities as they advanced along the River Dzvina, encroaching upon the territory of Polack. In a similar vein, the Teutonic Order also penetrated the lands around Polack. The 1240 attack from the east carried out by the Golden Horde Mongol-Tatars devastated Kyiv and most other principalities but left Polack unscathed, although by this time its power was in decline.

What role did Belarusian lands and culture play in the Grand Duchy of Lithuania?

The Grand Duchy of Lithuania covered a vast territory of Europe as an individual entity from the thirteenth to the sixteenth centuries. Even today it is still debated which of the two neighbors—Belarusians and Lithuanians—played a more important role in the creation and development of this medieval state. In addition to the lands of modern-day Belarus and Lithuania, it encompassed the Kyiv, Volyn, and Chernihiv regions of Ukraine, and a part of western Russia. Its ethnic composition also included Poles and Jews. Its foundation is usually attributed to Prince Mindaugas of Lithuania, an obscure figure—his date of birth is unknown—who nonetheless is widely considered to be the founder of the Lithuanian state. By the fifteenth century, the state was the largest in Europe. The common name for its citizens was "Litvins," a term widely used on the territories of Belarus. The city of Brest was called Brest-Litovsk (literally Lithuanian Brest) as late as 1918.

It is frequently pointed out by Belarusian scholars that the vast empire, while founded by Lithuanians, was heavily influenced by the ancestors of modern Belarusians, particularly by the Polack principality. One of the main reasons this large empire emerged was the common need for defense against foreign invaders who included crusaders from the west, the Mongols from the east, and the principality of Galicia-Volyn from the south. The lands of Rus', having accepted Christianity in the late tenth century, also became literate, in contrast to the pagan Lithuanians. Thus, the language used in official business, chronicles, courts, and chancelleries was Old Belarusian, a process that continued until Polish language replaced it gradually in the seventeenth century.

The expansion of the Grand Duchy made further progress under the reign of Alherd (1345–1377, Algirdas in Lithuanian), and now included Chernihiv-Seversk, Volyn, Pereyaslav, the Principality of Smolensk, and territories in the regions of the Dniester, Dniapro, and Buh rivers. Troops led by Alherd achieved a notable victory over the Mongol Golden Horde in 1363, thereby securing the southeast regions of modern-day Belarus, including the important Principality of Turaŭ.

In Belarusian historiography, the rule of Vitaut is believed to be the golden age of the Grand Duchy of Lithuania. Since those years the foundation of multicultural land, composed of Belarusians, Poles, Russians, Ukrainians, Jews, Tatars, and Lithuanians and encompassing the representatives of the large world religions—different confessions of Christianity, Islam, and Judaism—was laid. The Duchy expanded and became the territory "from the (Baltic) sea to the (Black) sea." The Battle of Grunwald of July 15, 1410, which united the armies of two brothers—Yahaila (Władysław II Jagiełło after his baptism in Poland) and Vitaut—defeated the Teutonic Order army and prevented their further expansion deeper into Slavic lands. Remarkably, Vitaut's army included battalions from current-day Lithuanian, Belarusian, Ukrainian, and Russian (Smolensk) lands as well as many Tatar warriors from Khan Tokhtamysh's army, part of the Golden Horde.

Subsequently, Tatars settled compactly in the Belarusian-Lithuanian-Polish borderlands, initially around Lida in Western Belarus, and then spreading further in different directions. Iuje and its vicinities are the most Tatar Belarusian area in the contemporary period. Many Tatars remained Muslims, but some converted to Christianity and became important families, such as the Bahdanoviches (Maksim Bahdanovich was the most important Belarusian poet at the beginning of the twentieth century) and the Sienkiewiczes (Henryk Sinkiewicz was a prominent Polish writer and winner of the Nobel Prize in literature). Thanks to the Tatar population of the Grand Duchy of Lithuania, Belarusian became the only Slavic language which was written using the Arabic script, Belarusian Arabitsa. Books written in that literary tradition were known as "Kitabs," the Arabic word for "books."

In 1385, Lithuanians embraced Catholicism under Grand Duke Yahaila (Władysław II Jagiełło in Polish, the founder of the Jagiellonian dynasty in Poland), who was required to convert in order to take up the Polish throne and marry the Polish queen Jadwiga and adopt the name Władysław II. In 1385, a formal alliance between the Grand Duchy and the Polish state was agreed at Kreva Castle. After some internal disputes, the treaty was modified in 1392 by the Treaty of Ostrava, which permitted the Grand Duchy to maintain its independence, with Prince Vitaut (Vytautas in Lithuanian) of Hrodna as its Grand Duke. Gradually, tension arose in the higher echelons between the Catholics and the Orthodox, though initially most of the Belarusian population adhered to Catholicism. The Grand Duchy underwent a period of civil war in the 1430s, leading to a brief division in the state, during which Polack became the center of a breakaway state under Grand Duke Svidryhaila (Švitrigaila in Lithuanian).

The Grand Duchy increasingly found itself at the center of tense relations between Russia and Poland and drew gradually closer to the latter. It also lost lands to the expanding Muscovite state as Polack and the Baltic States were captured by the Russians. By 1569, with the signing of the Treaty of Lublin, the Grand Duchy of Lithuania and the Kingdom of Poland formed a new state called the Polish-Lithuanian Commonwealth. A few years later, at the Union of Brest in 1596, a Uniate Church was formed, which was subordinated to Rome, meaning in effect that there were now three competing religions on Belarusian lands: Catholicism, Uniates (Greek Catholics), and Orthodox. Belarusian territories also experienced the arrival of Jesuits, who spread their teaching as the Counter-Reformation swept across Europe.

The seventeenth century saw a series of wars between the Commonwealth and Russia that led to devastation of Belarusian land. During the sixteenth century, the Muscovite Duchy attacked the lands of the Grand Duchy of Lithuania five times, physically eliminating local population, cities, and cultural heritage. The Russian Empire was threatening the independence of the Belarusian, Lithuanian, and Polish noble families who elected kings from their own ranks, while Russia was an absolute monarchy at that time. Russians used bribes, violence, and intrigues to drag many aristocratic families, especially those who were poor but still had a noble status and a right to vote, into promoting their interests and destroying the Commonwealth from within. The Livonian War of 1558–1583, when the Muscovites launched a war against the Grand Duchy of Lithuania over the Baltic lands, weakened the latter.

Sporadic wars with Muscovites continued in the seventeenth century. During the wars of 1609–1611 and 1617–1618 with Muscovites, the Grand Duchy managed to regain the Smolensk region. The Khmelnytsky uprising of 1648–1651 (known as the Cossack-peasant war in Belarusian historiography), ultimately leading to the inclusion of Ukrainian lands in the Russian Empire, caused destruction and numerous deaths on Belarusian lands. Only three years later, the Russian government launched another war, which lasted for thirteen years and resulted in the acquisition of Bryansk and Smalensk (Smolensk in Russian) by the Moscow tsars and the reduction of the population of the Belarusian lands by almost half, according to Belarusian historians.

During the years of the existence of the Grand Duchy of Lithuania, Belarusian cities, towns, and people played a crucial role in the development of the country. The noble families, living on the Belarusian territories, belonged to the elite of the rulers of the Duchy and later the Commonwealth, contributing to its intellectual, military, cultural, religious, and industrial evolution. Many of them became members of royal families through marriage, as in the case of Barbara Radzivil (Radziwiłł in Polish). The Sapiehas, the Radzivils, the Khadkevichs, the Ahinskis, and the Pats family formerly owned vast territories, cities and towns, manufactures, and factories. Thousands of Belarusians belonged to the sector of the aristocracy with smaller possessions, many of whom were predecessors of Belarusian national leaders and intellectuals of the early twentieth century. Belarusian was spoken informally in such families, whereas at public events many spoke Latin, and later Polish and other European languages. However, the Statutes of 1529, 1566, and Leu Sapieha's Statute of 1588, composed of legal rules and regulations of those times, were written in Old Belarusian. So, also, was the Bible of Francysk Skaryna, published in 1517 in Prague.

The devastation and degradation of the Polish-Lithuanian Commonwealth continued in the eighteenth century. The Northern War of 1700–1721 dragged the country into another massive military conflict, when the Commonwealth was in an alliance with Russia against Swedish invasions led by Charles XII. While the reasons and course of this war lie outside the scope of this book, suffice it to say that much of contemporary Belarus was subjected to heavy fighting between the various armies. In 1764, Stanisław August Poniatowski became king of Poland. In 1768, the Sejm (the Commonwealth Parliament) issued a resolution on freedom and equality of religion and banned the death penalty for serfs, measures that produced an armed uprising by magnates and gentry against the king, leading him to appeal to Russia for assistance. The move indicated the growing weakness of the Polish-Lithuanian Commonwealth, even though the rebellion was quashed. In 1772, Russia, acting together with Prussia and Austria, partitioned the Commonwealth between them.

The Polish-Lithuanian Commonwealth made several last attempts to resist the partitions. On May 3, 1791, the Commonwealth released the first constitution in Europe, and in 1794 Tadeush Kastsiushka (Tadeusz Kościuszko in Polish), born on what is now Belarusian territory, organized an uprising, uniting thousands of people fighting against the Russian and Prussian monarchies. He managed to escape the Russian tsar's punishment and later became a national hero in France and the United States. Further partitions in 1793 and 1795 ended the Commonwealth's existence permanently, and Poland, together with the Belarusian territories, was erased from the map of Europe until 1918. Belarusian lands thereafter were incorporated into the Russian Empire, where they remained until the First World War.

Who was Kastus Kalinouski and why did he lead a revolt against tsarist Russia in 1863?

Kanstantsin (Kastus) Vintsent Kalinouski was born in the Hrodna region, which is now Podlasie Voivodeship, in Poland in 1838. He originated from a middle-income aristocracy and was very much influenced by his older brother Viktar, who worked in the archives of St. Petersburg and was researching the roots of rich aristocratic families from the lands of the former Grand Duchy of Lithuania. Kastus joined his brother there and spent a lot of time in the libraries and was fascinated by the history of the Grand Duchy of Lithuania and its outstanding people. After Viktar's death from tuberculosis, a deadly disease at that time, the future revolutionist stayed in Saint Petersburg and started his degree at the Law Department of Saint Petersburg University.

Already at the university, Kalinouski was part of the underground anti-tsarist organization, but he managed to graduate with a law degree in 1861 and attempted to find work with the local authorities in Vilnia (now Vilnius), where he intended to start his liberation campaign, but was denied everywhere. He managed to create an underground organization in the Hrodna region and began to lay the groundwork for an uprising.

In 1862, Kalinouski, together with his colleagues Feliks Razhanski, Stanislau Sanhin, and Valery Urubleuski, started to publish the issues of the *Mužyckaja praŭda* (Folk's or Peasant's Truth) newspaper, aimed at peasant populations of the Belarusian lands. His nickname was "Jaśka, a landowner from near Vilnia." The newspaper was written in Belarusian *lacinka* (Latin alphabet) and criticized colonial policies of the Russian Empire toward Belarusians. Kalinouski called Belarus "Litva" and Belarusians "litvins" in his paper, connecting thus the lands and its people to the legacy of the Grand Duchy of Lithuania. The newspaper became very popular and was spread by many peasants, some of whom were, once discovered, sentenced to death by the tsarist Russia.

In autumn 1862, Kalinouski headed a Lithuanian province committee preparing an uprising against the tsarist regime in Belarus and Lithuania. Though a simultaneous uprising erupted in Warsaw in January 1863, Kalinouski rejected Polish control, insisting on independence. He belonged to a radical, "red" wing of the uprising, which wanted to hand all land to the peasants. More moderate, the "white" Warsaw-based wing of the uprising only fought for the re-establishment of the Rzeczpospolita (the Commonwealth in Polish) of Two Nations, led by Poland, in the borders that had existed before the eighteenth-century partitions. The white wing feared the peasantry and opposed a separate division of Belarus and

Lithuania; they managed to withdraw Kalinouski from leadership in 1863 after issuing a common appeal to the people of Belarus and Lithuania. Historians believe that Kalinouski ultimately wanted to establish an independent state as a revived Grand Duchy of Lithuania, an affront to the Polish wing of the uprising.

The tsarist authorities failed to catch Kalinouski until he was betrayed by Vitaut Parfiyanovich, who disclosed that he was living under the name of Ihnat Vitazheniec. His fiancée Maryia Yamant was also arrested, and banished with her family to Siberia for ten years. Kalinouski was imprisoned in Vilnia but managed to leak his "Letters from Beneath the Gallows." In a passage now quoted frequently by anti-Russian and anti-Soviet Belarusians, he wrote: "only then you will live happily, you [Belarusian] people, when there will be no Muscovite above you." On March 22, 1864, Kalinouski was hanged by the Russian authorities in Lukishki square in Vilnia.

For more than a century the figure of Kalinouski fascinated Belarusians. During the Soviet period his memory was glorified, as he was configured into a symbolic protector of the rights of peasants, and enemy of the tsar and the aristocracy. Numerous monuments to Kalinouski sprung up, and many streets were named after him. His legacy was rehabilitated after the fall of the Soviet Union as a hero of the fight for the independence of Belarus and Lithuania from both Russia and Poland. In 1996, the Belarusian authorities established a medal of Kastus Kalinouski, which was only later abolished. From 2006, when anti-Lukashenka protesters occupied the Kastryčnickaja square in the center of Minsk, they named it Kalinouski Square. The Kalinouski Scholarship Program was established at the University of Warsaw in 2006 to support young Belarusians.

In 2017, the remains of Kalinouski were discovered in Vilnius and the DNA match confirmed by the archeologists in 2019. On November 22, 2019, the recently unearthed remains of Kalinouski and the commanders and prominent participants of

1863 uprising were reburied, during a breakthrough ceremony that brought together the leadership of Lithuania, Poland, and Belarus, an event no longer (since 2020 revolution) acknowledged by the state. Kalinouski's legacy was the inspiration for the name of the Belarusian Regiment fighting against Russia's full-scale invasion in Ukraine.

What was the Belarusian People's Republic and how long did it last?

The Belarusian People's Republic (BPR) was a state proclaimed by the Council of the Belarusian Democratic Republic in its Second Constituent Charter on March 9 and declared independent on March 25, 1918, during the First World War. It arose as a logical step for Belarusian national elites who were striving for their autonomy or independence, depending on a political background, from the Russian Empire on the heels of the Bolshevik Revolution. People's republics were founded in Ukraine and Moldova, while the Baltic states declared their full independence with the support of the Germans, fighting the First World War against tsarist Russia at that point.

From 1914 onward, Belarusian territories once again became a battlefield for competing empires, as Germany fought against Russian troops. Many Belarusians were conscripted to military service by the tsarist authorities; and the local population was forced to endure the hardships of war, destruction, and economic decline. Tsar Nicolas II and his milieu tried to save a situation, in which most western territories of the Russian Empire were already occupied, and were powerless to resist the February Revolution of 1917. However, the Bolsheviks organized a coup later in the year, which led to their political victory, but also started a protracted civil war on the territory of the former Russian Empire.

The First All-Belarusian Congress, which included leading Belarusian organizations and representatives of Belarusian, Ukrainian, Russian, Polish, Jewish, and Tatar origin, was held in Minsk in December 1917. They announced the formation of a Belarusian democratic republic, connected to the Russian Democratic Republic. On December 31, they announced the establishment of a temporary Belarusian government, represented by the Executive Committee of the People's Council of Belarus. On January 3, 1918, Aliaksandr Tsvikevich and Symon Rak-Mikhailouski, representatives of Belarusian parties, traveled to Brest to take part in the initial peace negotiations between the Bolsheviks and the Germans, but were turned away. Their next goal was to establish a Belarusian independent army, but the Bolsheviks arrested members of the newly established Central Belarusian Military Council at the end of January 1918.

The Bolsheviks, with the financial support of the Germans, quickly initiated peace negotiations in Brest-Litovsk (today's Brest on the western border of Belarus). The German army was still de facto occupying Belarusian territories when the Bolshevik Party, representing the new government of the Russian lands, and Wilhelmian Germany signed a truce on March 3, 1918. The Ukrainian People's Republic had already declared its independence on January 22, 1918. Germany recognized Ukrainian statehood and signed a separate peace treaty with Ukraine on February 9, 1918. Belarusians, however, were not invited to any stage of the peace negotiations and lost the territories of Belarusian Palesie to Ukraine. According to the Brest peace treaty, the western part of Belarus remained under German occupation until its leaders signed a peace treaty with the Triple Entente.

From 1915 in Vilnia, many Lithuanian, Belarusian, Polish, and Jewish politicians supported the idea of reviving the Grand Duchy of Lithuania in the shape of a confederative Belarusian-Lithuanian state. In January 1918, Belarusian representatives organized a conference in Vilnia, where they proposed the establishment of the Belarusian-Lithuanian confederation. They elected the Vilnia Belarusian Council, headed by Anton Lutskevich. But the Lithuanians had already announced the re-establishment of the Lithuanian state in December 1917, and on February 16, 1918, Belarus declared its independence.

On February 19, 1918, the Bolsheviks fled from Minsk, and two days later the Executive Committee of the Council of the All-Belarusian Congress published its first Constituent Charter, whereby the Executive Committee declared itself the only source of power over Belarusian lands. However, German troops arrived in Minsk on the same day and took full control of the city by February 25. As the peace negotiations with the Bolsheviks were concluding, the Germans wished to stymie the activities of the All-Belarusian Congress. Nevertheless, on March 9, 1918, the Second Constituent Chapter, announcing the establishment of the Belarusian People's Republic (BPR), was published. The Council of the Republic declared its independence on March 25, 1918. The territory of the BPR included the Minsk and Mahilioŭ regions and parts of Vilnia, Viciebsk, Hrodna (including Białystok and Bielsk), Smolensk, and Chernihiv regions, as well as Suwałki, Kouna, and Pskov areas, populated by Belarusians.

Neither Germany nor Bolshevik Russia recognized the BPR. However, the Germans allowed its leadership to remain active, with the exception of the establishment of an independent army. By the autumn of 1918, the BPR was officially recognized by Lithuania, Latvia, Estonia, Finland, Ukrainian People's Republic, Czechoslovakia, Armenia, Georgia, and later Austria. Following the German Revolution and armistice of November 8, 1918, the German army retreated, leaving the Belarusian territory to the Bolshevik army. The final meeting of the Council of the Republic took place on November 28, 1918. Its government left Minsk on December 3, 1918.

Prior to its demise, the Belarusian People's Republic confirmed its temporary constitution and renamed the Secretariat of the Council of People's Ministers, among whom were important Belarusian intellectuals. Anton Lutskevich was council chairman and minister of foreign affairs; Arkadz Smolich, minister of education; Ales Tsvikevich, minister of justice; Vasil

Zakharka, minister of finance; Yazep Varonka, minister of interior affairs; and Liavon Zayats, minister of control.

They continued their political activities in Vilnia, before escaping Polish troops in 1919 and moving to Berin, and then moving to Paris in the summer of 1919. Ultimately most of the BPR representatives did settle in Prague by 1921. But many returned to Minsk, which was already under the Belarusian Socialist Soviet Republic, attracted by the "Belarusization" taking place at the time (see Chapter 4). In the 1930s most of the leaders were killed in Stalinist purges, and those representatives who survived fled abroad.

The memory of the Belarusian People's Republic was revived after Belarus became independent in 1991. Whereas previously school textbooks had omitted it, many historians began to more closely research the formation of the BPR. Before Lukashenka came to power, the BPR declaration of independence, known as "Freedom Day," was celebrated by the Belarusian Popular Front and its followers yearly. Later, these marches were prohibited and only in 2019, 101 years later, was the anniversary of the BPR celebrated as a major holiday on- and offline, in Belarus and abroad, including a huge concert in Minsk. Many historians still dispute the legacy of the BPR, but most perceive it as a first step to true Belarusian independence, established finally in 1991.

4

SOVIET BELARUS (THE BSSR)

How was the Belarusian SSR (Byelorussian Soviet Socialist Republic) formed?

The departure of the German army from Belarusian lands began after the end of the First World War, although it took several months to complete. In the wake of the Germans' retreat, the leaders of the Belarusian People's Republic followed initially to Vilnia (the Belarusian name for Vilnius). Their flight on December 3, 1918, created a void of power that was exploited temporarily by the regional variants of the Russian Bolshevik Party (then still known as the Russian Social Democratic Workers' Party). Nine days later, the Red Army occupied Minsk and took over the government, although a few members of the BPR remained behind, hoping it might be possible to work with the Russians to renew a Belarusian state. They included Yazep Losik, who had taken over as BPR president from Yanka Sierada on May 14, 1918, and remained its leader until the government disbanded.

A Workers' and Peasants' government known formally as the Soviet Socialist Republic of Belarus (SSRB) was declared at an All-Belarusian Congress in Smolensk on January 1, 1919, the date that the Soviet regime retained subsequently as the official founding date of the BSSR. In Soviet parlance, the VI Congress of the Russian Communist Party (Bolsheviks) of the

Northwest Province made the declaration. The Conference then renamed itself as the First Congress of the Communist Party of Belarus (CPB). Two days later, a manifesto of the Soviet Worker-Peasant Government announced the creation of the Soviet Socialist Republic of Byelorussia headed by Zmitser Zhylunovich. It encompassed a wide area, including parts of Smolensk, Vilnia, Chernihiv, and Kovno, and the entire regions of Minsk, Mahilioŭ, Hrodna, and Viciebsk.

Although ostensibly the idea of an independent Belarusian state remained prominent, there was considerable opposition among the rival groups in Vilna, Minsk, and Smolensk, with the majority in favor of remaining part of the Russian state. The initial BSSR therefore could be described as a rump state comprising only six districts of the Minsk region. Viciebsk, Mahilioŭ, and Smolensk regions had by this time been transferred to Soviet Russia. On January 8, the newly formed socialist government migrated from Smolensk to Minsk. The deputies created a constitution for the new state but also voted to merge with the Lithuanian Soviet Socialist Republic that had been declared two weeks earlier. In late February, the two republics formed a combined state known as LitBel, known more formally as the Lithuanian-Byelorussian Soviet Socialist Republic, led by the Lithuanian revolutionary Vincas Mickevičius-Kapsukas as chairman and minister of foreign affairs.

LitBel lasted for seven months before it became a victim of a new war between Poland and Soviet Russia. The newly emerged Polish state, restored after more than 120 years, and led by Józef Piłsudski, was anxious to regain its ancestral lands. The Polish invasion began on August 8, 1919, and the Poles occupied Minsk the following month. The Bolshevik regime fled, but the BPR leaders returned to the capital, hopeful that the Polish occupation would signify a revival of the People's Republic. Piłsudski appeared to be quite accommodating, but there were different opinions among the Polish leadership regarding the aspirations of the minorities now living under their military rule. Piłsudski's chief rival for power in Poland was Roman Dmowski, with whom he had clashed several times in the past. By 1919, Piłsudski was the provisional head of state and commander in chief of the armed forces, but Dmowski represented Poland at the Paris Peace Conference dealing with the end of the First World War and the allocation of European territories after the defeat of Germany.

The main difference between the two Polish leaders was, in simple terms, that Piłsudski possessed a more enlightened attitude and saw himself as the leader of a multi-ethnic state that harkened back to the Polish-Lithuanian Commonwealth and his own background in the Polish socialist party. In that state, all ethnic groups would have equal rights. Dmowski, on the other hand, perceived the future as a Polish state ruling over its ethnic and religious minorities. As a result of the ambivalent nature of Polish rule, Belarusians in the BPR not only began to question the benefits of Polish rule but became divided over policies. A rift emerged in the BPR Rada between those who sought cooperation with the Polish rulers and believed that the Belarusian state might be achieved through federation, and those who feared becoming a colony of Poland. In July 2020, as the Red Army mounted a counterattack and moved into Polish territories, the former group led by Anton Lutskevich retreated with the Poles to Warsaw; the latter faction under Vatslau Lastouski moved to Kaunas.

The Red Army failed to capture Warsaw, and the Poles once again marched into the main towns of Belarus. The eastern border of Poland became a topic for the Great Powers in the discussions in Paris. Making the debates even more complex was the question of Vilnia and whether it should be included in Poland or Lithuania. The city was also the cultural center of Belarusian life, and the Kaunas group was prepared to respond to the solicitations of the Lithuanian government for support against Polish demands. Lithuanians assumed that the future of Vilnius would be decided by plebiscite and appealed to the Belarusians for their support. The BPR faction based in the city agreed to support Lithuania's cause in return for financial help for their own government and autonomous status for Belarusian-speaking parts of Vilnia and Hrodna. The Poles had intended in turn to seek help from the BPR faction, but the plebiscite never happened. Poland incorporated the Vilnia region, and cooperation between the BPR in Lithuania and the Lithuanian government ended. The Lastouski group then moved from Kaunas to Prague.

For Belarusians in the democratic movement, the Paris Peace Conference was a huge disappointment because their territorial claims never received a hearing. The Great Powers—Britain, France, United States, and Italy—had little knowledge of Belarus and did not even consider the question of autonomous regions. Belarusians had no control over any territory and were thus ignored. The Polish-Soviet war ended with the Treaty of Riga of March 18, 1921, and Poland retained the western regions of Belarus. The border was drawn just to the west of the city of Minsk, and thus the cities of Białystok (Bielastok in Belarusian), Brest (Litovsk), and Hrodna were incorporated into Poland. Soviet Byelorussia reappeared on the European map, limited to six districts of the Minsk region, and comprising just over 1.5 million people. It was later expanded (1924 and 1926) by the addition of ethnic territories that had been incorporated into Soviet Russia, that is, in Homiel, Viciebsk, and Smolensk regions.

In December 1922, the smaller version of the BSSR, limited to the Minsk region, was one of the signatories of the foundation of the Union of Soviet Socialist Republics (USSR), along with Russia, Ukraine, and the Transcaucasian SSR. The republic was in a dire situation after the lengthy years of warfare, destruction of property, and curtailment of agricultural production. The demise of the BPR left a rump state under the control of Moscow, with a small, mostly illiterate population. However, the very fact of the formation of the BSSR as a founding member of the USSR was a recognition, by Lenin in particular, of the Belarusian aspirations for their own state.

And in the 1920s there was some hope that the BSSR could be a viable replacement of the BPR, as the Soviet authorities introduced milder economic policies and promoted Belarusian culture and language. Perhaps the most notable achievement of the 1920s was the establishment of the Belarusian Academy of Sciences, the introduction of the Belarusian language into schools, the production of Belarusian textbooks, and the rapid elimination of illiteracy. The progress was quite remarkable and the first injection of Belarusian content into society since the early years of the twentieth century (see below).

How were Stalin's purges implemented in Belarus and who were the main victims?

The Belarusian SSR was a relatively tolerant place in the 1920s as the period generally adhered to Lenin's dictum that national republics could be "nationalist in form, socialist in content." As a result, the BSSR became a form of nation building not seen before, one that recognized Belarusians as a distinct entity, perhaps as a legacy of the Belarusian People's Republic of 1918. The rise of Stalin and the change of economic policy to collectivization of agriculture and heavy industrialization took place amid a general atmosphere of suspicion. To some extent, these changes reflected Stalin's personality. He was ruthless toward his actual and perceived opponents. He created class enemies among the peasantry by dividing them into social strata, with the wealthier, and often more hard-working, peasants—the kulaks—as the main target of a war in the villages. The kulaks were accused of joining the new collective farms to destroy them from within. The accusation translated into a system of mutual suspicion, jealousy of those who had property or livestock, and denunciations abounded.

In the towns, now filled with migrants from the countryside, the atmosphere was similar. The party organizations and courts were not capable of taking on the thousands of cases of alleged Trotskyites, Zinovievites, spies working for hostile countries, priests and representatives of other religions, saboteurs, and members of fabricated political parties, yet all of these enemies "reportedly" sought to overthrow Stalin and the Soviet regime. In the towns, troikas were created and could try people without any legal defenses. The purges began at the start of the 1930s but escalated after December 1, 1934, when a jealous assassin shot Sergey Kirov, the party leader of the city of Leningrad and a close friend of Stalin, in his own headquarters. At least 5,000 people were rounded up in that city alone, all accused of the murder of Kirov. The main victims of the ensuing crackdown were Grigory Zinoviev and Lev Kamenev, two close associates of Lenin who had been part of the collective leadership that led the country after the death of Lenin in early 1924. Together with Trotsky, they had formed the last real opposition to Stalin, who now had eliminated them, but chose to target thousands who were supposedly associated with them. The peak of the terror was 1937–1938, when thousands were arrested and charged with unimaginable crimes.

The first purges occurred in 1930–1931 and were directed against a nonexistent anti-Soviet group called the Union for the Liberation of Belarus. The actual targets were leaders of the Belarusian cultural elite. Eight-six people were arrested, the most prominent of which was Usevalad Ihnatouski, president of the Belarusian Academy of Scientists. Without waiting for a trial, Ihnatouski committed suicide by flinging himself out of a fifth-floor window of the OGPU (then special secret services) building in central Minsk. Whereas these first victims were members of the intelligentsia, the next victims were from another fake group called the Peasant Liberation Party supposedly operating in the Pukhavičy district of Minsk region. A troika put 110 "kulaks" on trial, of whom 101 were sentenced to death, with the sentence carried out in April 1933. All the victims were to be rehabilitated in 1956 after Nikita Khrushchev's denunciation of Stalin.

A third target was the Communist Party of Belarus (CPB), almost 11,000 members of which were exposed as "enemies of the people" in the period 1934–1936. In the years 1937–1938, however, the numbers increased rapidly and over 40,000 were expelled from the party. The scourge of "Trotskyism-Zinovievism" (alleged followers of Lev Trotsky and Grigory Zinoviev) had clearly penetrated the highest echelons of the party apparatus, so it was not surprising that the party leaders themselves fell victims to the firing squads. Nikolay Gikalo (Mykola Hykalo), a former Ukrainian revolutionary who had joined the Bolshevik Party in 1917, had been party leader in the BSSR since January 18, 1932. On March 18, 1937, he was arrested, having been removed from his position a day earlier, accused of plotting against the Soviet state, and was executed over a year later on April 25, 1938.

His successor was Vasil Sharanhovich (Vasily Sharangovich), who was tasked with rooting out the "traitors" in the party; he began at the highest level, ordering the arrest of government leaders who were opposed to the purges. They included the head of the Belarusian government, Mikalai Haladzied, and the chair of the Executive Committee of the Supreme Soviet, Aliaksandr Charviakou. Haladzied died under interrogation, and Charviakou, after being denounced by Sharanhovich at the 16th Party Congress of the CPB, committed suicide. Both Second Secretaries of the CPB were also executed as the party declined in membership numbers from 47,000 to 31,500. Almost inevitably, Sharanhovich did not survive long himself. He was replaced on July 27, 1937, by the Belarusian Communist Yakov Yakovlev and forced to confess that he had been a Polish spy since 1921, as well as being a member of a Trotskyist-Bukharinist faction (thereby combining both the Left and Right Opposition). Sharanhovich was then among the accused at the Third Moscow Show Trial in 1938, where Nikolay Bukharin was the main target.

As for Yakovlev, he lasted precisely twelve days as party leader of the BSSR before he was recalled to Moscow. An enthusiastic supporter of all-out collectivization, he had served earlier as minister of agriculture, but he and Stalin had different views on how the sowing campaign should be organized. Yakovlev also supported Trofim Lysenko, an agronomist who had rejected the theories of Mendelian genetics in favor of his own pseudo-scientific studies. By mid-October Yakovlev had been arrested, and in December, expelled from the Central Committee of the Communist Party and accused of spying for Nazi Germany. He also featured in the Third Moscow Show Trial, by which time he was supposedly associated with Bukharin, the proponent of the New Economic Policy, the antithesis of Yakovlev's beliefs. His execution was delayed until July 29, 1938. Thus, the position of Belarusian party leader was one of the riskiest positions to hold in the Soviet Union. Stability returned with the subsequent appointment of Panteleimon Ponamarenko, an advocate of deeper purges, who remained in the office until 1947.

Events in Belarus did not occur in a vacuum but rather mirrored events taking place in Moscow and in other republics. Following the attacks on kulaks and party leaders, the NKVD state security department was itself purged. The official term for the accused was the "United Anti-Soviet Underground" (UASU) and the official narrative was that it had carried out sabotage of industry, espionage, terrorism, and insurgency. The UASU also allegedly embraced numerous organizations, very few of which existed in any form, including Trotskyists, Zionists, members of the Socialist Revolutionary Party, and Menshevik Party, the two rival socialist parties of the Bolsheviks since the early twentieth century, but which had been thoroughly defeated before the end of the 1920s. The process of accusations and trials by military tribunals and troikas continued through the period 1937–1938, in the former case most often with an invited audience of "Stakhanovite" shock workers, who jeered those in the dock and called for their execution.

Belarus was also the location for some of the NKVD operations against ethnic nationals, particularly the Poles and Latvians, although other groups were also targeted.

On August 11, 1937, NKVD chief Nikolay Yezhov signed Order 00485, which demanded the liquidation of the Polish Military Organization, but in practice carried out a sweeping series of arrests of Poles and others under suspicion who were living in the area between Minsk and the Polish border. Almost 140,000 Poles were arrested on Soviet territory, out of which over 110,000 received the death sentence. In the BSSR, the respective numbers were approximately 21,000 arrested and 18,600 executed. A further 1,500 were rounded up in the Latvian Operation, with some of the bodies uncovered after 2014 in the regions of Viciebsk and Orša. Some Poles were executed at Kurapaty (see below).

The total numbers of those arrested, executed, and/or deported have been debated by Western historians for years. Precise numbers are difficult to determine because of the secrecy with which many of the executions were conducted, and the fact that many of those deported remained in the areas of exile. If one looks at the entire period between the Bolshevik Revolution in 1917 until the death of Stalin, then in the territories that eventually formed the BSSR, about 250,000 people were arrested for political "crimes," most of them without due cause. Other sources have maintained that up to 1.5 million may have been arrested between the 1920s and 1950s on Belarusian territory. About 86,000 people were deported from the territory of the BSSR in the 1930s, with more deportations carried out in the newly annexed territories of Western Belarus (about 123,500 people), which was part of Poland before September 1939. Thus over 200,000 residents of the BSSR were removed from their homes, an astonishing figure, given the population of around 5 million.

The number of people executed was smaller, but still significant. Although sources vary dramatically on the number, the minimum figure is around 7,500, and if one includes the population incorporated after September 1939, it may have been up to 30,000. By some margin, the peak years were 1937–1938, but the totals in 1940–1941 are less well known or documented.

The closure of the KGB archive in Minsk since 1994 has meant that we are reliant on official government sources in Moscow and the Belarusian capital, which are inclined to downplay the totals. The discovery of a number of mass graves over the past decade has not resulted in official inquiries, and some of the historians in a position to uncover this information have lost their jobs since 2020 or have fled abroad.

In terms of social composition of the victims, perhaps nine out of ten were males between the ages of eighteen and fifty, and a similar proportion were from the peasantry, indicating that ethnic Belarusians were the main victims (around 65%), with a high number of Poles (17%). Only about 11% were members of the Communist Party, but as noted those came from the highest echelons of the party. Over one-third of the charges emanated from troikas rather than the main legal authorities. Over 82% of the cases involved treason, espionage, anti-state acts, or attempts to overthrow the Soviet government, and in almost all of these allegiance to Trotsky, Zinoviev, or Bukharin was cited as the reason for arrest. In the late 1950s and late 1980s, under the leadership of Khrushchev and Gorbachev respectively, most of those charged were rehabilitated.

What happened at Kurapaty?

The memorial site at Kurapaty in the northern part of Minsk—about 8 miles north of the city center—is believed to be the main killing ground of Stalin's NKVD. Originally, the nearby village was known as Brod. Although the history of the site was not completely unknown, it became prominent in the late 1980s during the peak of Gorbachev's *glasnost*, when a program of de-Stalinization was initiated that exposed many of the crimes committed under Stalin's rule, mostly those from the 1930s. An archeologist, Zianon Pazniak, and an engineer, Yauhen Shmyhaliou, wrote a major article entitled "Kurapaty: The Road of Death" in the Belarus Writers' Union newspaper *Litaratura i Mastatstva* (Literature and Art) concerning a major burial site they had uncovered in the Kurapaty Forest. Pazniak and Shmyhaliou had collected testimony of eyewitnesses to NKVD executions that took place between the years 1937 and 1941 at a killing site 2 miles north of Zialony Luh. Two schoolboys playing in the forest had been the first to (re)discover the graves; although they were found in the mid-1950s, Pazniak only became aware of them in the 1970s. The scientific work there was done in 1988 by the team of Zianon Pazniak, Mikalai Kryvaltsevich, and Alei Iou.

These eyewitness accounts, contributed by fifty-five people, recalled events as follows: The killings initially took place three times per day at dawn, 2 P.M., and sunset, but eventually occurred throughout the day. A former soldier reported that the victims received a bullet to the side of the head while standing in a line so that more than one was killed by the shot. The NKVD then threw the bodies into a pit and at some point constructed a fence around the site, which was already becoming flattened by the constant arrival of "black ravens" cars. The bodies continued to be piled into the pits until about sixty corpses had been flung there. Subsequently, the Soviet authorities planted pine trees on some of the graves. Having been alerted by the schoolboys, Pazniak and his colleague examined the site but were unsure how to proceed and how to publicize what they had found. For context, the discovery of mass graves was occurring across the Soviet Union. Around this same time a mass grave was discovered at Bykivnia, near Kyiv, for example.

Pazniak and Shmyhaliou had difficulty publishing their account of their findings. They received encouragement from Vasil Bykau, the renowned writer and chronicler of Belarus in the Second World War. Bykau agreed to write an introduction to the article. In the original version of the article, the two authors had speculated on the number of victims, assessing that based on the number of graves and corpses in each, the total of dead must have been somewhere between 150,000 and 500,000. We now know that such totals were greatly inflated.

They were also asked to delete sections of the article that referred to the execution of victims who were arrested after the annexation of Western Belarus in September 1939. The article's publication caused a sensation in the BSSR. The Council of Ministers in Minsk felt obligated to respond by setting up a government commission to investigate the findings of Pazniak and Shmyhaliou, who were included among the members.

The initial commission included many figures who would not have been expected to produce an objective account. Its chair was Nina Mazai, a deputy chairman of the BSSR Council of Ministers, and its other representatives were from the government and Communist Party, Nikolay Kovalev, deputy chair of the KGB, former heroes of partisan brigades, and well-known workers. Bykau was also allowed to join it, but Pazniak and Shmyhaliou were excluded. It completed its report between July and November 1988, a mere four months to deal with such a complex phenomenon.

Its findings, nonetheless, were remarkably clear. There were 510 burial sites, each containing 50–60 corpses, meaning that at least 30,000 victims were located in the forest. Bullet cartridges discovered were from Nagan revolvers and TT pistols, made in the Soviet Union between 1928 and 1939. Over 3,000 objects found in the graves were examined by scientific, medical, and legal experts, including shoe fragments, coins, and clothing. When the Nazis arrived in the region in the summer of 1941, they had cut down the forest and removed the fence. The returning Soviet authorities had replanted new trees in the 1940s and 1950s. The commission found out little about the identity of the victims but concluded that the NKVD was responsible for the crimes.

The report, though revealing, did not satisfy Zianon Pazniak, who insisted that the identity of the victims was known. Evidence of concealment is clear. The KGB representative on the commission, Kovalev, refused a request by Latvian investigator Vadim Shershov to access the KGB archives even though it was well known that before executions, the NKVD always solicited a confession from the accused and produced a certificate confirming that the sentence had been carried out. Kovalev also informed Shershov that the Nazis had established two concentration camps containing prisoners from the Soviet army quite close to Kurapaty. The comment raised doubt that the crime was the responsibility of the NKVD. As with the more famous NKVD executions of Polish officers carried out at Katyń and two other camps, Kurapaty could also be obfuscated by laying the blame on the invading army—admittedly it had carried out similar and even more heinous crimes on Belarusian territory.

For Pazniak, the response constituted a cover-up. He was convinced that the intention of the Soviet rulers was to eliminate Belarusians and that the events at Kurapaty were part of an organized "genocide." Even before the final report was published, he organized in response a group known as "Martyrology of Belarus," which was dedicated to the victims of Stalinism in Belarus. He and others also created a committee to establish an opposition group—the Belarusian Popular Front—led by Pazniak. The only material result of the commission's report was a small plaque and wooden cross at the Kurapaty mass grave site. The idea of a lengthier examination of the findings of the two authors of the article never emerged, and before long, members of the commission, including a former partisan commander Ivan Zaharadniuk and Hero of the Soviet Union Maryia Osipava, formed an independent commission that concluded the Germans and not the NKVD were responsible for the massacre. The dates for the deaths were thus advanced into the period of German occupation—summer to December 1941—and the issue of the guns was resolved by the statement that the Nazis had purloined the weapons from Soviet troops as they advanced.

Thereafter the very question of Kurapaty became associated with the opposition and the Belarusian Popular Front in particular. The Communist Party establishment set up more commissions to try to reinforce the interpretation that blamed

Nazi Germany for the massacres. One was led by Maryia Osipava, which once again focused attention on the Germans and the fact that many victims had mugs, bowls, razors, jewelry, and other goods that would not have been allowed for prisoners. However, by 1993, the State List of Objects of Historical and Cultural Value of the Republic of Belarus included the "Kurapaty tract" as a burial ground for the victims of the Stalinist repressions of the 1930s and 1940s. There was much conjecture about the origins of the name. Pazniak thought that it derived from young children who had observed white flowers growing on the mass graves in the springtime. The word "kurapaty" logically originated from "partridges," whose wings reminded local inhabitants of the shame of Kurapaty hills. Another version of the origin of the name is a changed version of "Karpaty" mountains.

The state prosecutor at this time was Aleh Bazhelka, who was highly critical of the initial commission, which he claimed was one-sided and facing pressure from "nationalists." He dismissed the testimony of eyewitnesses because of the passage of time and commented that some of them were under the age of six. He maintained in 2000 that the death toll was about 7,000, a figure that has also been cited by one of the Russian state's main historians, Aleksandr Dyukov. Such comments testify to the politicization of the Kurapaty question, and the corresponding difficulty to maintain it as a memory site on the same level as the official state memorial at Chatyń, dedicated to the victims of the Great Patriotic War and opened in July 1969. But even in 1988, Kurapaty was a highly controversial finding. The initial procession of commemoration on October 30, 1988 (also the date of the memory of ancestors and used in Belarus to remember the murdered poets in 1937; see below), was disrupted by troops of the Ministry of Internal Affairs, who used a gas spray to try to disperse the crowd. They also tried to block the path of the procession, at Kurapaty itself, but, led by Pazniak, thousands gathered in an open field near the forest and held a prayer service.

This symbolic act engraved Kurapaty as the national shrine for the victims of Stalin. But it also antagonized the authorities, who still comprised many hardline Communists. In 1994, when President Bill Clinton visited Belarus, he insisted on being taken to Kurapaty, to the consternation of some of his hosts. There, on behalf of the United States, he donated a memorial stone bench to the victims buried there, which became a target for vandals, likely with the encouragement of the Belarusian authorities. Clinton's visit came just a few months before Aliaksandr Lukashenka was elected president of the country, and just prior to the dismissal of his host, Stanislau Shushkevich, as chairman of the parliament. The new leader was plainly unenthusiastic about the memorial, which ran counter to his desire to elevate the Great Patriotic War as the defining symbol of the Belarusian state and the corresponding veneration of partisans and veterans generally.

In 2001, the Minsk authorities announced the construction of the Moscow Ring Road (M9) through the Kurapaty Forest. The Popular Front and other organizations held rallies and vigils to prevent road work. In 2001–2002, there were numerous clashes between riot police and those "defending" the Kurapaty site. Some were quite violent. On October 8–9, 2001, police applied tear gas and detained over forty people, who had objected to builders working in a zone that required the supervision of archeologists to ensure that none of the gravesites were affected by the construction. In October 2007, unknown vandals destroyed the "Cross of Suffering" at the center of the forest.

In the summer of 2018, several entrepreneurs, some of whom were not citizens of Belarus, opened a restaurant called "Let's Go Eat" on the boundary of the Kurapaty memorial. Pavel Seviaryniec, a prominent critic of Lukashenka, suggested that the protests against the restaurant should be held around the clock and based on a tent city. Many regarded the restaurant, which was a large entertainment complex, as offensive because of its location and the gaudy advertisement signs in the area around it, very close to the original plaque established for the Kurapaty site in the late 1980s. The main political parties that became involved in protecting the Kurapaty site included the Conservative Christian Party of the Belarusian Popular Front—the BPF divided into two separate groups from 1999—and the unregistered Belarusian Christian Democratic Party.

The main concession to the Kurapaty defenders was the establishment of an official monument on November 6, 2018, with the permission of the Ministry of Culture of the Republic of Belarus and the attendance at the official ceremony of an official from the Federation of Trade Unions, and adorned with a bell, standing between the main large crosses. No high government officials attended. One might have expected the normalization of Kurapaty as an official commemorative site subsequently. But the president was incensed that activist Zmitser Dashkevich and others had added more crosses on the borders of the forest. On March 1, 2019, Lukashenka made a speech in which he banned further demonstrations and erection of crosses around the Kurapaty perimeter. The Ministry of Forestry received instructions to demolish the additional crosses, which the government claimed had been installed without permission. On April 4, 2019, some seventy crosses were hacked down. Minsk Oblast State Construction evidently sent a letter to Dashkevich, who had collected money for the crosses, demanding the removal of thirteen crosses, but he received it a day after the crosses had been destroyed and two weeks prior to the deadline cited in the letter.

The destruction of crosses provoked worldwide condemnation, as well as from Belarusian human rights activists and churches of all three main denominations in Belarus. Pazniak referred to the actions as "open warfare against the Belarusian people," and Nobel Prize laureate Svetlana Alexievich condemned the lack of respect for memory of the victims executed there. The image of the destruction of crosses offended people of all religions and was an act of unusual insensitivity even for the hardline ruler of Belarus. Lukashenka, unabashed, next ordered the construction of a fence around the entire perimeter of Kurapaty, preventing further visitations to end not only the memorial site, but also discussions about the victims and their backgrounds.

After the uprising of 2020, many historians were removed from their posts, including the most prolific writer on Kurapaty, Ihar Kuzniatsou of the Belarusian State University. Kuzniatsou had ignited debates about the identities of the victims with his insistence on the inclusion of a significant number of Poles. Pazniak countered that Kurapaty is the site of the attempted genocide of Belarusians by the Stalinist state in Moscow. Both, however, concur that the number of victims is far higher than the 7,000 cited by the former Prosecutor-General Bazhelka, as well as the 30,000 established by the first Government Commission in 1988. In our 2020 article, we maintain that the 30,000 total may be closer to reality than the figures cited by either Pazniak or Kuzniatsou.

The bigger problems after 2020 are twofold: first, the removal and likely incarceration of anyone focusing on research on the Stalin Purges; and second, the continued closure of the KGB archives that could reveal information about the victims of these crimes. Comparisons are often made with the memorial site at Chatyń, which receives substantial financial support from the government and Lukashenka personally. By contrast, little progress has been made on uncovering all the victims of the massacres buried at Kurapaty. Yet they form part of the same era, the same violence, albeit conducted by two different totalitarian regimes. And while Chatyń represents a crime of the occupants and their collaborators, at Kurapaty, most of the corpses were executed by their own government.

What was the Night of the Murdered Poets, October 29–30, 1937?

The night of October 29–30, 1937, in Belarusian independent historiography is called the Night of the Murdered Poets or Black Night. On that day, 108 Belarusians representing the highest level of Belarusian intellectuals, including writers, poets, academics, scientists, and politicians, were shot in Minsk NKVD prison and at Kurapaty. Among the murdered people, twenty-two were poets, writers, and literary critics. Several of them, including Moyshe Kulbak, were of Jewish origin, writing in Yiddish, and had contributed to world Yiddish literature.

This night became one of the darkest moments in Belarusian history as it negatively influenced the development of Belarusian culture, literature, and science, after many of their brightest representatives were physically eliminated during the 1930s Stalinist purges and especially in 1936–1938, the climax of the purges in the USSR. The vast majority of the people killed in those years were rehabilitated and proven to be innocent after Khrushchev came into power in Moscow and denounced Stalin's crimes at the 20th Party Congress of the CC CPSU.

People killed on the Night of the Murdered Poets attracted special attention after the discovery of Kurapaty, as it was confirmed by members of their families and documentary proof that many of them had been killed there. Thus, Kurapaty obtained additional significance in Belarusian national history as the place of the physical destruction of people who were a driving force of Belarusianization in the 1920s–1930s and contributed largely to the crystallization of the Belarusian nation, being part of the USSR at that time.

The fact that many Belarusians of Jewish origin were killed there was taken into consideration when an official memorial was erected in 2018. The monument included words in all four languages that were official in the BSSR between 1922 and 1936—Belarusian, Polish, Russian, and Yiddish. A special stone commemorating Jews killed on that night is also situated at Kurapaty with inscriptions in Yiddish and Hebrew. In the period between the 1990s and the 2020s, musicians, artists, and writers devoted their works to the commemoration of that night and the NKVD victims killed at that time.

Popular interest in that date recurred in 2017, when a musical critic, Siarhei Budkin, together with a group of Belarusian musicians and researchers, launched the project Unshot Poetry. A special website dedicated to this project gathered all the elements of the activities carried out before the eightieth anniversary of that date. Researchers and literary critics gave a series of lectures about the life of the executed writers and poets, whereas the musicians wrote songs using poetry of the murdered poets. Simultaneously, a group of political activists, previously protesting at Kurapaty, such as Zmitser Dashkevich and Pavel Sieviaryniec and many others, started organizing an annual gathering at Kurapaty that night where all participants could volunteer and read out verses of the killed poets. People could also bring candles and leave them at Kurapaty, thus making it a night of commemoration of Stalinist victims, in addition to an annual Dziady march, which had been held since 1988 from the city center to Kurapaty on the day of Dziady, which is not fixed and, depending on the year, might be at the end of October or beginning of November.

After 2020, all the commemoration activities of the Night of the Murdered Poets moved abroad, due to the scale of repressions in Belarus and the special sensitivity of the topic of Kurapaty for Lukashenka and his associates. Activist Belarusians have set up a website, nochpaetau.com, where they document not only the details of the tragedy and biographies of the victims, but also commemorative events organized by Belarusians globally, starting from 2021. Thus, the memory of that night became digitalized and the responsibility of the Belarusian diaspora.

How were Belarusian lands reunified in September 1939?

The reunification of Belarusian lands and westward expansion of the BSSR occurred essentially without any local input. In the western regions, the population was not politically active to the same degree as its counterpart in Western Ukraine. Neither the Polish nor the Soviet government of the 1930s was interested in the development of a Belarusian national entity, and the leftist political elements on the Polish side of the border were left rootless after the dissolution of the Communist Party of Poland in July 1938 on Stalin's orders to the Comintern. At the same time, the annexation of Belarusian lands was received positively by much of the population, and for Belarusian Jews in cities like Bialystok, Brest, and Hrodna (and initially Vilnia/ Vilnius), Soviet rule was preferable to living under a Nazi regime.

The foundation for unification was the agreement between Hitler and Stalin on August 23, 1939, a controversial agreement that was presented to the world as a non-aggression pact to prevent a war breaking out between two states that were ideologically opposed. Much of the political narrative of the 1930s was taken up by anti-Soviet rhetoric from Berlin and anti-Nazi or anti-Fascist statements from Moscow. In 1936–1939, Stalin backed the leftist government in Spain in its efforts to prevent a takeover by Franco's Fascist forces. As at the Paris Peace Treaties, Belarus was no more than a pawn on the chessboard, though the foundations of the contemporary state owe much to these maneuvers of the two dictators.

The terms of the Secret Protocol of the Molotov-Ribbentrop Pact between Stalin's USSR and Nazi Germany divided the Second Polish Republic between the two totalitarian powers. As a result, Belarusian lands became unified once the Soviet Union annexed the northeastern part of Poland, which became known as Western Belarus. Soviet propaganda never referred to this invasion as a military takeover, but rather the "liberation of the western regions of the BSSR" from the former Polish state and the protection of its population, presumably from Nazi Germany, although the two states cooperated closely over the later months of 1939 and at least until the spring of 1940.

The operation was a sensitive one, not least because Britain and France had declared war on Nazi Germany the moment that Hitler directed his troops and air force to attack Poland.

From the Belarusian perspective, September 17 could be perceived as a positive event that unified Belarusian lands for the first time since 1919. Moreover, these lands had earlier been part of the Russian Empire, whereas much of Western Ukraine, annexed simultaneously, had only seen Russian occupation during the First World War and had earlier been part of the Austrian Empire and Polish state.

Under Polish rule, a census of the population was taken in 1931, although some sources have indicated that the numbers were weighted to exaggerate the number of Poles in the various regions. In this census, only four cities of Western Belarus had populations of more than 25,000: the largest was Białystok (Bielastok in Belarusian), with 107,650, followed by Hrodna (48,500), Brest (47,500), and Pinsk (32,000). Although the 1931 census only requested respondents' native language and not nationality, it nonetheless provides a good illustration of the ethnic makeup of these urban settlements, which were dominated by Poles and Jews. About 167,000 declared their native language as Yiddish or Hebrew, and 148,000 stated Polish. Belarusians were mainly confined to the rural areas and mostly on the eastern side of the region.

Soviet sources emphasized the bleak economic and cultural picture for Belarusians, noting that in 1937, over 400,000 residents of Western Belarus were unemployed, while 83,000 peasants were landless and a further 180,000 possessed less than 1 hectare (approximately 2.5 acres) of land. Almost half the population was illiterate, with the proportion among Belarusians being the highest. The Polish government had essentially treated its northeastern region as a colony, despite vague promises offered at the Paris Peace Treaties to provide autonomy for its huge population of Ukrainians and Belarusians in the east.

In the 1920s, accordingly, the local branch of the Communist Party of Poland (CPP), known as the Communist Party of Western Belarus, attracted a significant number of members, especially from the Jewish population. In July 1938, as noted,

Stalin, through the Comintern, dissolved the CPP and its affiliates, many members of which were accused of deviations such as following Leon Trotsky or Grigory Zinoviev, two former Bolsheviks who had been removed from offices by Stalin, and in the case of Trotsky deported, while Zinoviev had already been executed. Thus, Western Belarus suffered from the aftermath of the purges of 1937–1938, though the ramifications never matched those of the earlier period.

Under Poland, there was also cultural Polonization. Organizations such as the Belarusian Institute of Economics and Culture and the Belarusian School Association were banned between 1936 and 1938, and the Belarusian population was encouraged to assimilate into the Polish majority. Uniate believers, who were mostly Belarusians, were encouraged to switch to the Roman Catholic Church. In short, Poland treated Western Belarus as a region to be assimilated rather than be given autonomy. But while some Belarusians were willing to join the Communist Party, there were few nationalists in contrast to their neighbors in Western Ukraine.

When the Germans invaded Poland on September 1, 1939, they initially advanced into the territory that was part of Western Belarus according to the Nazi-Soviet Pact. Sixteen days then elapsed before the Soviet forces arrived and the population noted the contrast between the affluent-looking German soldiers and the bedraggled Soviet troops, who looked emaciated, as did their horses. Nevertheless, for many Belarusians and, especially, Jews, Soviet rule was a preferable alternative to that of Poland, and they welcomed the incoming army with bread and salt. Panteleimon Ponomarenko, the Stalinist party leader of the BSSR, also visited some settlements in the newly annexed territories and noted the friendly attitude of the local Belarusian peasants. A joint military parade on September 22, 1939, of the Wehrmacht and the Red Army in Brest marked the handover of the city of Brest and the Brest Fortress to the Soviet Union, an event hidden for decades in Soviet historiography.

For Belarusians in both West and Soviet Belarus, there was great disappointment when on October 10, 1939, Stalin and Molotov decided to transfer the Vilnia region, including its major city (Vilnius), to Lithuania, which was to be annexed in the summer of 1940 as a Soviet republic. Vilnia was a major cultural center for Belarusians, as it was also for Lithuanians, Poles, and Jews. The transfer left Western Belarus with five regions: Białystok, Brest, Pinsk, Baranavičy, and Viliejka. Subsequently, in November 1940, a territory in the north with a population of 81,750 was added to the territory of Lithuania. Regarding the southern border with Ukraine, the BSSR was also forced to make some territorial concessions following a meeting between Stalin and the respective party leaders: Ponomarenko and Khrushchev. The Kamen-Kashirskiy district and a small part of the Biełaviežskaja pušča were transferred to the Ukrainian SSR. The western border with Greater Germany had already been established by the Pact and another Protocol of October 4, 1939.

Given the innate suspicion of the Stalin regime that had been in place throughout the 1930s, it was not surprising that Western Belarus remained sealed off from the eastern region, despite propaganda extolling the "reunion" of Belarusian territories. Polish officials were removed from their positions and many were arrested, while the NKVD checked anyone crossing the border between the two parts of Belarus. Former members of the CPP and CPWB were permitted to apply for membership of the Communist Party of the Soviet Union (CPSU), although some were accused of Trotskyism and arrested. The CPWB was weighted in favor of Jewish members, who made up more than half the total.

The USSR established a Provisional Government based in Bialystok, which was designated as the capital city of Western Belarus. On October 22, 1939, in coordination with events in Lviv, Soviet officials supervised the election of a People's Assembly with ninety-one deputies, over 70% of which were Belarusians. The elections were not democratic. In each district there was only one officially appointed candidate—sometimes a member of the Soviet army—and the population received vodka and sausage at the polling station. The vote was almost unanimous and thus the elections were a ritual designed for foreign consumption to conceal the nature of the annexation. It convinced very few people outside the region.

The Assembly then began to create election commissions, again with many Jews in those in cities, who were better educated than the overwhelmingly Belarusian peasantry. A simultaneous election took place in Lviv in Western Ukraine. The key figure in Western Belarus, cited regularly in Soviet reports, was Siarhei Prytytski, then aged twenty-six, a prominent former member of the CPWB, who was to have a lengthy career in the Communist Party of Belarus and wartime partisan movement. Most deputies in the Bialystok assembly were non-Party members, however. Once the election was completed and the assembly in place, it immediately requested that Western Belarus become part of the Soviet Union and be joined to Soviet Belarus.

The region was politically sensitive because of its border with Greater Germany. The Soviet Union began to build up military forces there, fortifying the Molotov Line, which extended from the Baltic Sea to the Carpathian Mountains, including most of the newly annexed regions (the Baltic States, Western Belarus, Western Ukraine, and Bessarabia). It consisted mainly of pillboxes. Although in theory such installations could have delayed the German advance that began on June 22, the Line was never completed and did not pose a serious obstacle to the Wehrmacht once it crossed the border. By October 30, 1940, the border between the Soviet Union and Nazi Germany was closed and gradually fortified. Prior to its closure, many Jews fled from the German zone into Western Belarus.

The new authorities did not act with great alacrity, but gradually began to introduce Soviet institutions, culture, and education. There were no higher educational institutions prior to the annexation, and the only university in the region was in Vilnia (Vilnius), thus unavailable once that territory was added to Lithuania. Having initially targeted Polish officials, the new rulers carried out mass deportations of Poles in 1940–1941, particularly landowners and colonists (*osadniks*), and members of the Polish political and economic elite. Some of the refugees entering from Greater Germany were also subject to deportation, and by the summer of 1941, over 22,000 had been transported to eastern regions, with a further 2,000 arrested. A large proportion were from the Bialystok region, which would be removed from the BSSR in the postwar period and added to the revised territory of Poland.

A key difference between the populations of Western Belarus and Western Ukraine was the level of national consciousness, which manifested itself in resistance to Soviet rule. The Soviet authorities encountered little resistance as they nationalized local industries—they were not large scale—and abolished private trade. They did not attempt to carry out mass collectivization of agriculture, perhaps because of the need to maintain the sympathy of the local peasants, but also because their priority was to fortify the region and build up military forces. The annexation added about 4.5 million people to the BSSR, almost doubling its population, and establishing the foundations of the future republic after 1945. Once the Germans invaded, however, the Soviet forces rapidly abandoned the region, fleeing eastward. Only the Brest Fortress provided some resistance, although the Wehrmacht did not assign high priority to its immediate capture, preferring to pursue Soviet forces all the way to Smolensk, capturing large numbers of prisoners along the route (see below).

What happened at the Brest Fortress in the early weeks of the Nazi invasion?

The 1941–1945 war in Belarus is the most important event in the official narrative propagated by the president and government, which has exploited the attention given to the war in the former Soviet Union after 1965. The interpretations of the war have not changed substantially since the Soviet period, but rather they have become more rigid and closed for debate. These narratives combine both suffering and heroism, and focus on the "Belarusian people" almost exclusively, even though it is well known that the Red Army was multinational, and some of the main battles that are commemorated involved several national groups of the USSR. It has become difficult for historians to determine with accuracy how many of the events actually unfolded since they have become part of a general myth of the victory. It has been noted by several sources how the Holocaust in Belarus has been largely subsumed to the overall narrative of the losses of the "Soviet people," for example, and the studies of collaborationism are fairly limited, despite the appearance of some new studies devoted to this topic.

The changing depiction of the war can be illustrated by two film examples. Elem Klimov's *Idi i smotri* (Come and See; 1985) is a harrowing portrait of a young boy caught up in the war who attempts to join the partisans. Part of the screenplay was written by the noted Belarusian writer Ales Adamovich, who had published a collection of eyewitness testimonies from this period in 1977 and inspired by his work future Nobel Prize laureate Svetlana Alexievich. The film is difficult to watch and includes a massacre in a barn reminiscent of the massacre at Chatyń village. The second film, *Fortress of War* (in Belarusian and Russian—*Brest Fortress*), a joint Russian-Belarusian production from 2010, directed by Aleksandr Kott, also provides a script from the perspective of a fifteen-year-old boy at the Brest Fortress, and adheres closely to the official narrative of the heroic defense of the fortress against overwhelming odds for nine days. The movie is gripping and intense but does not explore the same depths of emotions or raise the same sort of questions as Klimov's movie. The film was released to coincide with the sixty-fifth anniversary of the end of the Great Patriotic War (celebrated on May 9 as opposed to the May 8—the end of the Second World War in Europe) and thus formed part of an intensive Belarusian propaganda campaign.

The war began at 4:30 A.M. on June 22, 1941, as three German army groups invaded the Soviet Union with over 3 million troops, with the support of about 650,000 additional troops from Finland in the north and Romania in the south. Army Group North moved in the general direction of Leningrad, Army Group South advanced into Ukraine moving toward Kyiv, and Army Group Center crossed the border into Belarus. The capital Minsk was occupied by June 28, just six days after the invasion, a distance of approximately 220 miles, indicating the lack of serious resistance. The route taken by Army Group Center was the same as Napoleon's Grande Armée almost 130 years earlier, and led by Fedor Von Bock, a sixty-one-year-old East Prussian who had played a prominent role in the 1940 invasion of France. By the end of August 1941, the entire republic was occupied, after which the Germans erased the BSSR by dividing the republic between different regions of Nazi occupation as follows:

The northwestern regions of Brest and Bielastok (now in Poland and called Białystok) including the cities of Hrodna and Vaŭkavysk were added to East Prussia; the southern regions of Brest, Pinsk, Paliessie, and Homiel oblasts along a line 12 miles north of the Brest-Homiel railroad were added to the Reichskommissariat Ukraine; the northwestern parts of Viciebsk became part of the District of Lithuania; the remaining districts of Viciebsk, as well as Mahilioŭ, most of Homiel Oblast', and the eastern regions of Minsk Oblast', constituted the operating rear zone of the Army Group Center; and the General District of Belorussia (Weissrussland) comprised Baranavičy, parts of Vilejka, Minsk, Brest, Pinsk and Palesie oblasts, about one-third of the prewar territory of the BSSR in its September 1939 expanded area. It was included in the Reichskommissariat Ostland and made up of ten districts. In this way, the Nazi regime avoided the questions of Belarusian statehood it had faced in 1918, but at the same time did not negate it completely.

The year 1941 therefore might be considered a disastrous year of retreat, encirclement of armies, and loss of territory. However, the modern narrative interprets the year differently and focuses on the "Brest Hero Fortress" on the border with Poland, arguing that its defenders performed an act of self-sacrifice and heroism in defending it. The basis of this account is a 1957 book by Sergey Smirnov, which appeared a year after Khrushchev's Secret Speech denouncing Stalin—who would not have heroized a defeat—and the creation of a Museum of the Heroic Defense of the Brest Fortress at the garrison of the House of Officers in the original building at the fort. Smirnov described the selfless actions of the main defenders: Pyotr Gavrilov, the military leader; Efim Fomin, an NKVD official; Vasily Bitko; and Andrei Kizhevatov. According to Smirnov, the defense constituted "one of the greatest feats in the history of man." Facing such hyperbole, a brief background of the fortress and its place in the early events of the German-Soviet war is merited.

The fortress was constructed in 1842 as a western outpost of the Russian Empire, and about 12,000 troops could be based there. By the First World War, although as a military object it had become obsolete, it changed hands several times as the Russian and Austro-German armies contested it. It contained, however, several underground passages and cellars, making it a complex task for an invading army to completely eradicate any defending force. Thanks to the changing borders that arose from the 1921 Treaty of Riga, the fortress ended up in the territory of eastern Poland in the interwar period. It is located just to the east of the city of Brest, known as Brest-Litovsk well into the twentieth century because of its Lithuanian origins. The first objective for the Germans after the invasion of Poland on September 1, 1939, was a Polish garrison, led by General Konstanty Plisowski. The borders changed again because of the August 1939 Nazi-Soviet Pact, when the fortress became part of Belarusian territory, and after the initial takeover the Germans pulled out, allowing the Soviet army to move in for the next twenty months.

Thus, the summer 1941 invasion saw a German army capture the fortress for a third time. Soviet reports correctly note that the survivors held out for some time, particularly Gavrilov. On the other hand, the invaders captured Fomin and executed him on June 28, less than a week after the initial attack. The main army then advanced to Smolensk by July 8 after subjecting the city to a heavy bombing campaign. The battle for Smolensk lasted until the end of July, a more significant impediment by far for the German Wehrmacht than the defense of the Brest fortress, which did not delay the German advance. After the war, the story of the fortress was forgotten as far as official publications were concerned. It was revived on the twentieth anniversary of the victory by the Brezhnev-Kosygin leadership in Moscow and enthusiastically endorsed by the Belarusian party leader Piotr Masherau. The feat of Gavrilov, an ethnic Tatar, was finally recognized and together with now deceased Kizhevatov, he received the award Hero of the Soviet Union in May 1965. At the same time, the citadel became the Brest Hero Fortress, a title that placed it alongside the Hero Cities of Minsk, Moscow, Leningrad, and Kyiv.

The site was then subjected to a massive campaign to build a befitting memorial complex of 170,000 square feet that dwarfs the old fort buildings. The two main monuments are huge statues entitled "Thirst" and "Courage," and at the rear of the latter are illustrations of the main battle. On the wall in one part is the inscription "We will die but we will not leave the fortress; I am dying but will not surrender. Farewell Motherland, 20 July 1941." The same inscription appears in the Museum of the Great Patriotic War in Minsk. Whether authentic or not, the impact of such a statement is not in question, and it illustrates the skillful use of propaganda by a government that had been in possession of the fortress for less than two years when the Nazi invasion began. The Brest Fortress is a regular choice of Aliaksandr Lukashenka on official occasions, and he has been visited there by Russian and other foreign leaders at various times.

How were the Germans able to occupy Belarus so quickly in 1941?

The German Army Group Center applied tactics of Blitzkrieg in Belarus as it had done elsewhere in Europe in 1940. In the regions of Brest and Bialystok, the German tank formations led by Generals Hermann Hoth and Heinz Guderian attacked the 4th and 9th Soviet armies that were defending the Western region. Having received orders from Moscow not to retreat, the armies had little response to the swift attacks. An attempt to counterattack near Hrodna in the north failed, and about 300,000 Soviet troops found themselves trapped in what the Soviet authors call a "cauldron" to the west of Minsk. The capital was soon occupied, too, with the defenders resorting to the use of "Molotov cocktails" as a main means of defense. The fighting then moved eastward, and on July 6, a large tank battle ensued known as the Lepel Counterattack between Orša and Viciebsk in the northeastern part of the original BSSR. According to the Soviet version of the war, the army managed to advance about 25 miles with the loss of some 830 tanks. But by July 11, Viciebsk had fallen to the invaders.

Further to the south, Major General Mikhail Romanov defended Mahilioŭ, the former headquarters of the tsarist army in the later years of the First World War. The fighting here was more intensive than in other parts of the former BSSR, and resistance lasted for about three weeks. The region had more time to prepare for battle, and it is possible that public sentiment was more in favor of the Stalin regime than the western borderlands that had been annexed so recently. The city of Homiel in the southeast fell on August 19, 1941. Although pockets of resistance endured until September, essentially the loss of the eastern cities signified the beginning of the Nazi occupation regime that was to last a full three years.

The official accounts of the war on both Soviet and contemporary Belarusian textbooks for schools and universities tend to gloss over the remarkably swift conquest of the republic. On the contrary, they have developed a different version of events, namely that strong resistance in Belarus slowed down the German army, thus delaying the attack on Moscow and allowing time to call up reserves from the east to defend the Soviet capital. The Stalin Line Museum at Zaslaŭje, near Minsk, a historical cultural center, depicts the defense of the fortified line from German attacks, using tanks, planes, and other weapons, in an elaborate conception of the myth of firm resistance. Its entrance contains a large bust of Stalin. In such ways the disastrous year of 1941 has emerged from ignominy to heroism. In truth, there was little to stop the Army Group Center's charge through Belarus as the initial stage of Operation Typhoon, the conquest of Moscow.

Aside from the inept responses from Moscow, the lack of enthusiasm for the Stalin regime in the western regions should also be considered. Though the initial targets of Soviet arrests and deportations were members of the Polish community, Belarusians were also subject to the same process by 1940–1941. The purges that had been prevalent in 1937–1938 were now extended into the newly annexed regions. The result was that many Belarusians—though not Jews, who feared the invaders—were either sympathetic or ambivalent toward another invading force, this time coming from the west. Moreover, the memory of the German occupation of 1918 was still relatively recent, and locals could recall the period and equate, mistakenly, Nazi Germany with Wilhelmian Germany, while some more committed Belarusian nationalists hoped that collaboration with the invading forces would lead to a return of a Belarusian state and the breakup of the Soviet Union.

But one can also attribute the slow reaction to the invasion to the personal idiosyncrasies of Stalin, as Khrushchev revealed at the 20th Party Congress as well as in his memoirs. Stalin adhered faithfully to the pact with Nazi Germany, so much so that on the very morning of the invasion, Soviet raw materials were still being transported on trains to the neighboring state. The Soviet leader also feared that the duplicitous British were trying to inflame the situation and encourage a war between the two totalitarian powers. Therefore, he dismissed warnings about the coming conflict, ignoring a warning from British prime minister Winston Churchill that the attack was imminent, as well as another from Richard Sorge, his spy in Tokyo, who even provided the date of June 21 (one day early).

As a result of Stalin's strong position, overruling his own military leaders, Soviet planes on the border were left in the open rather than being concealed, troops were not on full alert, and the invasion came so suddenly that there was no response in Moscow for several hours. And when it came, it was left to Foreign Minister Viacheslav Molotov to address Soviet citizens on the radio, an occasion now replicated at the entrance to the Brest Hero Fortress on the western border. Of the three fronts, the most significant advance was at the center, en route to Moscow, which initially was the main target. Thus, the BSSR was on the direct path to the Soviet capital and its defenders were simply overwhelmed. After the occupation of Kyiv, Minsk was the biggest prize of the Nazis' attack on the Soviet Union and was to remain occupied for the next three years.

Did Belarusians support the Nazi occupation?

The Hitler regime's plans for the east were clearly laid out in theory. Belarusians, as Slavs, were anticipated to lose about 75% of their population and be treated as slaves in an expanded Nazi Aryan Empire. The current Belarusian leadership since 2020 has expounded a theory of a war to carry out "genocide of the Belarusian people." In truth, there is very little evidence that the purpose of the Wehrmacht's march eastward was directed specifically against Belarusians, at any point.

The first task was to round up Communist leaders and Jews. But the difficulty is that the Nazi government was multidimensional and included several structures that worked in parallel with each other but not necessarily in unison.

Thus, the Reich Minister for the Occupied Eastern Territories, Alfred Rosenberg, the Nazis' main racial theorist, despite his general contempt for "*Untermenschen*," was quite prepared to collaborate with Eastern Slavs—meaning in this case Ukrainians and Belarusians—to help establish a buffer zone to the east of Greater Germany and offer these peoples independent states. His ideas did not meet with the support of Hitler or SS Reichsführer Heinrich Himmler, whose ideas ultimately prevailed, but they provided some encouragement to Belarusian nationalists anxious to establish an independent state with the help of an invader. In Ukraine, the occupants had refused to countenance the state announced by a branch of the Organization of Ukrainian Nationalists that followed Stepan Bandera on June 30, 1941. In their view, this movement was too independent for Berlin's purposes. The Belarusians, however, were more malleable, and their numbers much smaller.

On October 6, 1941, the new authorities established a Belarusian People's Defense (BPD) organization, led by a former member of the BPR, Ivan Yermachenka, which had a variety of assigned duties, including military assistance to the Germans, school education, health care, and culture. Later it also helped the system whereby local Belarusians were sent to Germany for forced labor. Initially, however, it appeared to be a concession to Belarusian cultural aspirations. It helped organize trade unions and a legal system, and to recreate the Belarusian Central Council (Rada in Belarusian). Overall responsibility for the BPD was in the hands of Gauleiter Wilhelm Kube, the General Commissar for Belarusian territories, a ruthless anti-Semite, who at the same time complained about the inclusion of German Jews in the Holocaust and who was also prepared to provide some concessions to the Belarusians who opposed the Communist system. The Germans disbanded the BPD by the spring of 1943.

The ideas of Rosenberg were more fully implemented during the period of the German retreat from Russia, from the end of the battle of Stalingrad in February to the summer of 1944. On June 22, 1943, the occupants created the Union of Belarusian Youth (UBY) and began to open leadership training schools for those aged ten to twenty. Five days later, they added the Belarusian Council of Trust, which included the leaders of several organs working for the occupation regime, led by Vatslau Ivanouski, the Burgomaster of Minsk. The Council, among other duties, assisted with the formation of police battalions in the Minsk, Slonim, and Niasviž regions. By March 1944, there were seven battalions with over 3,600 participants.

In December 1943, Ivanouski was killed. Belarusian historian Yury Turonak believes this was organized by Radzislau Astrouski, who competed for the power with Ivanouski. At the end of 1943, the authorities allowed for the re-emergence of the Belarusian Central Rada, under the leadership of Astrouski, former principal of the Belarusian Gymnasium in Vilnius. He was responsible for the convocation of the Second Belarusian Congress, which took place in the summer of 1944, just a few days before the Soviet army arrived in Minsk. These various organizations were not insignificant, but they were not numerous compared to the number of Belarusians fighting in the Red Army. They created problems for the Diaspora because the exiles of the 1918 BNR government never recognized their authority. Further, their use of the white-red flag and Pahonia symbol (a coat of arms featuring a white knight on a white horse, chasing forward on a red field), following the example of the BNR, provided Aliaksandr Lukashenka with propaganda in his campaign to equate wartime collaborators with the contemporary opposition, particularly the Belarusian Popular Front. Astrouski became prominent in a far-right emigration group called the Anti-Bolshevik Nations, which issued pamphlets during the Cold War from the United States.

Still, one should not dismiss the collaborators outright. They represented a segment of the population alienated by the purges of the Stalin period and the mass executions of Belarusians by the NKVD, particularly in 1937–1938. Had the Nazis adopted policies more conciliatory to the population from the outset, local support for the invasion would have been wider. On the other hand, much of the republic unified against a foreign invader that proved even more pitiless than the Communist Party leadership in Moscow. For the Germans, the much-despised collective farm system imposed by Stalin was quite convenient in a wartime setting since it tied peasants to the land and villages to the state. They changed the name to "cooperative farm" but essentially used the same system to ensure the supply of grain for the troops.

Importantly, some of Belarusian nationalists were saving Jews, like Ivanouski's wife Hanna and his daughter Sabina, who saved two Jewish women in 1941 and received the Righteous among the Nations title in 2001. Many surviving members of the Belarusian national forces, working under the Nazi occupation, fled to the United Kingdom, Canada, the United States, and other countries of the democratic West. Individuals like Barys Kit, Jan Zaprudnik (born Siarhei Vilchytski), Vitaut and Zora Kipel, and Father Aliaksandr Nadsan continued to collect manuscripts, documents, medals, and other exhibits of the Belarusian People's Republic and Belarusian Central Council period. They also contributed extensively to the preservation of the Belarusian traditions among the diaspora. Others were brutally repressed, like Larysa Heniush, who was released by the government of socialist Czechoslovakia to the USSR and spent many years in GULAG camps.

How did the Holocaust unfold in Belarus?

It would be impossible to describe all the details and nuances of the Holocaust in Belarus in one section. As the Shoah in Belarus is highly understudied and relatively little has been published about it, especially compared to the situation in Poland or western Europe, it would need its own book. This section will outline the main stages and most important issues specific to "the Catastrophe" in Belarus.

Since the attack of the Nazis on Poland, followed by the invasion from the Soviet Union in September 1939, the BSSR became a larger state, with the Brest, Hrodna, and Białystok regions joining the territory of Soviet Belarus. Historically, these were the territories with the most multicultural population with Belarusian, Polish, Jewish, Tatar, and Ukrainian populations.

Many Jews were happy with this transformation and complained to the Jews from Eastern Belarus about Polish anti-Semitism. Most of them were more religious and traditional than those from the Eastern Belarusian regions who had been forbidden to practice Judaism, alongside other religions under the atheistic Soviet regime. Hence, at that point, the only official repression Jews as an ethnic and religious group were encountering was punishment for practicing their religion. Quotidian anti-Semitism was also an issue. However, Jews, like all other nations in the Soviet Union, were subjected to harsh measures for any anti-Soviet and anti-Stalin criticism.

The USSR Census of 1926 stated that 8.2% of the BSSR population was Jewish, amounting to 407,059 people. Due to the large concentration of Jews in the cities and towns (*shtetls* from Yiddish), as well as their better average education level than that of Belarusians, many Soviet Belarusian Jews before 1939 were very much embedded into the Soviet state. They worked at the Soviet state apparatus, factories and plants, in hospitals and in universities. And ultimately, many of them became victims of the Stalinist purges, accused of being connected to Trotsky or Grigory Zinoviev (real name Ovsei-Gershon Rodomyslsky), who were Jewish. The years of 1937–1938 became especially harsh for the Belarusian Jewry; many were killed or sent to Soviet GULAG camps for lengthy periods. The only two victims identified at Kurapaty by Zianon Pazniak,

Yauhen Shmyhaliou, and Aleh Iou were Jews—Mordekhai Shuleskes and Moishe Kramer. As Yiddish had not been an official language in the BSSR since 1937 and Judaism was forbidden and went underground, the majority of the Jewish population was trying to integrate as much as possible to the Soviet system, raising their loyalty to it and trying to avoid any possible repressions from the Soviet regime. Many mixed marriages took place.

When the Western Belarusian Jews and Eastern Belarusian Jews encountered each other, they had undergone different experiences in the 1920s and 1930s, but they still belonged to the same ethnic and religious group and spoke Yiddish. Western Belarusian Jews, who had been part of the Communist and socialist underground in interwar Poland, quickly climbed the social ladder and became leaders of the local Communist parties and governments in Western Belarus. In September 1939, many Poles leaving the towns of their former state accused Jews of being too welcoming to the Soviet authorities, and some even initiated pogroms in Hrodna and other cities and towns with large Jewish populations.

Very often the local Jews would take revenge on those Poles in Western Belarus who had anti-Semitic views when this territory was still Polish. The Soviet authorities targeted thousands of landowning Polish families, Polish state officials, and small and large businesspeople, as well as peasants, most of whom were sent to Siberia and Central Asia. The tension was very high as very often newly recruited members of the local NKVD were of Jewish origin, as they were better educated than Belarusian peasants. Thus, in the eyes of many Poles, Jewish NKVD workers were the ones sending many Poles to death, which further fueled the hatred between different ethnic groups in the region and had consequences when the Holocaust unfolded on those territories. Hitler's regime tended to instrumentalize the tensions among the ethnic groups on the occupied territories and used that for its benefit.

Another important group of Jews—Jewish refugees—were coming to the now enlarged BSSR from Poland, occupied by the Nazi regimes. After Nazis established ghettos throughout Poland in 1939–1940, many Jews experienced an ongoing deterioration of the conditions and started to flee to the neighboring Soviet Union. This is the main reason why estimates of the number of Jews killed during the Shoah in Belarus are questionable. The newcomers would bring terrifying stories to the Jews of the Soviet Belarus about the Nazis, but the Jews felt safe in the BSSR, thanks to Soviet propaganda.

When Nazi Germany attacked the Soviet Union in Brest and other places from land and air on June 22, 1941, this news was a surprise for the Jewish population of Belarus. Many of them refused to listen to the Jewish refugees from Poland that they were in danger and remained on the occupied territories. They could still remember the Germans' behavior during the First World War. Those who were involved in the work of big factories and plants, as well as the Communist Party, were able to evacuate to Central Asia and deeper Russia and mostly survived. In line with the evil irony of that time, many Jews who were serving prison terms in Soviet concentration camps in Siberia and Central Asia survived the war, thanks to the Soviet repression they had experienced before 1941.

As the occupants were already experienced in organizing ghettos for the Jewish population in their occupied territories to the West from Belarus, the first Belarusian ghetto was quickly established in July 1941 in Minsk, according to that pattern. It was the fourth biggest ghetto on Nazi-occupied territory, after Warsaw, Lviv, and Łódź. Other large Belarusian ghettos include Brest, Hrodna, Baranavičy, and Pinsk—all cities from the Western Belarusian territories, acquired by the Soviet Union in September 1939.

The Nazis quickly established a network of bigger and smaller camps on the Belarusian territory, dispersing the atmosphere of total control and fear with the help of their Lithuanian, Latvian, Ukrainian, Hungarian, Russian, and

Belarusian collaborators. Many Belarusian anti-communists collaborated closely with Belarusian Generalskomissar Wilhelm Kube, hoping for an independent Belarus under Nazi rule. Unlike western Europe, in central and eastern Europe everyone helping or assisting Jews was subject to immediate death. Yet, several hundred Belarusians saved Jewish adults and children during the war and received the Righteous among the Nations title after the war.

As the Soviet nomenklatura was completely unprepared for Hitler's attack, most of them left their possessions in Belarus and fled to Russia. With the absence of the leadership and in the light of cruel Nazi policy toward Jews who could be killed for no reason, Jewish activists started to organize themselves into an underground resistance in many cities and towns. One of the outstanding groups was the Minsk ghetto underground led by Hersh Smolar, who arrived in Minsk from Bielastok (Białystok in Polish) after Hitler's attack. Thanks to his extensive experience of the socialist underground's fight in Poland earlier, he managed to organize an efficient network to smuggle Jews to the forest from the Minsk ghetto, especially after the major pogroms by the Nazis in March (Purim) and November (October Revolution) 1942. The Germans and their collaborators scheduled their most brutal actions for Jewish and Soviet holidays on purpose, playing on the Nazi propaganda stereotype that Jews and Communists were the same people.

Belarus's large forests and swamps, well known to the local population, turned into the main areas of resistance for the anti-Nazi movement and posed traps for the Nazi troops. The Soviet authorities realized in 1942 that they needed to take control over the partisan movements, and Jewish resistance groups were among them. However, in practice, it was not so simple. Many Jews organized Jewish partisan units, having faced anti-Semitism among the Soviet partisans already functioning in the forests. The latter units did not want to accept Jews, fearing they might come under greater threat because of the Nazi policy against Jews, but some carried anti-Semitic views themselves, thinking Jews could not fight.

A remarkable feature of the Jewish partisan units run by the Bielski brothers or Sholom Zorin and his supporters was the fact that they had many women and children. Zorin's unit was even called the "family" partisan unit, as it hosted around 400 individuals, who were mostly refugees from the Minsk ghetto unable to fight and 141 fighters. Jewish women were proudly fighting alongside their male partners in ghettos, the underground, and partisan units. "Aryan-looking" Jewish women and those who dyed their hair and spoke multiple languages were especially valuable for the Jewish resistance. They were able to collect valuable information and were not perceived as dangerous as men. They were also harder to identify as Jewish compared to the Jewish men who were circumcised.

There are some remarkable stories of cohabitation in those towns and cities, which were populated by Belarusian Tatars. In Minsk and Iŭje, and some other places, Tatar families were saving Jewish circumcised boys, claiming that they were Muslims and members of their families. Hopefully one day more light will be shed on these stories.

In 1941–1944, Belarusian territory became a site of suffering not only for Belarusian and Polish Jews, but also for German Jews who began to arrive in the Minsk ghetto already in November 1941. This first transport came from Hamburg. Transports from Bremen, Berlin, Vienna, Düsseldorf, Frankfurt am Main, Cologne, and Königsberg (now Kaliningrad in Russia) followed. Several transports arrived from Brno and a famous ghetto of Terezin (Theresienstadt in German) of occupied Czechoslovakia. The transports of German and Czech Jews continued until October 1942.

Ironically, as pointed out by Aliaksandr Dalhouski, the initial victims of the Holocaust were Jews in those territories that were part of the Soviet Union prior to September 1939. The reason is that the rapid advance of Germany's Army Group Center precluded the pacification of many smaller settlements.

The army leaders thus sought to eliminate all Jews in the immediate rear. It was followed by the extermination of Jews in General District "Belorussia" in the first half of 1942. Those in the western regions—as far west as Bialystok and south to the General District "Volhynia" in the fall of 1942. The occupants began to destroy ghettos and labor camps from February 1942 until the fall of 1943. In the following winter, any Jews who had survived were moved to concentration camps.

Nazis were initially killing the German and Czech Jews by shooting them in Blahaŭščyna, which was directly east of Minsk in November 1941. The rows there were already prepared by the prisoners of war from Masiukouščyna camp near Minsk. Soon the Nazis decided to transform this killing site into a death camp—Maly Traścianiec, the biggest such camp after Auschwitz, Majdanek, and Treblinka. It is the only death camp of this scale on the former Soviet territory. Belarusian Jews from the Minsk ghetto, Belarusian partisans, and thousands of the European Jewry perished there. Unlike in Poland, the Nazis mostly shot or poisoned Jews in gas vans before burying them or letting others do this for them. This death camp was unique for a Soviet territory in this regard. It operated until July 1944, when Nazis, in the light of the approaching Soviet troops, burned alive the remaining 6,500 prisoners of Minsk prisons and the Šyrokaja street concentration camp in Minsk as well as all the camp papers.

Maly Traścianiec was also a labor camp with a farm growing food for the SD and Gestapo. But mainly it has become infamous for around 100,000–207,000 people killed and buried there: the exact numbers are hard to estimate. Two main reasons contribute to the obstacles to carry out proper research of Maly Traścianiec victims and its further recognition as a killing camp. The first one is the fact that the Soviet leaders did not mention this camp during the Nuremberg trials, as before 1941 it is believed to be a killing site of Stalin's NKVD, so they did not want an international investigation to take place and closed the camp at the earliest opportunity. The second reason is the closeness of the Belarusian regime to that period and their fear to move the focus from the "genocide of the Belarusian" people to the Shoah tragedy. One such burial site of Stalin's victims is close to the entrance of the memorial to the camp along the highway between Minsk and Mahiliou.

Minsk city was retaken by the Soviet army in July 1944, and thus Soviet troops were the first to uncover evidence of the death camps as they advanced westward as part of the massive Operation Bagration campaign.

Jews were not the only victims on the territory of Belarus. Belarusian Roma were largely exterminated by the Nazis in a similar manner—shootings, gas vans, burning people alive, and putting them to death in concentration camps. As most of the Roma in Belarus were illiterate, it is almost impossible to trace the scale of the tragedy—those few who survived could not write their testimonies and often did not speak any language other than the Roma local dialect.

After the end of the Second World War, it took decades for many Jewish partisans and resistance fighters to be recognized by the Soviet state. As soon as it became possible, many of them left for Israel, fearing Stalin's anti-Semitism campaign of 1948–1953. Because of the complicated movements of the Jewish population in 1939, it is impossible to estimate the number of the Jewish victims on the Belarusian territory, especially taking into account European Jewry killed in the Minsk ghetto and Maly Trascianiec. The rough number is from 600,000 to more than 1.2 million Jewish victims, according to different sources and estimates.

The Holocaust deeply affected Belarusians by exterminating the Jewish population whose role in the country had been remarkable for more than five centuries. After the 1930s, many representatives of Belarusian and Jewish intellectuals were repressed and killed; the Nazi machine liquidated the remaining cultural and scientific elites, workers, and peasants of Jewish origin. The scale of the tragedy can still be felt in Belarus. The absence of state support for the commemoration of Jewish victims and Jewish legacy, which was maintained until 2020 by the few remaining NGOs and some European embassies, only makes the tragedy larger. The state's endorsement of the "genocide of the Belarusians" after 2021 has only exacerbated this lack of recognition for the Jewish Holocaust.

Why was the partisan movement so effective in the occupied territories?

The Nazi regime turned the former BSSR into a land of ghettos and death camps. But its foci were not immediately obvious other than the rounding up of Jews and Communists as the occupation began. After the failure of the attempt to occupy Moscow in the fall and winter of 1941, Hitler turned his attention to the south, east of Kharkiv and Belgorod, and the summer of 1942 saw the beginning of the great battle of Stalingrad, which would be his first major defeat on any front. The limitations of manpower soon became evident, and Hitler's state could only control major towns in the areas it had occupied. Moreover, there were gaps in the front line, particularly in the eastern part of Belarus in the Viciebsk region that allowed the intrusion of partisan formations.

Partisan units sprang up in Belarus from the very start of the war. The party leadership, upon realizing the swiftness of the invasion and that party members would be the immediate targets in Minsk, fled the city and moved to Moscow, led by Communist leader Ponomarenko, the main architect of the later purges in the republic. Thus at first, there was a possibility of non-party partisans leading the struggle against the invader. Once the central leadership recovered, however, the local partisans were arrested, and the Communist Party took over command. Perhaps the first fully established partisan formation was in the settlement Pudat in Surazh region at a local cardboard factory, led by the factory's director Minai Shmyrou, referred to as *Batska* Minai ("Father" Minai in Belarusian). Another early and much celebrated formation was the unit under Vasil Korzh in the Palesie region in August 1941, a vast area of swamps and forests that proved very difficult for the Germans to control.

Any sort of organized movement, however, took some time to develop. The first opportunity occurred because of the 25-mile gap in the front lines known as the Viciebsk Gate. The Soviet advance after the failure of the Nazis to occupy Moscow brought the Army of the Kalinin Front close to the Belarusian border, allowing sabotage groups to move behind the enemy lines with weapons and military equipment. The gap remained open from February 10 until September 1942. By this time, a number of partisan brigades had formed, including one led by the future Communist Party leader Piotr Masherau, who also formed an underground Komsomol organization in Viliejka, to the west of Minsk. As the numbers increased, and the military situation was looking less dire, the Soviet authorities began to take control of the movement and adopt a more organized form.

In mid-1942, the State Defense Committee in Moscow created a Central Headquarters of the Partisan Movement led by Ponomarenko, with a regional version in Belarus, which became the central part of the movement. The choice was logical since the former republic had extensive areas of forests and lakes that would provide both water and concealment. It also had an important railroad network. On the other hand, the partisan regions lacked an adequate food supply and were heavily reliant on local villagers for sustenance. For the rural communities, some of which were not heavily affected by the war, the presence of the partisans was a double-edged sword. They were defending their homeland against a cruel invader, but their appearance often signified assassination attempts on local German officials or auxiliary police and the village would then suffer retribution through executions of residents or even the burning of their cottages.

For some, such as Jews now forced to live in ghettos, the partisans offered an opportunity to survive if they could manage to escape. There are many examples of Jews fleeing to the forests and even forming their own partisan units. In the Nalibaki forest in Western Belarus, for example, a group of Jewish partisans led by Tuvia Bielski formed after the Germans set up a ghetto near their home in Stankiewicze (Stankievičy). Tuvia, Asiel, and three other brothers fled to the forest, but the other family members were killed in the ghetto. The Bielski partisan group focused on rescuing Jews from ghettos and reportedly saved over 1,000 during the war. (British actor Daniel Craig played the role of Tuvia Bielski in the 2008 movie *Defiance*.) Another famous battalion fighting there was the unit of Shlomo Zorin, which saved many Jews from the Minsk ghetto.

Another name that is prominent among partisan heroes of Belarus is Kanstantsin Zaslonau, a railroad worker from Belarus who moved to Moscow from his native Orša at the start of the German advance into Eastern Belarus. With other railroad workers, Zaslonau volunteered to move behind enemy lines where he created a local band of guerrillas and adopted the pen name Dyadya Kostya (Uncle Kostya). He and his colleagues used a method first deployed by the Confederate Army in the American Civil War, placing explosives in iron casings that could be concealed within coal used for the trains. The result was severe explosions that often killed the train crew as well as derailing the train. In three months, Zaslonau's team blew up a reported ninety-three German trains. Wanted by the Germans, Zaslonau left Orša to form a partisan movement that operated in the eastern regions between Viciebsk, Orša, and Smolensk. Zaslonau was killed during a skirmish with the Germans in November 1942 and was awarded the title of Hero of the Soviet Union posthumously.

Soviet sources stress the growth of the partisan movement from an initial handful of troops to a mass body with tens of thousands as the Germans began to struggle following their defeat at Stalingrad. But the swell in numbers also created ever-greater problems of food supply, meaning more pressure on village communities. By the end of 1943, partisans controlled about 60% of the territory of the prewar BSSR in twenty partisan zones, which established community organizations, newspapers, schools, and libraries. By this time, the Nazis' defeat in the tank battle at Kursk Salient opened up the western borderlands to the Soviet army.

Partisan control allowed for more elaborate attacks on German railroad communications. The so-called war of the railroad tracks took place in three stages: after August 1943, when the Soviets advanced at Kursk, the partisan movement reduced supplies to the German army by as much as 40%; Stage 2 was between mid-September and October 1943 when the Red Army crossed the Belarusian border; and Stage 3 started on June 20, 1944, on the eve of the Operation Bagration, which brought the liberation of Belarus from Nazi occupation.

The later years of the war also saw the greater mobilization of the underground, particularly in the major cities such as Minsk. On September 22, 1943, a combined plot of the underground and partisans succeeded in a plot to assassinate Gauleiter Wilhelm Kube using a timing device hidden in his mattress. The chief perpetrator was his Belarusian mistress Alena Mazanik, who worked as his maid. Though Mazanik had been persuaded to lay the bomb, there were numerous plans to eliminate Kube on the orders of Moscow. The murder resulted in the deaths of about 1,000 male residents of Minsk in reprisal. Mazanik became a Hero of the Soviet Union on October 29. Ironically, the news of Kube's death did not cause great consternation in German leadership circles because the Gauleiter was regarded as too sympathetic to the local population. Mazanik began a career as a librarian after the war and died in Minsk in 1996.

For outsiders, it is difficult to comprehend the modern influence of partisan myths in Belarus. Through memorials, monuments, and museums in major cities and towns, their memory is preserved, and no doubt exaggerated and distorted over the years. The official figure of 374,000 partisans at the peak of operations in summer 1943, for example, seems improbable if one object is concealment in the forests. There would have been no way to feed an army of such a size. The figure is an example of how Soviet propaganda finds its way into modern interpretations without being properly analyzed. The task of feeding and equipping such a large number of insurgents would have been impossible.

The end of the Soviet Union did not appreciably change the commendations, and they are as pervasive today as they were sixty years ago when the war became officially venerated. Critical accounts from within Belarus are dismissed as historical revisionism, though they exist. For the occupying forces, the partisans caused considerable problems, making it difficult to supply their distant armies, and suffering harassment when they retreated, just as Napoleon's army over a century earlier had experienced. The partisan story ends in the summer of 1944 when the main narrative of the war in Belarus is taken over by the massive invasion armies.

Similar stories abound about Belarusian pilots, particularly female ones. Their exploits form part of the historical narrative of resistance and conquest. In their case, the more notable feats only took place after the tide of the war turned in early 1943 and afterward as prior to that the Luftwaffe had command of the air. One often cited example is the all-female 46th Guards Night Bomber Regiment made up women aged 17–22, which carried out about 22,500 combat sorties. The Regiment's navigator, Halina Dakutovich, who was born in Homiel in 1921, died on the night of August 1, 1943, returning from a mission. She received the Order of the Red Star posthumously. The Nazi occupants referred to the female pilots as "night witches" because prior to their attacks they turned off their engines and approached the enemy planes silently.

On August 15, 2024, the Belarusian version of *Sputnik* announced the death of ninety-nine-year-old Halina Brok-Beltsova, the navigator of a Pe-2 dive bomber, who had participated in Operation Bagration, the massive assault on

Army Group Center that removed the occupants from the territory of Belarus. She was part of the 125th Women's Aviation Regiment, had made thirty-six combat sorties, and received a number of official awards, including the Order of the Great Patriotic War.

How was Belarus liberated from Nazi occupation?

On May 30, 2024, the Russian Foreign Ministry on X (formerly Twitter), commenting on the forthcoming D-Day commemorations in the West, stated that "Of course, nothing is said in the West about the fact that no D-Day would have been possible without the Red Army's success." The comment is accurate. Coinciding with D-Day was the start of Operation Bagration against the depleted Army Group Center, most of which took place on the territory of the prewar BSSR. Timed for the second anniversary of Hitler's attack on the Soviet Union, it involved four armies of the First, Second, and Third Belorussian Fronts and the First Baltic Front under the overall command of Georgy Zhukov and Aleksandr Vasilevsky. The initial targets were Viciebsk, Orša, and Babrujsk, with the former taken on June 26, followed by nearby Orša. The armies then turned toward Minsk, which was liberated on July 3, one week later. Minsk had been destroyed by bombs and missiles, so little was left of the prewar structures. Only 40% of its prewar residents remained.

The second stage of Operation Bagration saw the liberation of Brest on July 28, after which the engagements moved beyond the borders of the BSSR. Soviet sources estimate that 1.3 million Belarusians fought in the Red Army. At the main memorial site located on the territory of the destroyed village of Chatyń 30 miles from Minsk, burned down by auxiliary troops of the Schutzmannschaft Battalion 118 on March 22, 1943, one finds the statement that it was one of 9,200 settlements destroyed by the invader. The BSSR reportedly lost over half its national wealth as a result of the war. After the war the government of the republic demanded in reparations from Germany a sum of \$1.5 billion, but that sum only covered a fraction of the costs.

There is no doubt that the losses were catastrophic and the psychological impact of the period of occupation on Belarusians could only be imagined. Belarus lost a minimum of 1.8 million people, about one-third of whom consisted of its Jewish population. Even the international community gave some recognition to the republic when it agreed that the two republics that had suffered most from the German occupation, Belarus and Ukraine, should be given seats at the newly established United Nations—Stalin had demanded seats for each republic. The war remained in the minds of the public, but ironically the memory was perpetuated even more in the twenty-first century than at any time after the defeat of Nazi Germany. It was portrayed dramatically and with painful realism in the works of the former junior lieutenant Vasil Bykau (born 1924) and the child soldier Ales Adamovich (born 1927), both of whom became critics of, and exiles from, the regime of Lukashenka in their later lives.

In Minsk in particular, but in all cities and towns of Belarus, the war monuments began to replace Lenin as the defining symbol of the past. The Museum of the Great Patriotic War was a project undertaken almost immediately in 1944 following the recapture of Minsk. It occupied a prominent place in the corner of Kastryčnickaja (October) Square next to the Trades Union building until 2014. In that year, a new museum opened that was far more ornate and modern, some distance away next to the location of the stela denoting Minsk as a Hero City on the Avenue of the Victors and taking up a space of 45,200 square feet in Victory Park. It has become the most popular place to visit in Belarus and has a special "Museum for Children," which is free of charge and caters to school excursions. The scale of the museum renders it perhaps the most elaborate museum to the war worldwide. Other memorials include Victory Square with an obelisk on the main highway, the Mound of Glory just outside the city, made up of soil from each Soviet republic, the Chatyń Memorial, and the Stalin Line Museum. Statues of partisans and a partisan monument close to the subway station of the same name are also notable.

What were the main features of cultural and political developments in the postwar years?

The years of war and occupation brought both economic and demographic devastation to the lands of the BSSR, which were quickly reunified following the Soviet advance in the summer of 1944. The worst destruction was caused by the major battles between the two great armies, particularly by Operation Bagration, which led to the virtual destruction of the German Army Group Center. The overall losses to the Belarusian population were estimated by the partisan (and later party) leader Piotr Masherau at one in four of the population, or between 1.8 and 2.2 million people. As the years of the war, and the Great Patriotic War itself, became heavily politicized during the third decade of the Lukashenka presidency, the number of losses began to increase, to as high as 3 million, and to one in three of the population. New sites of the dead were suddenly discovered, and at the time of writing, new investigations are under way.

In 2012, Belarusian historian Immanuel Ioffe outlined the official approach to the question of war losses. In an article entitled "Truths and Myths about War Losses," published in the pro-government newspaper *SB Belarus Segodnya*, he provided figures on the number of children born on Belarusian territory during the war and estimated the losses in each region, in death camps such as Maly Traścianiec, and among those sent to Germany for forced labor. His total for the number of losses is just over 1.8 million, which included 715,000 Belarusian Jews, leaving 1,130,155 mortalities in the BSSR. As about 80% of those were ethnic Belarusians, then 904,124 Belarusians died during the years of the Great Patriotic War, in addition to an estimated 173,200 in forced labor abroad. Thus, his total for war losses is 1,077,324 people, out of his calculated total of 6.47 million ethnic Belarusians on the eve of the war, or between one-sixth and one-seventh of the total number. But in calculating human losses on all fronts, including the destruction of about 55,000 collaborators, those who died abroad, fighting in Japan and on other fronts, the human losses amounted to one-third of the prewar population or 2.2 million people.

It seems illogical to exaggerate the human impact of such a cataclysmic tragedy in which the people of the Soviet Union suffered more than other parts of Europe and Asia, except for China. About one-third of the mortalities occurred among the Jewish population, once a thriving community in the cities of Belarus. Its presence was not completely eradicated, but it was reduced to a shadow of its former self. Cities like Hrodna, Brest, and Minsk were once prominent in the Russian Empire's Pale of Settlement to which Jews had been confined during the reign of Catherine II, with many confined to small shtetls rather than the larger cities. The later years of Stalin saw Hitler's work compounded with a harsh campaign directed against so-called rootless cosmopolitans, focused on Jews in all capacities, from cultural figures to doctors. On January 13, 1948, an assassin murdered Solomon Mikhoels, the leader of the wartime Jewish Anti-Fascist Committee, in the center of Minsk, along with theater critic Vladimir Golubov-Potapov. Their deaths were officially attributed to a traffic accident.

In the early postwar years, the atmosphere of suspicion that had been so prevalent in the 1930s returned to the Belarusian lands. Since they had been occupied longer than most other parts of the Soviet Union, Stalin and his fellow leaders were suspicious that they had fallen under Nazi influence. And some had surrendered, or, worse, had collaborated with the occupiers, particularly at the start of the war. That suspicion even extended to the defenders of the Brest Fortress, and its leader, Piotr Gavrilov, was deprived of his Communist Party card and sent to run a prisoner of war camp for Japanese prisoners in Siberia in the early war years. His membership was only restored four years after the death of Stalin, in 1957, when he received the award Hero of the Soviet Union and the Order of Lenin for his bravery during the initial Soviet invasion.

The rebuilding of cities became a priority, and the formerly rural landscape quickly became urbanized, while the rural regions were neglected during the early postwar Five-Year Plans. Industrial output in the first postwar year was 20% of that of 1940, so most of the investment of the Fourth Five-Year Plan was devoted to the restoring industry. Given the beginning of the Cold War and the fear of a coming war with the United States and Great Britain, the priority was to be military industries, particularly given the geostrategic position of Belarus as a western borderland. That need gradually eased once the states of eastern Europe acquired Communist rulers and were fully subject to the leadership and policies of the Soviet Union in the late 1940s.

Superficially, the BSSR gained in prestige after the war ended. It became a founding member of the newly established United Nations, with its own seat, in recognition for the suffering it had endured during the years of Nazi occupation. But that recognition did not provide any national cultural revival to compare with the 1920s. The party leader after the war remained Pantaleimon Ponomarenko, the Stalinist who had supervised the partisan operations and remained a close associate of Stalin, as he had during the 1930s purges. Ponomarenko was known not only for his cruelty but also for his corruption, as he used his party position to promote his own cult of personality and to aggrandize himself through property and wealth. Although there were some attempts to investigate his activities, none prevented his advancement, as his later career shows. In March 1947, he was replaced as First Secretary of the CPB by Mikalai Husarau, but eventually Ponomarenko was added to Stalin's Presidium as a full member in 1952–1953. Even though he came under suspicion after the death of Stalin, he soon recovered, becoming the party leader of Kazakhstan in 1954 and ambassador of the USSR to Poland in 1955–1957.

In July 1956, Kiryl Mazurau became the First Secretary of the BSSR, only the second ethnic Belarusian to hold this position since the short and ill-fated leadership of Sharanhovich. A former Komsomol leader whose reputation had been made as a partisan during the war, Mazurau supported Khrushchev in his conflict against the hardline Stalinists who tried to remove him from the Soviet leadership in Moscow in 1957 (Malenkov, Kaganovich, Molotov). He combined fanaticism for the Communist cause with attempts to restore the use of the Belarusian language and the industrial development of the republic. Under his leadership, in 1958, the Navapolack oil refinery was established, as well as the "Palimir" chemical plant. He also initiated the exploration and development of diamond deposits in the republic, although the factory for the industry only appeared in Homiel in the 1970s.

Another major enterprise that appeared at this time was Belaruskali, the Belarusian Potash Company, established in 1958, which grew into one of the world's largest potash companies, and the most profitable factory in the country. Most of its exports went to China by the twenty-first century. Belarus also saw the construction of weapons and rocket factories as its towns began to grow into industrial centers and much of the population began to migrate from villages into towns. Belarus became well known for the production of tractors, machine building, and potash fertilizers to enhance agricultural production. The best-known tractor company—Minsk Tractor Works (MTZ)—was established in 1946, with its well-known MTZ-1 and MRZ-2 caterpillar models in production from 1953.

In 1965, the first production at the Hrodna "Azot" Company started its operations as a nitrogen and fertilizer plant that was transformed by 1975 into the Hrodna Production Association Azot called Siarhei Prytytski (named after the former Western Belarusian Communist leader of the 1930s and later a prominent partisan chief). Other industries that developed in the postwar Soviet period included the production of TV sets, oil processing, trucks, and metal-cutting lathes, giving the BSSR the reputation as the workshop of the Soviet Union. In agriculture, the main products grown were grain, potatoes, sugar beets, flax, vegetables, and dairy products.

While such development might have facilitated intellectual development of the titular group as Belarusians became urbanized, Soviet policy precluded much progress in culture and language, despite the efforts of Mazurau and his successor, another former partisan leader Piotr Masherau (who headed the BSSR in 1965–1980) to promote the Belarusian cause. As Belarusians moved from the countryside to the industrializing cities, they encountered a Russian-speaking environment that included migrants from all parts of the Soviet Union. There was little chance of the majority Belarusians having a major impact on their fellow citizens because the Moscow leadership has imposed a policy of Russification since the early postwar years. The migration in turn drastically reduced the village population, the traditional base of the Belarusian language. Russian migration into Belarusian cities also occurred such that by 1970, about one-fifth of city residents were ethnic Russians.

The biggest changes in composition of the population took place in the 1970s, when the rural population declined by about 700,000 and the urban dwellers increased by about 1.7 million, signifying that a majority of those moving into the urban areas were from outside the republic. By 1979 the rural population had dropped to 3.5 million. Unsurprisingly, the elderly were generally the ones who remained behind, whereas their children sought employment in the towns. The villages were quite primitive, with poor roads, and the collectivized agriculture barely sustained the population. The cities, on the other hand, were growing rapidly as new industries developed.

Some analysts as a result have perceived the period as a success story for economic development, but in terms of national culture, it was one of gradual but clear decline of Belarusian: in publications, business, schools, and careers, Russian became the dominant language. More than 60% of the books published in the BSSR in the 1970s were in the Russian language. In the city of Minsk in 1970, more than 50% of the population declared Russian to be their native language and only 3% spoke Belarusian on a daily basis. The period saw the peak of the eastern direction of the republic, which even in the 1920s and 1930s could boast an impressive number of scholars using the Belarusian language in their works.

The policy of Russification can be dated back to the earlier days of the Russian Empire, but the 1920s had provided realistic hope that Belarusian could eventually replace it. The partisan leaders provided some credibility to the notion of a Belarusian nation while adding to the myths of the wartime heroics. Mazurau moved to Moscow in 1965, and his replacement and protégé, Piotr Masherau, was the most charismatic leader in the position of the First Secretary or Communist leader of the republic. From a humble background in the Viciebsk region, popular rumors suggested that he derived his name from a soldier in Napoleon's Grande Armée of 1812, who had remained behind after the failed efforts to defeat the Russian army of Tsar Aleksandr I. Reportedly, the soldier converted to Orthodoxy and married a local peasant woman, and Masherau was his great-great-grandson.

Masherau's early years were perhaps typically tragic for the 1930s era. The family was chronically short of food, and his father Miron was arrested in 1937 and given a ten-year sentence in a labor camp for "anti-Soviet agitation." He died before fulfilling the sentence but was fully rehabilitated in the 1950s. Piotr studied mathematics and physics at the Kirov Viciebsk Pedagogical Institute, graduating in 1939, after which he taught these two subjects at a secondary school in Rasony, in the Viciebsk region. When the Nazis invaded the Soviet Union, Masherau volunteered for the Red Army and his initial role was in a "destruction battalion," whose task it was to target deserters and spies or prevent the retreat of Soviet units.

Subsequently, he formed an underground Komsomol unit in the Rosson region before acquiring command of his own partisan unit named after N. A. Shchors. The unit operated in Viciebsk region as well as over the former Soviet borders of Latvia and Russia, all in the rear of the advancing German army. During his partisan years, he was twice wounded, became a full member of the Communist Party in 1943, and by 1944 received the prestigious title of "Hero of the Soviet Union." His chief achievement as a partisan was blowing up a major bridge on the Viciebsk-Riga highway, an operation he led under his pseudonym, Dubniak.

The fifteen years of Masherau's leadership are regarded as something of a golden era for the BSSR, and it is difficult to discern the extent to which the leader was an initiator or simply a witness during what were the peak years of the Soviet Union. Elena Gapova has described this period as one of "rebirth of living socialism" and sees it as a romantic shift in "imagining the native lands of Belarus." Many historians, though, condemn him for further Sovietization of Belarus. During his rule, BSSR infamously became "the most Soviet [i.e., nationless] Republic" among all other ones. There is no doubt that Masherau was a populist style politician, a good communicator, and an economic reformer—to the extent that the Soviet Union was committed to such a path. Certainly, he embraced the efforts of Kosygin to enhance the power of factories to distribute profits, and he presided over a period of rapid industrial expansion in his own republic.

In this period, too, in line with the narratives emanating from Moscow, the BSSR began to recognize and commemorate some of the feats of the war, such as the creation of the Brest Memorial Fortress, with its elaborate sculptures, a massive park to the east of the city. Masherau had spent some of his early career in Brest, where he had been the party secretary between 1955 and 1959 and responsible for the opening of the museum at the memorial site. He also promoted the development of Western Belarus and the fostering of education and culture.

There are also reports that it was Masherau who pleaded with Brezhnev for the construction of Minsk metro as a priority project and took part in the discussions over its design. It was operational only from 1984. It was in this period also that the construction of the Niamiha area replaced the older historical buildings in this part of Minsk, although the final product did not please the leader, who had wanted Minsk to have an equivalent area to Warsaw's Old Town. Ironically, perhaps, it was in the Lukashenka period that such a design materialized. The image of a booming republic under a smiling, much-loved leader is persuasive though not convincing, but his attempts to revive agriculture were less successful.

By contrast, Masherau was also a prominent figure supporting the 1968 Soviet invasion of Czechoslovakia, fearing that the sentiments of the Prague Spring might spread to his republic. That is not surprising, given Masherau's dedication to Marxism-Leninism, but one should note also that by the 1970s, he was beginning to distance himself from the corruption pervading the leadership of Leonid I. Brezhnev, and what were becoming ritualistic celebrations of the achievements of the Moscow leader and the Soviet state. Like Gorbachev a few years later, Masherau was a believer in the principles laid down by Lenin, a "pure Communist" who was appalled by the corruption he saw among the party hierarchy in Moscow.

We know more about Masherau's personality than that of any other Belarusian leader prior to Lukashenka. He projected an image of a kind, smiling man of the people, one who traveled around his republic by helicopter—another practice adopted deliberately by Lukashenka in emulation—attending sporting events, ballets, operas, and visiting the forests, especially Biełaviežskaja pušča (Belavezha Forest), which crosses the border into Poland. He did not drink alcohol but smoked incessantly, and in the late 1970s flew to Moscow to have his kidney removed, perhaps an indicator that the local hospitals were not considered adequate for such an operation. Masherau evidently suffered from high blood pressure because of the stressfulness of his position. The way he departed from the world shortly afterward may have defined his legacy in Belarus, and it also provides an apt illustration of the nature of his leadership.

On October 4, 1980, Masherau set off from Minsk to Žodzina in a Gaz-13 Chaika car in a cavalcade of three cars. At the front was a white Volga car and a traffic police car in the rear. The cavalcade was traveling at about 80 miles per hour on the Minsk-Moscow highway. Improvements had been made to the road in preparation for the 1980 Olympic Games, but the lanes were still not clearly defined with white lines. Also, several official rules were broken. Masherau sat in the front seat next to the driver, Yauhen Zaitsau, with Major Valiantsin Chasnakou of the security services in the rear. By tradition, the party leader should not have been sitting in the front. The lead vehicle had no flashing lights, so it was less obvious to other cars that they should move to the side of the highway.

Reports suggest the lead car was also about 500 feet ahead of the car carrying Masherau when in theory it should have been much closer. The object of the journey had not been officially announced beforehand but that was not unusual with the Belarusian leader who flouted formalities. At the entrance to a farm near Smaliavičy, a MAZ truck approached the motorcade. Seeing the approach of the three cars coming at high speed, it began to slow down but in turn it was overtaken by a dump truck full of potatoes driven by Mikalai Pustavit. The front car of the cavalcade accelerated to avoid the dump truck, which then collided with the car carrying Masherau at a speed of around 60 miles an hour.

The crash resulted in the death of Masherau, his driver, and the security officer, and the Chaika was filled with potatoes. The dump truck driver survived but tried to commit suicide when he realized what he had done. At a trial in December 1980, the court found Pustovit guilty and sentenced him to fifteen years in a penal colony, but the sentence was later reduced under an amnesty, and he served only three years. The circumstances of the accident seemed preventable had Masherau and his aides followed the usual rules and in the appropriate vehicles. But rumors began to circulate that the crash was not an accident, that the authorities in Moscow had targeted Masherau for his independent policies. Masherau was known to be on bad terms with Brezhnev's ideology secretary Mikhail Suslov. On the other hand, there were some unverified suggestions that Masherau was about to be appointed chairman of the USSR Council of Ministers. One person who benefited from Masherau's early demise was Suslov's protégé Mikhail Gorbachev, who was appointed a full member of the ruling Politburo at this same time.

The sudden death of a popular leader had a major impact on Belarus, which adorned several streets and factories in Masherau's name. One of the main streets in Minsk, starting in the Niamiha area, was named Prospekt Masherau until Lukashenka decided to rename it as Victory Avenue in 2005 (Masherau retained a street name in a less prominent part of Minsk). When Masherau's funeral was held in Minsk four days later, the CC CPSU Politburo was notable for its complete absence. The only senior figure in attendance was the Belarus-born secretary of the Central Committee Mikhail Zimianin, a former editor of *Pravda*. Given that Masherau was a Candidate Member and leader of a national republic, the absence was astonishing, a deliberate rebuff and a suggestion that he had become a persona non grata. Taken alone, that does not indicate that he was deliberately targeted, and one would have thought that the KGB would in such a case have deployed a more sophisticated device than a potato truck.

Given the direction of contemporary Belarus and its focus on the Great Patriotic War, Masherau will remain a figure of significance in Belarusian society. Like the writer Vasil Bykau, his name is synonymous with the wartime period and partisan activities. Whereas the former resorted to the pen to express himself, Masherau, in his own words, "loved the people" and spent as much time as possible among them. None of the leaders that followed made remotely the same impact, nor did they last as long. Strictly speaking, Masherau was the third partisan leader to be appointed the Communist Party leader in the republic, after Ponomarenko and Mazurau, but the former was a leader in the Stalinist mold, who fled to Moscow at the approach of the Germans. Though he headed the headquarters of the partisans, he operated from a distance. Mazurau and Masherau, by contrast, both fought in the occupied territories and both were linked with the Komsomol underground as well as partisans. After the war, they faced an uphill battle to get recognition for their wartime operations prior to the death of the suspicious Stalin.

What was the impact of the 1986 Chernobyl disaster in Belarus?

Although the Chernobyl disaster in Ukraine took place only 10 miles south of the Belarusian border, it took some time for the repercussions on the republic to become evident. The initial explosions at the reactor in the early hours of April 26, 1986, led to the release of numerous radioactive isotopes to the northwest, directly over Belarusian lands, for about a week before the wind changed direction and blew from the north, moving the radioactive cloud over the Ukrainian capital of Kyiv. Belarus, then known as the Byelorussian Soviet Socialist Republic, received the largest portion of the radiation fallout, though its leaders had no authority over the Chernobyl plant and no independent means of addressing it since all decisions about response were elaborated in Moscow. Like Ukraine, the official secrecy over the scale of the accident, especially in the first days, was responsible for the impact that followed.

About 90% of the republic was irradiated with short-lived radionuclides, particularly Iodine-131 with a half-life of eight days, deposited by the radiation cloud that was formed after the two steam explosions at the fourth reactor unit of the "Lenin" nuclear power plant at Chernobyl in the early morning of April 26, 1986. The reaction of the republican authorities was delayed by the lack of information about what had happened from both the Soviet authorities in Moscow and the Ukrainian party leadership in Kyiv. But there were no efforts to provide the population with safety measures, such as potassium iodide tablets, or warnings to stay indoors.

Turning to specifics: in May 1986, the Soviet authorities evacuated about 45,000 people from the Belarusian side of the designated 18.5-mile zone. The decision followed the creation of a Government Commission to investigate the consequences of the disaster, which included the academician and future parliamentary chair Stanislau Shushkevich. The Commission received instructions from Moscow to conceal the main findings, to which Shushkevich objected. He was then dismissed. As in Ukraine, the May Day celebration on May 1, 1986, went ahead as normal. Unlike his Ukraine counterpart V. V. Shcherbytsky, the Communist Party leader in Belarus, Mikalai Sliunkou did visit the contaminated regions of the Homiel region that were located inside the evacuation zone. But that was an isolated event in a leadership marked by ritualism and lack of action. And in contrast to the much-publicized evacuation of Prypiat (population 54,000) on the Ukrainian side of the zone, the republican leaders opted to decontaminate Brahin, the most affected population point, without evacuating the population.

In 1989, the Soviet central media published maps illustrating the extent of radioactive fallout for the first time. The maps, which also appeared in the republican press, contradicted earlier statements about the path of radiation fallout. The public information had suggested that the radioactive cloud created by the explosions moved to the west and northwest, but between May 1 and 5, the wind changed direction, carrying particles to the northeast of the plant as well, and these days were the most dangerous for Belarus. One of the chief scientists involved in monitoring the situation, Yauhen Kanaplya, commented that radioactive hotspots had been detected in the west and far eastern parts of the republic. The city of Homiel, Belarus's second largest city, reported a rise in the natural radiation background of 130,000 times, far higher than in the capital Minsk.

The total area of Chernobyl-linked contamination in the Soviet Union was reportedly 10,750 square miles, of which 6,400 square miles (59%) were located in Belarus. At higher levels—usually measured by the content of Cesium-137 in the soil—the proportion was higher, at around 62%. At 40 curies, the amount that required immediate evacuation of the population, the Belarusian segment was almost 70%. Altogether, 400 villages received over 15 curies, compared to 206 in Russia and 49 in Ukraine. Seventy Belarusian settlements received over 40 curies of Cesium-137.

The situation in the BSSR was worsened by the extensive area of sandy peat oil, which retains radioactive particles. Peat soil, in contrast to heavy clay soil, can contaminate agricultural products at exposure levels of only 2–4 curies. Belarus also contains a wide area of swampland in the southwest and southeast, the Palesie marshes, and in peat swamps radionuclides were detected at levels as deep as 1 foot. At the height of the Chernobyl aftermath in the late 1980s and early 1990s, about 20% of Belarus lay in the contaminated zone, which contained a population of around 2.2 million. The accident also removed from agricultural production about 635,000 acres of agricultural land and 3.31 million acres of forest (15% of the total forest area of the republic). Thus, the impact of the explosions on the territory of Belarus constituted an unprecedented environmental catastrophe.

Radioactive iodine—Iodine-131—took a serious toll that took some time to discern. By the early 1990s, it resulted in about 4,000 cases of thyroid gland cancer, almost a quarter of them in young children, and in most cases contracted after 1989. The long-term effects were equally serious. Over the seventeen-year period 1986–2003, doctors carried out surgery on almost 2,000 young adults and children, and 19 had died because of the progression of the tumors. About 23% of the BSSR was contaminated with Cesium-137 and Strontium-90, which have half-lives of 30 and 29 years respectively. About 2% of the territory was affected with radionuclides of Plutonium, which has a half-life of 24,000 years. Most of the affected regions, of which Homiel, Mahilioŭ, and Brest were the worst afflicted, did not take any preventive action until 1989, when it was revealed in Soviet media that they formed part of the contaminated zone.

In the first five years after the Chernobyl accident, there was a threefold increase in illnesses among the Belarusian population. These were not all related directly to Chernobyl or radiation but arose from a combination of factors, one of which was enhanced monitoring of the population's health, and another a general fear of radiation that prevented the consumption of nutritious foods. Further, the amount of funding dedicated to Chernobyl problems decreased dramatically after Belarus became independent in 1991. Belarusian doctors discovered not only thyroid cancer among children, but also a huge rise in cases of diabetes; neither had been a factor in this age group prior to the disaster.

In addition, the establishment of a presidency and the election of Aliaksandr Lukashenka proved detrimental to a prolonged attention to the health and economic situation in the 1990s. The fact that the Popular Front had embraced the effects and victims of Chernobyl and taken a strong stance against plans to build a nuclear power plant in the republic politicized the situation. It also increased the lack of confidence in the government of the general population, particularly as the advice of scientists was ignored, several were arrested, and the government insisted that economic life should not be affected. Land should be cultivated and products consumed. The long-term effects thus remained in Homiel, Brest, and Mahilioŭ regions for many years afterward.

Thus, in April 1992, the Belarusian organization Public Opinion carried out a survey of 826 residents in the areas contaminated by Chernobyl radiation. Over 40% responded that there had been no improvements in state aid over the previous three years. In reply to the question regarding which entities had provided the most effective assistance, 64% chose the nongovernment Belarusian Charitable Fund "For the Children of Chernobyl," led by a university professor and member of the Belarusian Popular Front, Henadz Hrushavy (Gennady Grushevoy in Russian), whereas only 11% selected government organizations and 10.5% local and district authorities. The Children of Chernobyl group had by this time sent over 12,000 children from the contaminated zones abroad for recuperation to Germany, and other European countries, as well as Canada and the United States.

By 1997, the government began to harass the Fund, sending KGB officials to its headquarters, conducting audits, and eventually evicting it from its location. Its leaders fled to Germany, accused of financial improprieties. Other charities such as the Irish Chernobyl Children's Fund, by contrast, opted to cooperate with the government, transferring some of the sick children to hospitals in Ireland for treatment. The charitable funds worldwide had the effect of bringing Belarus to world attention while providing an opportunity for the children to experience life in different societies. In terms of the health benefits for the children, the impact is questionable, particularly in locations like Cuba, where lengthy airplane flights would only increase the amount of radiation for the passengers. But for children from small villages, often without roads, the impact was considerable.

Chernobyl was a key concern of the Belarusian Popular Front, which helped organize an annual protest march on April 26 each year in central Minsk, often organized by the "For the Children of Chernobyl Fund." The Fund held summer camps in the forests where it was freer to allow more political expression and denounced nuclear power and the Lukashenka regime. As a result, the question of the accident and its consequences became politicized. The tenth anniversary march in 1996, in which over 50,000 people took part, ended in violence as riot police broke up the march using truncheons. Afterward, armed police wearing masks stormed the headquarters of the Popular Front. Pazniak and several colleagues escaped through the back door and fled over the border into Poland and later to the United States, where they requested and received political asylum. Thereafter, the authorities insisted that all problems related to Chernobyl had been dealt with, and the affected lands could once again be cultivated and used for agricultural purposes.

How was the Belarusian Popular Front formed and what was its role in promoting culture and democracy in the period after 1988?

The prequel to the formation of the Belarusian Popular Front (BPF) was a club to protect monuments known as Talaka (society), formed in 1985. It involved itself in excavations and the protection of historical and architectural monuments. It also pursued cultural and educational pursuits and the revival of folk traditions and customs. Its creators included Siarzhuk Vitushka, Vintsuk Viachorka, Viktar Ivashkevich, and Ales Susha. Its emblem was Minsk City Hall, which at the time needed restoration. It was one of the first informal organizations in Belarus and became influential by the late 1980s. Its publications included a wall newspaper *Ratusha* and the humor publication *Bruk*, released on the Day of the Soviet Army, February 23, 1989. Its activities also included large crowd events such as the "Dvinsk Rally '87," in defense of the Upper Town; Pripyat88, related to the Chernobyl disaster; Kurapaty, the memorial site to Stalin-period NKVD victims; and an anti-missile campaign at the Eastern Cemetery.

On the initiative of Talaka, its adherents readopted the slogan "Long live Belarus," as well as the white-red-white national flag and the Pahonia coat of arms. Although hundreds took part in its activities, it retained a core membership of fifty, with Vitushka invariably at the helm.

The BPF, which followed Talaka with an overlapping membership, was a public organization formed also from an earlier formation known as Martyrology of Belarus, which focused on the repressions in Belarus under Stalin, particularly in 1937–1938, but generally during the entire time of the dictator's rule between 1928 and 1953. It had two other prime raisons d'être: the first was the fate and future of the Belarusian language, which had been badly neglected in the postwar period, when both education and public life prioritized Russian; and the second was the Chernobyl disaster and its repercussions in the republic.

All three causes were part of the platform of the BPF when it was founded in 1988 under its original name of Belarusian Popular Front for Perestroika "Revival." (The "for Perestroika" was removed from its title in 1990.) The time saw parallel popular fronts formed in Soviet republics, starting in the Baltic States and spreading to Ukraine (the Rukh), the Caucasus, and Central Asia. In contrast to the other republics, however, the founding congress of the BPF could not be held in Belarus and was ultimately convoked in Vilnius, Lithuania. Its creation was initiated by Zianon Pazniak, along with Liavon Barshcheuski, Vasyl Bykau, Viktar Ivashkevich, Henadz Hrushavy, Vintsuk Viachorka, Ales Bialatski, Ales Adamovich, and others. It had about 10,000 members and gained the support of around 1 million voters during the parliamentary elections of 1990. They were people who advocated change, more steps to democracy, and investigations into past killings like Kurapaty and the nuclear catastrophe after Chernobyl.

Following the lead of Pazniak, the BPF's early focus was on Stalin-era repressions, and it initiated the "Dzyady" protest at Kurapaty, the main site of the victims of 1937–1941 on October 30, 1988, which the authorities eventually dispersed. Nine months after its founding congress, the organization took part in elections to the Supreme Soviet of the BSSR in March-April 1990, electing twenty-five deputies, with several other sympathizers. The results brought significant minority status, and the group became a vocal faction in the assembly promoting the Belarusian language and culture, as well as national consciousness. As the Soviet Union struggled with an economic crisis and republics began to assert their sovereignty, the BPF was able to advance the question of Belarusian as the state language, along with the white-red-white national flag, the Pahonia emblem associated with the Grand Duchy of Lithuania, and focus on the mass graves at Kurapaty. By 1993, it had formed a political party of the same name, under the leadership of Pazniak.

Both the declaration of state sovereignty on July 26, 1990, and the declaration of independence on August 25, 1991, were largely the result of BPF activity. Pazniak, a native of Hrodna region, who had a degree in art history and followed with training in archeology, had been a senior research fellow at the Institute of Ethnography, Art History, and Folklore of the Academy of Sciences of the BSSR. He had taken part in most of the rallies in 1989 and 1990, and in one rally in the latter year, Pazniak and Lukashenka spoke on the same platform in Mahilioŭ, a time when the political direction of the future president was uncertain. By March 1991, the BPF sought independence for Belarus, the formation of a national army, Belarusian citizenship, and holding an all-Belarusian Congress to determine the future direction of the republic.

The BPF originally supported Gorbachev's March 1991 referendum to rework the Soviet Union as a Union of Soviet Sovereign Republics. In August 1991, when reactionary elements of the Soviet leadership attempted a putsch and arrested Gorbachev at his dacha in Crimea, the BPF was one of the few organizations in Belarus to oppose it openly. Once it failed, the BPF used the opportunity to push much of its program through a session of the Supreme Council, resulting in the independence vote that essentially ratified the earlier declaration of sovereignty.

However, the BPF was never a majority party. The Communists still dominated the Supreme Soviet, which had been elected before the end of the USSR. Thus, Pazniak and his colleagues worked hard to secure signatures for a referendum to hold new elections, for which 350,000 was the minimum number. The BPF gathered 442,000 signatures, which it forwarded to the Central Election Commission (CEC) in April 1992. Neither the CEC, the chair of the parliament Stanislau Shushkevich, nor the Supreme Soviet of the 12th Session was willing to accept the notion of new elections. The Communists feared losing their majority. Their obdurate attitude signified that the only way forward was a presidential state, the position favored by the pro-government majority who anticipated that the current prime minister Viachaslau Kebich would be the likely victor. The BPF advanced Pazniak as their candidate for president, a position its members had not supported because they believed it might presage a dictatorship.

As noted elsewhere, Pazniak officially came third in the election with 12.8% of votes, although there seem to have been some falsifications to swell the vote of Kebich, though not enough to forestall the second-round victory of Lukashenka. The BPF continued as an opposition party, and in April 1995 Pazniak and eighteen other deputies went on a hunger strike inside the parliament building to protest Lukashenka's 1995 referendum (see above). After Pazniak's 1995 election to the parliament was declared invalid because of negative votes against the two candidates, he left Belarus in 1996. The BPF formally split into two parties by 1999 after a debate over tactics, with the more radical wing forming the Conservative Christian Party of the BPF under the exiled Pazniak and the Party of the BPF, initially led by Vintsuk Viachorka. But both wings of the party remained active in support of Belarusian language and culture until their formal abolition in July 2023. Both supported the cultural and national revival of the Belarusian nation, although membership inside the country had fallen to around 3,500 at the time of its dissolution by the authorities

What role did Belarus play in the Belavezha Accords in December 1991?

Belarus's head of state and chair of the Supreme Soviet (Parliament) Stanislau Shushkevich hosted the December 1991 meeting at Biełaviežskaja pušča (Belavezha Forest) with Russian and Ukrainian presidents Boris Yeltsin and Leonid Kravchuk, which created a Commonwealth of Independent States to remove Mikhail Gorbachev and bring an end to the Soviet Union. The planning of the meeting involved some subterfuge because Gorbachev was unaware that it was taking place and it ran counter to the Soviet leader's lengthy quest to bring about the signing of a Union Agreement with most major republics of the Soviet Union—the Baltic States, Georgia, Armenia, and Moldova did not take part in the so-called Novo-Ogarevo process that followed a referendum in March 1991 to establish a new Union of Soviet Sovereign Republics.

Although some progress was made toward the Union Agreement, it was undermined by the putsch in Moscow starting on August 19, 1991, and the establishment of an Emergency Committee led by Vice President Gennady Yanayev, police chief Boris Pugo, and head of the KGB, Vladimir Kryuchkov, and several others, all of whom were Gorbachev appointees. The Committee was set up to try to reverse the changes of recent times, prevent a Union Treaty that would allow sovereignty to the national republics, and re-establish Communist Party authority. Gorbachev, who was vacationing at his mansion in Soros, Crimea, together with his wife and daughter, were placed under house arrest. The committee declared that he was ill and unable to carry out his duties. Following the failure of the putsch two days later, Gorbachev returned to Moscow, facing a situation in which those he had added to the leadership had betrayed him.

His rival Boris Yeltsin brought him to the Russian Parliament (Congress of Deputies), where he was obliged to support a ban on the Communist Party and resign from his position as General Secretary of the party's Central Committee. Yeltsin, who had been voted Russian president in June 1991, was now able to dictate what happened next.

Both Ukraine and Belarus decided to use the vacuum of power in Moscow to declare independence on successive days. In Belarus's case, the declaration of independence on August 25, 1991, was to give legal status to the declaration of sovereignty on July 27, 1990. The document was thus only one page in length and echoed what had been written a year earlier. Though badly weakened and shocked by the declarations, Gorbachev persisted in trying to form a new Union Agreement. The leaders of the three Slavic republics therefore took matters into their own hands by agreeing to negotiate between themselves, using the independence declarations as the basis for asserting such authority. Shushkevich was the host, but the key figures were the leaders of the two larger republics, Yeltsin and Kravchuk.

Yeltsin's main goal was to remove Gorbachev; Kravchuk, bolstered by the referendum in Ukraine on December 1, 1990, in which over 90% supported the independence declaration, was content with Russia's recognition of an independent Ukraine in its existing borders. Shushkevich's position was like that of Kravchuk, but without the support that the latter enjoyed. It was by no means clear that Belarusians would unequivocally back the declaration of independence if it severed the republic from the Russian sphere and Moscow. Moreover, Shushkevich personally had stepped into the leadership position without the endorsement of a political party or even a significant faction in the parliament. He represented a republic that was far from united on what it needed for the future.

At the Viskuli Palace in Biełavieža (Belavezha), the three leaders signed a document establishing the formation of a Commonwealth of Independent States, leaving open many of the questions that would later lead to conflicts between Russia and Ukraine in particular. Of the three signatories, Belarus was the least nationally conscious and much of its population felt the need to remain close to Russia, its main source of energy supplies and past political leadership. The Communist Party remained the strongest political force even after the formal ban placed on the party for its support for the failed coup in Moscow. Whereas both Russia and Ukraine had nationally elected presidents, the Belarusian leadership was split between the Communists and a fringe of figures who leaned toward social democracy but lacked a firm political platform. Shushkevich himself, an academician and physicist, was a compromise figure, who emerged only because his predecessor as chair of parliament had supported those who took part in the August 1991 putsch.

Nevertheless, his association with the signing at Viskuli weakened him politically, particularly among those political leaders who could not conceive of a future for Belarus without Mother Russia. They would accuse Shushkevich of playing a key role in destroying the Soviet Union, which had the immediate effect of causing economic difficulties because of the sudden severance of ties that enabled the Belarusian economy to run smoothly. Initially, Belarus had firm boundaries, but no permanent currency, no energy resources, and continued an economic recession that had begun in the latter years of the Soviet Union. The future was uncertain, although one could also argue that with the collapse of the Moscow center, the republic had no choice but to forge its own path.

5

THE INDEPENDENCE PERIOD

Who were the main political leaders of Belarus at the time of independence?

The main leaders of Belarus until July 1990 were the leaders of the Communist Party (Yafrem Sakalou) and government (Mikalai Dzemiantsei), and the leader of the Popular Front (Zianon Pazniak). Sakalou was born in 1926 in the village Reviačyna in the Orša region. He served in the Soviet army from 1944 to 1950 and later graduated from the Belarusian Agricultural Academy in 1956, having become a member of the Communist Party (CPSU) the previous year. In 1977, he was appointed the party leader in the Brest region, where he gained a reputation as honest and measured, yet uncharismatic. He devoted himself to the production of pork and improved infrastructure throughout the region; he was promoted in February 1987 to the position of First Secretary of the Central Committee (CC) of the Communist Party of Byelorussia (CPB). From July to December 1990, he also had a seat in the ruling USSR Politburo in Moscow. Sakalou retired the day after the BSSR declared sovereignty, the first step on the road to independence; he died in Minsk in April 2022.

A more controversial figure was Mikalai Ivanovich Dzemiantsei (born May 25, 1930), a native of the village Chotlina in the Viciebsk region, who enjoyed a lengthy career in the party establishment. He began his career in 1958 as Second Secretary of the Viciebsk regional party committee with a joint appointment in the department of agriculture. In 1974, he became the leader of the Viciebsk party organization, and between 1979 and 1989, a secretary of the CC CPB. By July 1989 in the Gorbachev era, he had risen to the position of deputy chairman of the BSSR Supreme Soviet and was promoted to chair on May 18, 1990, the position he held when Belarus declared its sovereignty on July 27, 1990. On August 19, when an Emergency Committee took power in Moscow, declaring that Gorbachev had been taken ill, it received the full support of Dzemiantsei; thus, he became associated with that unpopular act of treachery. That fateful decision proved his downfall. The putsch failed, Gorbachev returned to Moscow, and the Belarusian Supreme Soviet convened on August 22 to discuss the events of the previous days. He therefore offered his resignation and was replaced by Stanislau Shushkevich. Dzemiantsei died in August 2018.

Perhaps the most pivotal figure in the period that led to Belarusian independence was Viachaslau (patronymic Frantsavich) Kebich, a native of Navahrudak district, which, at the time of his birth, was a settlement in Poland, a multiethnic region close to the BSSR border. Kebich graduated from the Belarusian Polytechnical Institute in Minsk in 1958, and after a career as an engineer at the Minsk Automatic Lines Plant and Minsk Kirov Machine-Tool Plant became the latter's director from 1973 to 1978. His political ascendence began when he was appointed Second Secretary of the Minsk City organization of the Communist Party, and between 1985 and 1990, he served as deputy chairman of the BSSR Council of Ministers and chair of the BSSR State Planning Committee. He took over as chair of the Council of Ministers (in Western terminology, the prime minister) in April 1990. In elections to the Congress of People's Deputies the previous year, he had won a seat, narrowly defeating a younger rival, Aliaksandr Lukashenka of the Mahilioŭ Electoral District.

Kebich might be considered a traditional Communist who retained his conservative views throughout his career, although he was astute enough to resign from the CPSU after the failure of the Moscow putsch in August 1991. He became the first government leader in independent Belarus on August 25, 1991. Four months later, he accompanied Shushkevich to the Brest region to assign the Belavezha Accords, signaling the end of the Soviet Union. Later, he was an enthusiastic supporter of a common currency with Russia and the military-security union with Russia, hoping for the eventual full restoration of the Soviet Union. However, Kebich has been accused of corruption, accusations that seem valid. Siarhei Navumchyk maintains that in subsequent presidential elections, Kebich lost out in the first round, but exerted his influence over the Election Commission to fabricate higher totals for himself and lower for Pazniak. After the 1994 presidential election, Kebich became a supporter of Lukashenka and a deputy in the House of Representatives from 1996 to 2004.

Some of Kebich's political stances have already been noted. He regarded Gorbachev as a traitor who betrayed his country (by the same token, Kebich's appearance in Belavezha was unavoidable and undertaken, he claimed, to save Belarus) and rejected democracy as a political concept. He dismissed the opposition that emerged against Lukashenka as "loudmouths," criticized the Belarusian Rada in exile, and advocated a closer union with Russia. After 2014, he praised the idea of a Russian World, a narrative propagated by Vladimir Putin when Russia annexed Crimea from Ukraine and fomented war in the Donbas. And his about-face on his rival Lukashenka was completed by 1996, when Kebich fully backed Lukashenka's referendum, enhancing the powers of the president and reducing the parliament to a virtual talking shop with only 120 deputies, compared to the original 260. The two political leaders were essentially in agreement by that time, although one would have to grant Lukashenka more flexibility in his political outlook than the older man. Kebich was a Communist by ideology and belief, rather than one who simply promoted his own power and influence.

Paradoxically for one who offered Lukashenka such unequivocal support, it was the latter's decision to ignore the COVID-19 virus (see below) that helped bring about Kebich's death. In November 2020, as the pandemic began to exert its full influence in Belarus, Kebich became hospitalized with the virus and died from cardiac arrest the following month at the age of eighty-four. He remains one of the key personalities of the independence period, representing the nomenklatura and party establishment.

The two other figures who emerged, Shushkevich and Pazniak, are more complex and exerted more influence over 1990s Belarus. We will cover Shushkevich in the next section but first, Pazniak.

Pazniak's career is that of a restless intellectual with a deep commitment to Belarusian statehood. Of all the political leaders of Belarus on the eve of independence and the immediate years following, he stands out for his outspokenness, honesty, and passion. And if one examines closely the discussions about Belarusian statehood, language, and culture, Pazniak is almost always playing the role of advocate. Virtually every move Belarus made toward democracy in this period can be attributed to the efforts of Pazniak from his seat in the Supreme Soviet, as the leader of the Belarusian Popular Front, or as an author, historian, and archeologist. That he lacked finesse, patience, or tolerance for his opponents is undeniable.

Zianon (patronymic Stanislavavich) Pazniak was born on April 24, 1944, in the village of Subotniki in the Hrodna region into a Roman Catholic family. Subotniki is a small settlement that originally belonged to the Radziwiłł family, and in 1921, its population of just over 500 was entirely made up of Poles (90%) and Jews (10%). Like Lukashenka, Pazniak lacked a father in his life, as his father went missing when he was only eight months old, although he remarked that he was there in spirit when he was growing up. The village was friendly and neighbors knew each other, but in the 1950s outsiders entered from the east, he recollects, who did not attend church, imbibed vodka, and mouthed obscenities. In his recollection, they were pariahs and the locals did not communicate with them.

His first passion was for astronomy and in 1962 he left for Moscow with the intention of studying astronomy at the university level, but he left after only a month. His other passions included the theater; after his short sojourn in Moscow, he enrolled at the Minsk Theater and Art Institute later the same year. He did not last long there, either, and was expelled for "political unreliability." (This was in the relatively benign period of Khrushchev's leadership.) He remained in Minsk, staying at a dormitory and relying on the hospitality of his fellow students. Eventually he obtained a job at the State Opera as a stagehand and earned some money as a photographer at the Yanka Kupala Museum. Thanks to the help of the poet and chairman of the Supreme Soviet of the BSSR, Maksim Tank, he entered the Department of Theater Studies at the Belarusian State Theater and Art Institute but was expelled before he could sit his final exams, reportedly for ripping down a wall newspaper that was in the Russian language.

Tank again came to his rescue, possibly because earlier in Western Ukraine he had worked alongside Pazniak's grandfather, and the expulsion was revoked. Pazniak finally earned his degree in 1968 and entered the Institute of Ethnography, Art History, and Folklore as a graduate student in 1969, writing a thesis on the history of the theater. Because of disagreements with his supervisors, however, he did not receive his candidate's degree until 1981 and defended his thesis in Leningrad. By then, in 1976, he had been fired from the Minsk Institute, and after some appeals, he moved to the Institute of History, where his field switched to archeology, studying the later Middle Ages. His turbulent and colorful career up to this point set him apart from the leading figures that emerged in the late 1980s.

During the Brezhnev period, Pazniak became a dissident, writing in *samizdat* under the pseudonym Henrykh Rakutovich. His main concern was the destruction of Belarusian culture since the 1930s and the need to rehabilitate Belarus's writers, poets, playwrights, and national political figures. (Combined with his expertise in archeology, his writings led to the uncovering of the mass burial site at Kurapaty.) On October 18, 1989, he cocreated the group Martyrology of Belarus, tasked with gathering information on Stalin's persecutions in the republic. He also cocreated the Belarusian Popular Front, which dedicated itself to Stalin's victims, the promotion of Belarusian language and culture, and confronting the chaos and fallout of the Chernobyl disaster.

The Supreme Soviet of the Republic of Belarus of the 12th convocation is the Belarusian parliament, which was elected in 1990 as the Supreme Soviet of the Byelorussian SSR of the 12th convocation. It became a national parliament of Belarus after the proclamation of independence. In 1990, Pazniak won a seat in the Supreme Soviet, representing the Anharskaja constituency No. 9 in the city of Minsk. The Front formed a significant faction with about thirty seats in the parliament, although it was a minority in the Communist-dominated assembly. By the spring of 1991, after Belarus had declared its sovereignty, Pazniak and his colleagues demanded full independence, a Belarusian army, Belarusian citizenship, and an all-Belarusian Constituent Congress that would discuss the form of government the new state should assume. These firm positions were initially superseded by Gorbachev's referendum on forming a new Union State, accepted by 83.7% in the BSSR, but they were to form the basis of statehood after the failed putsch in Moscow.

The defeat of hardliners in Moscow justified Pazniak's position, and his faction immediately introduced a host of bills after Belarus declared independence on August 25, 1991. In addition to the demands mentioned, they added the privatization of agricultural land and the creation of Belarusian border and customs offices. (Only land privatization failed to be adopted.) In September, the white-red-white flag and Pahonia became official state symbols—remaining in place until 1995. Many attribute these achievements with Pazniak's leadership and advocacy.

One should add that his presence in the political spectrum generated opposition at almost all levels outside the Popular Front. Lukashenka was initially supportive until he recognized Pazniak as a threat. Others were opposed and even shocked by the potential radical changes, especially the Communists Kebich and Dzemiantsei. There was no obvious clash with Shushkevich, who had become the chair of parliament by August 1991, but there was significant variation in personalities between the radical BPF deputies and the somewhat distant and pedantic academic who was too cowed by Boris Yeltsin's use of army tanks in Moscow in 1993 to quell an uprising in the Russian parliament to push reform.

How and why was Stanislau Shushkevich removed as chair of parliament in early 1994?

In January 1994, the Belarusian Supreme Soviet voted to remove Stanislau Shushkevich from his position as chair of the assembly. Shushkevich, who passed away in May 2022 at the age of eighty-seven, had been in office for about thirty months, but he had presided over some of the most remarkable events in the history of the republic.

Shushkevich was born in Minsk on December 15, 1934, into a family of schoolteachers. His father was placed under arrest in the 1930s and imprisoned until 1956, but not completely cleared of the charges until the 1970s. As a child, Shushkevich lived through the war in Minsk with his mother and grandmother in poverty for many years, as his mother was unable to find a stable job because her husband had been politically repressed. In 1951, he completed high school as a star pupil and enrolled in the Belarusian State

University's Faculty of Physics and Mathematics. Initially tempted to become a philologist and writer, like his father, he was discouraged from studying the Belarusian language at the university by his mother. She feared he, like his father, might be repressed for his devotion to the Belarusian language. After graduation, he entered the Institute of Physics at the Belarusian Academy of Sciences to study radio electronics. (Later, while working at an electronics company, he taught Russian to Lee Harvey Oswald, as noted both in his own biography and CIA records.)

Shushkevich received a doctorate in mathematics and physics, and the rank of professor and corresponding member of the Academy of Sciences. By appearance a small, balding man, he was highly intelligent and energetic, but with a streak of stubbornness that often led to conflict once he entered politics. That he did so can be attributed to the nature of Belarusian society in the period of glasnost and perestroika, which allowed people of different profiles or experience to run for office. He supported reform and social democracy.

He assumed the position of chair—effectively the head of state—on an interim basis after his predecessor, Mikalai Dzemiantsei, was forced to resign because of his support of the failed Moscow putsch in 1991. On the same day (August 25), the Byelorussian Soviet Socialist Republic (BSSR) declared independence. In September 1991, under his chairmanship, the BSSR was renamed the Republic of Belarus. He is therefore associated with some key moments in the birth of the independent state.

Shushkevich entered the republican leadership as something of a political neophyte, a renowned physicist and academician, but one without strong political support. Shushkevich found himself in a parliament divided between a strong majority of Communists (302 seats) led by Prime Minister Viachaslau Kebich and a small opposition of 27 MPs headed by the leader of the Belarusian Popular Front (BPF), Zianon Pazniak, and about 8–10 MPs sympathetic to the national cause. The Soviet comprised 360 seats at that time (it was later reduced to 260), 310 of which were contested, although it took several elections before it could become quorate.

Pazniak's goal, like that of the BPF as a whole, was to hold new elections to replace the 1990 Supreme Soviet and to ensure that the new constitution retained a durable parliament to watch over any future president. The BPF, which became a formal political party only in 1993, gathered signatures in support of a petition for a new election, but they had little impact on the conservative legislature. As to who should hold the esteemed position of president, Kebich appeared the natural choice, as most deputies backed him.

By the summer of 1993, Shushkevich faced a vote of no confidence, having failed to gain the support of either the majority Communists or the Popular Front–led opposition. But the vote was delayed by his illness and ultimately fell six votes short of the required majority. He soldiered on.

Shushkevich's main concern was a proposed military-security union with Russia that he feared would erode Belarusian sovereignty. He had already agreed to send Belarusian nuclear weapons to Russia for dismantling, reinforcing the idea to enshrine a clause in the Constitution to declare Belarus a non-nuclear and non-aligned state.

Enter deputy Lukashenka from the Škloŭ district of the Mahilioŭ *voblast*, a former state farm leader and KGB border guard who sought a name for himself after his election to the Supreme Soviet in 1990. Although he was reportedly the only deputy not to support the dissolution of the Soviet Union (this rumor turned out to be false), he had seemed close to the Social Democratic deputies and BPF, and in 1990 had even appeared alongside Pazniak at a political rally in Mahilioŭ. Earlier, he had sought BPF support to be deputy chair of the parliament but could not find enough backing to make an impact. His desperation was self-evident.

His breakthrough came after he was elected the temporary head of a parliamentary commission on corruption; he used the position to successfully make accusations against state leaders. Parliamentary sessions were broadcast live on state television, and his charisma and showmanship contributed to his popularity among regular Belarusians. One of his main acolytes was Viktar Hanchar, who would run his 1994 election campaign and later become deputy chair of the parliament. These so-called young wolves also included Henadz Karpenka, the mayor of Maladziečna, another rising scientist and inventor. In short, future oppositionists were largely responsible for Lukashenka's sudden rise.

Kebich was content to allow Lukashenka's actions as head of parliamentary corruption, believing correctly that one of the main targets would be Shushkevich. But he miscalculated. Lukashenka did indeed focus on Shushkevich, but he eventually singled out Kebich, astutely recognizing that the public was concerned about corruption in the party and particularly in the leadership.

For many years, the BSSR had gained a reputation for the incorruptibility of party leaders in contrast to the numerous abuses of power by the Brezhnev leadership in Moscow. Piotr Masherau, a former wartime partisan leader and popular figure who led the republic between 1965 and 1980 prior to his death in a car crash, was known for his uncorrupted leadership. By Masherau's standards Kebich fell well short.

According to some observers, Lukashenka's commission focused less on corruption than on the personal foibles of the current leadership and sensationalism. In Shushkevich's case, he had used state funds to finance the repairs at his dacha, and specifically the purchase of some nails for which he had not yet paid fully. It was a minor issue. The deeper reason was that Shushkevich desired to keep Belarus separate from Russia, while still acknowledging the necessity of close economic ties. The psychological need to maintain links with Russia pervaded every part of Belarusian society, beset by economic woes after the dissolution of the USSR.

Shortly before Shushkevich was forced to resign, US president Bill Clinton visited Belarus on January 15, 1994, a sojourn of only a few hours but one that had a lasting impact. Clinton praised the republic for giving up nuclear weapons, insisted on meeting with opposition figures, and bonded with Shushkevich, who had been his guest in Washington, DC, the previous year. The United States offered aid to build a democratic state. Despite opposition from the powerful Communist bloc in the Supreme Soviet, Clinton visited Kurapaty, the site of mass graves to the victims of Stalin in 1937–1941, and donated a stone bench.

In the buildup to the chair's removal, Lukashenka would accuse Shushkevich of being an American stooge. The Clinton bench has subsequently been destroyed numerous times during Lukashenka's presidency and patched up by opposition members. The perpetrators are never identified, but one can assume that the authorities encourage the vandalism. For the pro-Russian sector of political life, Clinton's visit was a humiliation, but it was also an indicator to many Belarusians that there was an alternative to adhering to Russian-led structures.

On the right of the political spectrum, Zianon Pazniak and the BPF were far more radical than the head of state and frustrated by his lack of action to define a clear path to sovereignty. As noted, most of the initiatives toward an independent Belarusian state were taken by the Popular Front. However, the positions taken by the Front were too radical for Shushkevich, who eschewed radicalism, and consistently declined to support the Popular Front's wish to hold new elections for the Supreme Soviet. The Front gathered over 440,000 signatures to support its campaign, but Shushkevich refused its demands. Shushkevich lost an opportunity to combine forces with the national democrats and to move Belarus on a different path. Lukashenka's commission saw the opportunity and pounced, but Shushkevich lacked political backing to keep himself in office for long anyway.

Who took part in Belarus's first presidential elections in 1994?

At the time of its independence, Belarus was a parliamentary republic under the Supreme Soviet. Though hotly contested, on March 15, 1994, the deputies established a presidency, which was to be closely monitored by the parliament and Constitutional Court. They also established a Central Election Commission, which set presidential election dates of June 23 and July 10 for a run-off election if needed. Between April 15 and 24, election commissions were created, and the candidates formed initiative groups to gather signatures in their support.

A minimum of 100,000 signatures was required for the candidate to run. Of the nineteen original candidates, only six managed to gather that amount, but Hienadz Karpenka's candidacy was declared invalid even though his campaign collected 108,354 signatures. Others were declared invalid, while some withdrew their support. The six remaining were Aliaksandr Dubko, leader of the Agrarian Party; Viachaslau Kebich, the prime minister; Aliaksandr Lukashenka, people's deputy and director of the Haradziec state farm in Shkloŭ district; Vasily Novikau, secretary of the Party of Communists of Belarus (PCB); Zianon Pazniak, leader of the Belarusian Popular Front "Adradzhennie"; and Stanislau Shushkevich, the recently removed chairman of the Supreme Soviet of Belarus.

When the election campaign began in the spring, Kebich was expected to win, particularly since his campaign team gathered over 400,000 signatures in support of his candidacy, far more than any other contender. But Lukashenka's popularity was rising. He was pro-Russian and *seemingly* devoid of any corruption. Belarusians wanted change. Young activists like Viktar Hanchar and Anatol Liabedzka were prepared to give Lukashenka a chance, while to the electorate he seemed to pose the least danger: he was not equated with the Communist hierarchy or Belarusian nationalism. He was young, thirty-nine years old, and a popular figure on television. What was there to lose?

On June 23, 1994, Lukashenka received 44.82% in the first round of the elections, ahead of Kebich (17.33%), Pazniak (12.82%), Shushkevich (9.91%), Dubko (5.98%), and Novikau (4.29%). Of the 5.9 million votes cast, Lukashenka received 2.64 million, with a voter turnout of almost 79%. Supreme Council deputy Siarhei Navumchyk, a close associate of Pazniak, and others have testified that the results were doctored. In his opinion—and that of Pazniak—Lukashenka won outright in the first round with around 54–56%, with Pazniak second, Shushkevich third, and Kebich fourth. It is plausible that Kebich used his parliamentary backing to secure a place in the second round, but he lacked the support to challenge Lukashenka.

Although Lukashenka was popular everywhere in 1994, his support varied considerably between the various regions from a high of 63% in his own region of Mahilioŭ to a low of 26.5% in the city of Minsk, where his backing was shared almost equally with Shushkevich (21.2%), Pazniak (20.9%), and Kebich (18.2%). Had the two democratic candidates unified their campaigns, it likely would have been enough for either Pazniak or Shushkevich to enter the second round rather than Kebich, but the two candidates were incompatible and had little in common other than their shared conception of an independent Belarus, rather than a state that shared power with Russia.

On June 17, Lukashenka claimed that the Mercedes he was in, together with his sponsor Ivan Tsitsiankou, was shot at. Quickly, as the news spread, he grew to become a martyr fighting corruption to the public. The criminal investigation never found out the alleged perpetrator, but Lukashenka's opponents were convinced this incident had been staged to attract attention to his campaign and acquire more votes.

Round 2 followed on July 10, with Lukashenka winning easily with 80.34% to Kebich's 14.17%. The die was cast. There were to be no free elections and no new leader from that point forward. Notably, Lukashenka exploited the organizational system in future elections, ensuring that the election commissions were filled with his supporters and barring many opposition candidates from running by declaring many of their collected signatures to be invalid. But in 1994, at least, he won a democratic election.

What do we know about Lukashenka's personality?

Aliaksandr (patronymic Hryhoryevich) Lukashenka was born in the urban settlement of Kopyś in the Viciebsk region, but his mother moved to the village of Aleksandria, not far from the city of Škloŭ, in the Mahilioŭ region. Little is known about his father other than that he left home either before Aliaksandr was born or while he was an infant. In the 1950s, Belarus was still recovering from the war and restoring industry was prioritized over recovering villages by the Soviet government. Growing up fatherless in a poverty-stricken region likely strengthened Lukashenka's survival instincts.

Accounts of Lukashenka's youth suggest he led a fairly typical life of a Soviet man who worked within the existing Communist system. He entered the Komsomol (Young Communist League) while studying in the Department of History at the Mahilioŭ Pedagogical Institute. He edited a student journal. Later, placed in charge of a canteen, he was known for strictly weighing every morsel of meat, intimidating the staff. He was known as energetic and possessing a forceful and aggressive personality that liked to exert control. One report indicates that, while working as a commander of a state farm, he frequently beat workers who were found imbibing alcohol (as was common in villages).

He became a full member of the Party and joined the army, and served as a KGB border guard, but his ambition was to be chair of a collective farm. Every report about his pre-leadership career highlights the fact that he talked endlessly, and about any topic.

His ambition was boundless, but he operated within existing structures. Opportunities for advancement emerged during the Gorbachev period (1985–1991) and Gorbachev's reforms. Lukashenka ran for the Supreme Soviet. He was known to hold Gorbachev in contempt for his perceived weakness and lack of a strong hand. It is unclear still how committed he was to Marxism-Leninism or for Belarusian nationalism.

Two other characteristics merit attention. One was self-assurance, and once in power, he not only represented the Belarusian people, but transcended them beyond reproach. On many occasions he appeared to perceive himself less as a figure elected democratically in 1994, but as someone who epitomized the state: a father figure caring for his children, and those children, should they defy him, must be punished. Added to a natural truculence and ruthlessness, he could be capable of great cruelty and vindictiveness. Those whom he saw as betraying him—figures who resigned from the government, the opposition, young people carrying the white-red-white flag in defiance, even speaking the Belarusian language in the street—were the enemy.

The second feature of his personality was his ability to communicate with "the people"—workers, peasants, and pensioners. In the period before the advent of social media, such a gift was crucial. In some villages, the elderly kept icons of Lukashenka in their cottages. He was equally effective on television, with his high-pitched nasal voice and clipped phrases, simplifying complex events, often by focusing on who was to blame for some shortfall or problem and promptly firing that person. This connection to the population was largely broken by the 2020 presidential elections and by the advent of social media, which he ignored as a means of communication.

Lukashenka was born nine years after the Second World War ended, but he has latched on to that war, the occupation, and the victory as a source of personal survival and legitimacy. Official propaganda reflects this sentiment: monuments, memorials, commemorative holidays, Independence Day, Victory Day, ceremonies, medals, and above all, narratives about the period 1941–1945, pervade every facet of public existence, beginning with elementary schools and what is termed "military-patriotic education." It is impossible to discern whether there is any real feeling attached to such propaganda, but the image of Lukashenka shedding tears in memory of "dear veterans" and building a major museum to the "Great Patriotic War" close to the center of Minsk suggest that there might be.

Other observable facets, which are secondhand, are his need to reflect an image of physical strength and masculinity: playing hockey, rollerblading, escorting young attractive women to dances or balls, hugging female tennis players at a tournament in Belarus, nurturing his third son Mikalai, born out of wedlock, emphasizing the image of a devoted father. Although Putin has recently emerged as the greater strongman, Lukashenka still accompanies him riding a snowmobile through the streets of Sochi. Observers witnessed only two elderly men trying to maintain what is now a fading athletic image.

And like other twenty-first-century politicians, it is easy to detect elements of narcissism, of complete preoccupation with his own needs. One cannot detect any overriding political belief or goal for the state other than remaining in power and protecting himself from a prison sentence. Lukashenka has not achieved what may have been his ultimate ambition, to be the head of a Russia-Belarus Union. But he has survived, partly through his adaptability, and partly because of an innate cunning and ability to outmaneuver his counterparts, especially those in the West who believe it might be possible to open a dialogue with him or coax him toward democracy.

Ultimately, Lukashenka is a Soviet man lost in time. His era has ended, but he has remained through the loyalty of his closest associates: the KGB and his security forces. In the latter case, it is a union of "thieves," in that once the forces commit crimes on his orders, they are bound to him. Lukashenka's downfall would bring them with him, and the self-acknowledged dictator is only too aware of that fact.

Why did Lukashenka hold referendums in 1995 and 1996 and what constitutional changes took place as a result?

Lukashenka became the head of a democratic state with an independent parliament, constitutional court, and diverse media. The country was in a difficult economic situation, and he had to be responsible or creative to fulfill his pre-election promises. The Supreme Council (the Belarusian parliament) diligently supported him; while the opposition, led by the Belarusian Popular Front, called out his failures to the independent media and the tribune of the Supreme Court. This marked the beginning of Lukashenka's confrontation with the Supreme Council deputies.

This confrontation coincided with the start of the First Chechen War in Russia, which was strongly criticized by the members of the Belarusian Popular Front, who supported the Chechens and labeled Russia's intervention a war of "the empire." At the same time, Lukashenka initiated and obtained a rapprochement with Boris Yeltsin. He secured Russian gas and oil at discounted prices and thus prolonged the life of Belarusian factories, and maintained a Russian market for Belarusian products.

In February 1995, the chairman of the Supreme Court switched off Zianon Pazniak's microphone as he criticized Russia's intervention in Chechnya, Boris Yeltsin, and Lukashenka's politics favoring Russia. At that point Lukashenka and his cohort had already started to abuse executive power. Aliaksandr Fiaduta ordered state newspapers to remove the excerpts of the BPF deputy Siarhei Antonchyk's report about corruption in Lukashenka's administration, which he delivered openly.

They put pressure on the Belarusian Print House in Minsk, which terminated all contracts with Belarusian independent newspapers. But the opposition did not go quietly and continued to protest and speak up at the parliament's session.

In March 1995, Lukashenka openly criticized the Supreme Council, BPF, and journalists in public speeches. He desperately wanted to deepen integration with Russia. He knew changing the national symbols and elevating the status of the Russian language, which was not official at that time, would make him more favorable in Russia's eyes. Parliamentary elections were imminent and he needed to ensure a new Supreme Council would be loyal to him. On March 18, *Zviazda*, a state-run newspaper, published signatures of seventy-four deputies who called for a change of the national symbols. All of them were former Communists and some later claimed they had never signed the document. Still, the statement, addressed to Lukashenka, referred to the fact that the national symbols, white-red-white flag and Pahonia coat of arms, were used during the Second World War by the Nazis and their collaborators. (The same argument would be used by Lukashenka thirty years on, although national flags were used in the war by the Nazis on most occupied territories in central and eastern Europe.)

Lukashenka's clash with the oppositional deputies culminated on April 10, 1995, in a hunger strike by nineteen deputies from the Belarusian Popular Front following the announcement of a referendum. The referendum posed questions about changing the national symbols to those resembling the Soviet symbols, introducing Russian as a second national language, and approval for integration with Russia and early termination of the terms of the parliamentary deputies.

The hunger strike of the BPF deputies and Aleh Trusau from the Belarusian Social Democratic Hramada was brutally stopped on the night of April 11–12 when special KGB forces under Lukashenka's orders beat all nineteen deputies and dragged them from the parliamentary building. The official reason was that a bomb had been placed in the building. The injured deputies went to a hospital to verify their injuries, but doctors were too terrified to intervene. Lukashenka spread false stories that the deputies had run through the building wielding knives and he had stopped them. No one was ever held responsible for the attacks.

The president's team was demonstrating its growing impunity. Despite such adversities, the BPF Deputies initiated a trial in the Constitutional Court where they asked the Court to analyze recent decisions connected with the monopolization of media and referendum vis-à-vis the Belarusian contribution. The Court ordered Lukashenka to stop his campaign, but he ignored it.

The referendum held on May 14, 1995, violated the Belarusian Constitution and a number of earlier adopted laws, including the Law on Language. Belarusian writers and poets, including prominent writers Nil Hilevich and Vasil Bykau, had asked the Constitutional Court to offer an opinion on the legality of the questions of national symbols and official language in the referendum, but the Court, run by Valery Tsikhinia, was too intimidated to intervene. With only one month left for the pre-referendum campaign, Lukashenka took advantage of his control of state media to direct all possible propaganda tools at the Belarusian Popular Front and its deputies. The state TV aired the film *The Children of Lies* made by Yury Azaronak (father of Ryhor Azaronak, who became one of the most notorious of Lukashenka's propagandists in the 2020s), which compared Zianon Pazniak to Nazi collaborators. Pazniak won a trial against Azaronak for defamation, and the latter was obliged to apologize on state TV. Another myth spread then was that Pazniak's father was a *politsai* (collaborator with the Nazi military forces) during the Nazi occupation of Belarus.

Independent observers noted the violations that took place; observers from the BPF party were denied entrance to many polling stations. Nevertheless, the president claimed victory and that Belarusians supported him and his political course. On May 19, Lukashenka's head of administration, Ivan Tsitsiankou, together with his supporters, tore a white-red-white flag into pieces and signed every piece. The Pahonia coat of arms was removed from the building of the Supreme Court, which dropped to the ground and shattered. The Belarusian language gradually became even more marginal, fewer books in Belarusian were published, all subjects were taught in the Russian at Belarusian schools, and higher education in Belarusian was scattered among a few humanities departments at a handful of universities.

The new parliamentary elections took place on May 14 and 28, in two rounds, but turnout was very low. The Constitutional Court announced that the elections should be repeated in November in those constituencies with low voter turnout. In his 1995 book, Siarhei Navumchyk, then an active member of BPF, pointed out that elections were claimed to be invalid in most of the constituencies in which BPF members were most likely to have won. Many violations were registered by Lukashenka's opposition, but their claims were ignored. No BPF Deputies were elected, and only eighteen deputies were re-elected from the previous parliament. Siamon Sharetski, from the Agrarian Party, was elected chairman of the Supreme Council.

Deputies of the previous convocation who were beaten during their hunger strike tried to bring their case before the newly elected parliament, but they failed, as many deputies were either Lukashenka's supporters or hoping to earn his support. The Belarusian Popular Front still retained the right to organize protests and rallies as a registered party. They used many opportunities to do so, especially during the commemorations of the anti-Communist dates, such as Freedom Day (March 25, the day of the proclamation of the independence of the Belarusian People's Republic). During the commemorative event on March 24, 1996, politicians strongly condemned Lukashenka's intention to integrate further with Russia. A crowd of tens of thousands came to support the event, many holding banners criticizing Belarusian State TV and other instruments of Lukashenka's power.

The BPF leaders desired to address Belarusians on national television. On March 24, 1996, they brought protesters to the TV station hoping to make a live broadcast, but no one from management was present. Protesters had reached the building of the Belarusian State TV and Radio Station when special forces arrived and beat participants. This was the first time that special police applied excessive brutality; after that point, such behavior from state police would become the norm. Bound by extreme loyalty to Lukashenka's regime and multiple social benefits for them and their families, the police would eventually emerge as a social stratum, fundamental to the consolidation of Lukashenka's authoritarian rule.

The next day, Lukashenka announced that BPF had attempted a coup d'état, and that it was his responsibility to stop them. Zianon Pazniak was followed by unidentified cars. On March 26, Navumchyk and Pazniak fled Belarus fearing for their lives, and on the 27th they arrived in Kyiv. Pazniak would never return to Belarus. Navumchyk would return in 2016, after receiving political asylum in the United States and living in Czechia. Other active oppositionists would face repression in the following years, and many would leave the country.

On April 2, 1996, Lukashenka and Yeltsin signed an agreement on the creation of the Community of Belarusian and Russian States. The opposition strongly criticized this step fearing the incorporation of Belarus into Russia. Suddenly, the situation in the country grew unfavorable for Lukashenka. The newly elected Supreme Council openly criticized him and his government. Lukashenka decided to hold another referendum, which would transform the legislative branch of the Belarusian state by introducing several changes to the Belarusian constitution.

The parliamentary chairman, Siamion Sharetski, appealed to the Constitutional Court asking them to scrutinize the legality of changing the constitution based on the outcomes of the referendum. The Court claimed that such a referendum was indeed unconstitutional, but Lukashenka insisted on holding the referendum in November. On November 14, the chairman of the Central Election Commission (CEC), Viktar Hanchar, declared that the CEC would not acknowledge the results of the referendum if it was unconstitutional. Lukashenka dismissed him, though this also was illegal, as the CEC Chairperson was appointed by the Supreme Council. Hanchar was replaced with Lidziya Yarmoshyna, Lukashenka's former colleague and friend who would eventually oversee falsifications of all upcoming elections until 2020.

Seventy-three deputies initiated an impeachment against Lukashenka on November 19, 1996. The Constitutional Court scheduled a hearing on November 22, but already on November 21 Russian prime minister Viktor Chernomyrdin, head of Russian Duma Gennadi Selezniov, and Chairman of the Federal Council Yegor Stroyev arrived in Minsk and persuaded Belarusian deputies to reconcile and postpone the session of the Constitutional Court to November 26, when the results of the referendum, held on November 24, would be announced.

The outcomes of the referendum redesigned the branches of power in Belarus and strengthened the scope of the president's authority. Belarusian opposition, independent media, and lawyers detected an unprecedented number of violations and biased campaigning, where previously state media were used to affirm Lukashenka's point of view. Most people were not familiar with the new constitution before the referendum.

As a result, the Belarusian parliament was divided into two chambers, where only 110 deputies would be elected during direct vote by the Belarusian people. The Council of the Republic, the upper chamber, would consist of 64 members, whereby 56 would be elected by the local deputies and 8 would be appointed by the president. Direct elections of mayors were discontinued. The Constitutional Court lost its function; all judges became loyal to Lukashenka and never challenged his decisions thereafter. Lukashenka's regime became even stronger and spread its power over all branches of government. He extended his term in office until 2001, claiming that the new version of the Constitution had "re-started" his presidency.

Who were the main victims of the state repressions of 1999–2000?

After 1996, there were effectively two parliaments in Belarus: the first comprised members of the National Assembly with 110 deputies, almost all Lukashenka loyalists; the second was made up of original members of the previous Supreme Soviet who lost their seats after the 1996 referendum that overhauled the 1994 Constitution. The situation resembled somewhat that in Russia in the summer and fall of 1993, when the Russian parliament tried to impeach President Boris Yeltsin, but ultimately succumbed after the Russian army intervened. In Belarus, the confrontation appeared to be eased when Russian prime minister Viktor Chernomyrdin traveled to Minsk as a mediator, but ultimately supported Lukashenka, his changes, and his usurpation of supreme power.

But the situation remained tense and in 1999, the date when presidential elections would normally have been held, it was particularly so. Lukashenka maintained that the constitutional changes allowed him to restart his presidency from 1996, meaning that the next elections would not be held until 2001. His opponents, however, contested that position, arguing that Lukashenka was no longer the legitimate president and elections would be held regardless, under the supervision of the chairman of the parliament. Henadz Karpenka, who had previously attempted to initiate impeachment against Lukashenka in 1996, unexpectedly died on April 6, 1999. Karpenka had been thought to be the most probable candidate at the alternative elections. His supporters and friends never believed the cause of the death was natural.

On July 21, 1999, the rebel deputies adhering to the 1994 system appointed Siamion Sharetski, former chair of the Supreme Soviet in 1996, as acting president in place of Lukashenka. Sharetski was the founder and leader of the Agrarian Party, one of the most popular political parties in the country. Recognizing the vulnerability of his new position, Sharetski promptly fled to Lithuania.

His deputy was Viktar Hanchar, one of the original "young wolves" who had run Lukashenka's 1994 election campaign before realizing that he was moving in a clearly authoritarian direction. Hanchar was also the acting chair of the Central Election Commission and decided to hold a presidential election in the nontraditional way of taking ballot boxes around apartment buildings to gather votes. The two candidates were the exiled Zianon Pazniak and former prime minister Mikhail Chyhir, who was in prison. The result was an absurd process, made even more so by Hanchar's claim that more than half the electorate had cast votes. The results of the vote counting were never revealed. For Lukashenka, however, the whole process cast doubts on his continuing tenure.

What happened at this juncture in Belarus is subject to conjecture, but there is enough evidence to state that the official response was drastic. Andrew Wilson writes that a "secret death squad" was in operation from the 1990s that killed over thirty people, including five executions in a single day. Belsat TV (July 3, 2023) reveals that Viktar Sheiman created the Death Squad in 1997 to eliminate crime bosses before engaging it later in kidnapping Lukashenka's political rivals. Reports by State Prosecutor Aleh Bazhelka, Colonel of the Ministry of Internal Affairs Oleg Alkaev (who defected to Germany), and the head of the Main Directorate of the Ministry of Internal Affairs, Mikalai Lapatsik, cited in a Euroradio report of September 17, 2023, provided official documents that allow for a more detailed picture of the operations conducted by the authorities in this critical period.

In April 1999, Sheiman, by now elevated to the post of State Secretary of the Security Council, ordered the Minister of Internal Affairs Yury Sivakou to bring Dzmitry Paulichenka to the No. 1 Detention center to conduct executions. Paulichenka was commander of the "Almaz" Special Rapid Response Unit and a loyal acolyte of Lukashenka. On May 6, again on the instructions of Sheiman to Sivakou, Paulichenka received authorization to use a special execution pistol that had to be signed out for the purpose. The pistol reportedly was used to shoot the most prominent victims of the 1999–2000 purges.

The first victim was the former minister of defense Yury Zakharanka, who had been removed by Lukashenka in October 1995 and subsequently became a member of the United Civil Party. In 1999, he was the leader of the campaign to make Mikhail Chyhir president after the expiration of Lukashenka's legal term. On May 7, 1999, Zakharanka disappeared. A day later, the execution pistol was returned to the pretrial detention center. In September, the pistol was signed out again and the time coincided with the disappearance of Hanchar and businessman Anatol Krasouski on September 16, 1999. The two regularly visited the same *banya* on Thursday evenings and Hanchar's wife expected him to return for a scheduled phone call. After their disappearance there were reports of a red BMW car in the area, the same vehicle known to be driven by Paulichenka.

The next prominent victim was a cameraman for the Russia Television Station Dzmitry Zavadski, who disappeared on July 7, 2000. Zavadski used to work as personal cameraman of Lukashenka before starting work on the Russian television station ORT. He was last seen driving to the Minsk-2 International Airport to meet his friend Pavel Sharamet (Sheremet in Russian). His car was later found at the airport. It is not known whether the case was linked to those of Zakharanka, Hanchar, and Krasouski. Zavadski's film reports featured the revelation that some members of the Belarusian security services were fighting on the side of the Chechen rebels in the war against Russia. By this time, some senior figures in the administration were beginning to investigate the previous kidnappings.

In a statement made to a Belarusian opposition newspaper after he left the country, Alkaev recalled that he saw photographs of the missing political leaders in the newspaper and compared the dates when the official execution pistol had been signed out and returned. He also stated that the reason for using this particular weapon—which was only accurate at point-blank range—was to give the executioner a sense that he was carrying out the assassination as an official duty rather than a random killing. In November 2000, the head of the KGB Uladzimir Matskevich ordered the detention of Paulichenka, and it was sanctioned by Bazhelka on the grounds that Paulichenka was the leader of a criminal group involved in kidnappings and the "physical elimination of citizens." The incarceration lasted only a few days before Paulichenka was released. Matskevich and Bazhelka then lost their jobs. By 2001, all investigations into the disappearances were shelved by the authorities.

In 2003, the Council of Europe investigated the disappearances and linked them to the name of Colonel Dzmitry Paulichenka. Another sixteen years passed before any further major developments. In December 2019, Yury Harauski, a former member of the same Special Response Unit as Paulichenka, who had left the country, revealed in an interview with *Deutsche Welle* that he was a member of the team that kidnapped Zakharanka, Hanchar, and Krasouski. Paulichenka had shot each victim in the chest. In a confusing sequel, however, Harauski was tried for the crimes in a Swiss court in early 2023, and acquitted because the judge found his testimony and demeanor unconvincing. Harauski had denied using the pistol himself or handing it to Paulichenka. Valeryia Krasouskaya, daughter of Anatol, criticized the judgment as lacking any sense.

Other political opponents of Lukashenka may have suffered similar fates as those who went missing in 1999 and 2000. On July, 20, 2016, Pavel Sharamet, Zavadski's friend and long-term companion, with whom he had covered Belarus and criticized Lukashenka in the 1990s when Russian television was not censored, was killed by a car bomb in central Kyiv as he was driving to work. His death has never been resolved, and it is unclear whether it was related to the kidnappings in Belarus, politics in Moscow, or the Donbas conflict in Ukraine. Sharamet was an uncompromising writer who had critics in each of the countries, including the Lukashenka regime.

Though the macabre and grisly executions of 1999–2000 defined an uncertain period in the Lukashenka presidency, little has changed in subsequent years. Paulichenka is now retired but featured as part of the security forces that carried out arrests and beatings of 2020 protesters. Sheiman has occupied various positions at the very heart of the leadership—they include prosecutor-general and head of the presidential administration—and even after dismissals from some, he has always been reappointed. He is also involved in business interests and offshore companies, particularly in Zimbabwe, and some of his dealings have been on behalf of the Belarusian government. He is the creator of the Death Squad and gave the orders for the executions to his underling Paulichenka.

Notable also is that Paulichenka was cited in March 2023 (Belsat TV) as condemning fellow security officer Valery Sakhashchyk (former defense minister in Sviatlana Tsikhanouskaya's United Transitional Cabinet) and other "traitors who had betrayed the Motherland in 2020." He maintained there should be an investigation of all those who took vacations or sick leave in 2020 to avoid combating those protesting the fabricated election results. "We need to root them out," he declared, "and put them in their place." The comments suggest that he regards himself, at least, as a key figure in the regime despite his official retirement.

Was Lukashenka responsible for all these deaths? We do not know. Former British ambassador to Belarus Brian Bennett notes that four men were arrested for the death of Zavadski from the "Ignatovich gang." The gang was connected to Paulichenka, but the four accused were widely thought to have been framed. Bennett observes an "atmosphere of fear" in which those with information were safer not to speak out. Zavadski's wife emigrated to Germany and the regime harassed the Association for Legal Assistance to the Population that was also dealing with the families of those who died in the Niamiha metro tragedy in 1999.

Which were the main opposition parties in Belarus in the period 1991–2010?

The list of opposition parties is a lengthy one. If one looks at the early 1990s, then the following parties were active in Belarus: the Belarusian Popular Front (BPF), the Party of Communists of Belarus (PCB), the Social Democratic Party Narodnaya Hramada (People's Assembly) (Biełaruskaja Sacyjał-Demakratyčnaja Partyja [Narodnaya Hramada]), and the Social Democratic Party Hramada (Assembly) (Biełaruskaja Sacyjał-Demakratyčnaja Partyja [Hramada]). The Women's Party, the Labor Party, and the Liberal Democratic Party were also registered but should not be included as part of the active opposition to the Lukashenka regime. In 1995, the United Civil Party was founded and formed from the United Democratic Party and the later Civil Party.

In addition, there was the unregistered Christian Democratic Party and a few public organizations that played political roles, such as the Belarusian Helsinki Committee, Viasna 96 human rights organization, and the pro-European Union group Charter-97. Two Trade Union movements—Free and Official—can also be considered part of the opposition. These parties were usually small in membership but had clearly recognized leaders who were well known in public life.

Until the late 1980s, the Communist Party was the only official party in the BSSR. As in other republics, the period of *glasnost* under CCCPSU General Secretary Mikhail Gorbachev facilitated the creation of alternative political forces. But in Belarus changes came very slowly. Though the Communist Party was officially banned after the failed putsch in Moscow in August 1991, it was reinstated in the Republic of Belarus in February 1993. Its replacement in 1991 was the Party of Communists of Belarus (PCB) and in May 1993, the two parties decided to unite under the PCB name.

In November 1996, however, the Communist Party of Belarus held its 23rd Congress, linking it to the original CPB of the Soviet period, and reversed the decision to unite with the PCB. This created two new registered Communist parties. The newly formed CPB included those former PCB members who had remained loyal to President Lukashenka as well as some original members of the Soviet-era party. Yafrem Sakalou, First Secretary of the CC CPB between 1987 and 1990, and a former member of the All-Union Politburo, became the chair of the Party Council. The PCB therefore became an opposition party under Siarhei Kaliakin and eventually changed its name to "A Just World."

In the early 1990s, as noted, a bewildering number of parties operated in Belarus, the vast majority of which fell into the category of "opposition" to the Lukashenka presidency and government. We have already mentioned the Belarusian Popular Front (BPF) led by Zianon Pazniak, a national democratic party, which had its counterparts during the last years of the Soviet Union in the Popular Fronts of the Baltic States and the Rukh Popular Movement in Ukraine. After it was founded in late 1988, the BPF held its founding congress in Vilnius and derived from the movement Martyrology of Belarus, which focused on the repressions of the Stalin period, including the executions at Kurapaty. It also sought the revival of the Belarusian language, which was declared the state language of Belarus in

1990, and support for the victims of the 1986 nuclear accident at Chernobyl. The BPF's goal was an independent, sovereign Belarus, free from the influence of Russia. Pazniak maintained that after the rediscovery of the mass graves at Kurapaty, he lived in fear for his life.

The Communist authorities immediately turned on the BPF after its creation, and its representatives in the Supreme Soviet attacked the Front delegates as "fascists," linking them with the Nazi occupation regime of the Great Patriotic War. Pazniak was a senior figure in the movement, but was only one year old when the war ended. Initially, he was optimistic about the possibility of a nationalist revival in Belarus, particularly as the BPF acquired a significant presence in parliament in 1989, winning over thirty seats. In these early years, the BPF's policies appeared to be paving the way toward a democratic sovereign state: the declaration of independence; the change of the name of the state to Republic of Belarus; the adoption of Belarusian as the state language. But it quickly found itself the primary target of Communist leadership, and isolated in its initial goal of holding new elections to overhaul the membership of the Supreme Soviet.

In 1996, Pazniak fled Belarus, citing a potential arrest by the forces of Lukashenka. He was granted political asylum in the United States after staying at different periods in Ukraine and Europe. (His departure followed the historic demonstration on the tenth anniversary of Chernobyl nuclear accident, in which over 50,000 people participated.) On June 19, 1997, the Belarus prosecutor's office opened a criminal case against Pazniak accusing him of incitement to ethnic hatred against the Russian people. Pazniak later divided his expatriate life between New York City and Warsaw, as the latter was closer to Belarus and his colleagues from the party. In addition, his daughter started to work in Warsaw. and after the 2020 revolution he fully moved there, reviving his activities and attracting new supporters among the now large Belarusian diaspora, where it was easier for him to do so.

The BPF members who remained after 1996, led by Vintsuk Viachorka, tried to cooperate with other parties in the opposition, something that Pazniak had always refused to do. In 1999, the BPF split into two parties: the original party with headquarters in Minsk and led by Viachorka; and the Conservative Christian Party (CCP) of the BPF led by Pazniak, with a membership both abroad and at home. The politics of the BPF in Western terms might be described as center-right, pro-market and pro-Western, and nationalistic with a firm commitment to the Belarusian language and culture. The CCP BPF has been prominent in uncovering mass graves of NKVD victims from the 1930s, and the party generally has taken a strongly anti-Moscow line for much of the independence period.

The two Social Democratic Parties and the United Civic Party represent the middle ground—the former leaning leftward and the latter to the right—and have been prominent in trying to find a consensus during election periods for a unified candidate to represent them. In 1991, the Social Democratic Assembly was established and linked its roots with the 1903 Belarusian Socialist Hramada, one of the first Belarusian national political organizations. It considered itself part of the Socialist International and a viable alternative to the disgraced Communist Party following the failed Moscow putsch.

The diverse opposition parties have attempted on different occasions to form united fronts, particularly to contest elections. The earliest example in the Lukashenka years was in 2000–2001, when a single candidate was chosen with the assistance of the OSCE Advisory and Monitoring Group in Minsk, led by the former German ambassador to the USSR, Hans Georg Wieck. After an unsuccessful attempt to secure a dialogue between the main opposition parties and the president, Wieck supported the candidacy of Uladzimir Hancharyk, chairman of the Federation of Trade Unions of Belarus, as the candidate for the united opposition. Official figures gave Lukashenka 77.4% of the vote to Hancharyk's 16%, though the results were not considered free and fair by international observers. Hancharyk's support in Minsk was particularly strong at around 30%, but he had very little preparation time.

After the election, the Belarusian authorities refused to allow Wieck to renew his visa, and subsequent leaders of the OSCE office were not allowed to challenge the leadership in this fashion. Nevertheless, the idea of unifying the political opposition for the period of elections remained. In 2005, five parties joined together to select a candidate: the Popular Front, the Women's Party, the Social Democrats, the United Civic Party, and the Party of Communists. In this difficult period in which so-called color revolutions had taken place in several eastern European states, the Minsk leadership was on full alert to prevent any such occurrence in Belarus. Initially, the two main contenders for the unified candidate were Anatol Liabedzka and Professor Aliaksandr Milinkevich, a native of Hrodna. Ultimately, Milinkevich won the nomination.

By December 2005, a total of four candidates registered for the election, though seven canvassed initially, including Lukashenka and his ally Siarhei Haidukevich, chairman of the Liberal-Democratic Party, with the latter running as a guarantee that there would be more than one candidate should the opposition decide to boycott the campaign. The others were Milinkevich as the united democratic candidate; Aliaksandr Vaitovich, the former president of the Belarusian Academy of Sciences; Valery Fralou and Siarhei Skrabets, former members of the Respublika faction that had emerged briefly in the Belarusian Parliament; Pazniak (a nonresident); and Aliaksandr Kazulin, the former rector of the Belarusian State University, who represented the Social Democratic Party (Hramada). Ultimately, the authorities refused permission to register all but Milinkevich, Kazulin, Lukashenka, and Haidukevich.

The campaign took place at a time when Lukashenka's popularity was quite high, and the country was enjoying a stable economic period. Also, the chosen date of March 19, 2006, was well before the anticipated July deadline, leaving the unified campaign little time to prepare. But the presence of two democratic candidates diverted from the opposition cause. Kazulin, believed by some to be Russia's candidate, was far from passive. He used his thirty-minute time on national television to rip up a portrait of Lukashenka and stamp on it and was arrested trying to gate-crash Lukashenka's People's Assembly. Lukashenka received almost 2 million signatures in support of his campaign, or about one-third of the total electorate, rendering the results announcement a formality. Many workers were forced to add their signatures to receive salaries.

Lukashenka officially received 82.6% of the total vote, Milinkevich 6%, Haidukevich 3.5%, and Kazulin 2.3%. Protests followed in what was termed the "Denim Revolution," and a camp was established in Kastryčnickaja Square for several days before riot police dispersed it. The Denim Revolution can be considered one of the color revolutions that occurred in various states around the turn of the century (Serbia, Kyrgyzstan, Ukraine, Georgia, and others) to remove corrupt leaders and install more democratic regimes. They received support from the United States and EU countries through subsidies and NGOs, though their success proved to be short-lived.

On May 27, 2007, the Second Congress of United Democratic Forces was held at the Minsk Automobile Factory, and carried out an about-face, removing Milinkevich as the unified leader and adopting a system of cochairs. The Congress included eight political factions, highlighting the complexity of the opposition forces: Regions for Freedom (Milinkevich), with 201 delegates; the Party of Communists of Belarus A Just World, with 124; the United Civil Party, 119; the Party of the Belarusian Popular Front (PBPF), 98; the Union of Labor, 95; the Social Democratic Hramada, 94; the European Coalition, 50; and the Party of Freedom and Progress, 28. All the factions with over 92 delegates merited a seat on the Presidium of the Political Council. The Council consisted of 44 members, with, originally, 5 chairs: Milinkevich, Siarhei Kaliakin (A Fair World—Communist Party), Vintsuk Viachorka (PBPF), and Anatol

Lyaukovich (Social Democratic Hramada). Milinkevich, however, objected to the change of system and declined to put his name forward.

Mikalai Statkevich, a leader of the Social Democratic Hramada, and recently released from prison, advocated a different policy modeled on the European Coalition movement in alliance with youth activists and social democrats. Milinkevich, likewise, placed more emphasis on street protests and meetings with the public as opposed to discussions in roundtables behind closed doors. Neither Milinkevich's nor Statkevich's faction could muster enough votes to alter decisions. The ultimate outcome was the splintering of the opposition, with the outcome that by the time of the 2010 election, there were no longer calls for a unified candidate. Moreover, the prospects for the opposition always depended on the country's economic situation, Russian oil and gas prices, inflation, and other factors. In 2007, there seemed to be little hope for any pressure on the Lukashenka regime; that situation changed dramatically in 2008–2009 because of an international recession.

Unsurprisingly, in September 2010, nineteen candidates expressed their intention to run for president in the December elections. There were high hopes in the countries of the European Union that the elections would be freer than those earlier. With the Eastern Partnership membership in place and the release of some political prisoners, the atmosphere seemed to be more tolerant. Though some candidates dropped out, nine remained until election day, embracing a broad spectrum of the opposition. In addition to Lukashenka and Haidukevich, they included the leader of the Popular Front Ryhor Kastusiou; Yaraslau Ramanchuk (United Civic Party); Ales Mikhalevich (Movement for Modernization); Mikalai Statkevich (Social Democratic Hramada and European Coalition "Free Belarus"); Vital Rymasheuski (Christian Democratic Party); Uladzimir Niakliaieu (Tell the Truth); and Andrei Sannikau (European Belarus). Milinkevich decided not to run, arguing that the rules did not allow for a free and fair contest. Stanislau

Shushkevich, former chair of parliament, enthusiastically joined the Sannikau campaign.

Polls conducted before the election showed Lukashenka ahead but with far less than 50%, with Sannikau performing strongly, and Niakliaieu, the former leader of the Belarusian Writers' Union, also prominent. On the evening of December 19, as part of a regular ritual, Lidziya Yarmoshyna, head of the Central Election Commission, announced that Lukashenka had received 79.67% of the vote. Sannikau in second place officially received only 2.45%, or just over 156,000 votes, compared to Lukashenka's 5.1 million. Such results had been anticipated, and a demonstration took place in Kastryčnickaja Square at which about 40,000 people gathered. The authorities made it difficult to gather by transforming the square into a skating rink with music blaring out from speakers. Thus, a decision was made to move the protest to Independence Square further into the city center, the site of the government, parliament, and Election Commission.

The violence that occurred there shocked the international community and ended the dialogues that had occurred between European leaders and Lukashenka. At some point, some participants—drunken infiltrators, according to Rymasheuski—broke two windows of the government building and riot police intervened, beating demonstrators with truncheons. Of the presidential candidates, seven headed for the square: Kaliakin, Sannikau, Niakliaieu, Statkevich, Kastusiou, Rymasheuski, and Mikhalevich. Niakliaieu and Statkevich were intercepted en route, carrying speakers, and they were made to lie face down on the ground and beaten severely before being taken to prison. In a short but savage intervention, the militia arrested over 600 people, including all seven presidential candidates. Sannikau and his wife were singled out, and the candidate lay on the ground in the square, his legs broken.

Lukashenka claimed that the protesters wished to take power with Western backing, and thus he had been obliged to respond harshly. But the arrests continued and turned into a purge of the opposition. The teams of Sannikau and Niakliaieu, which had belatedly joined forces, found themselves pursued and arrested. Subsequently, Sannikau received a five-year prison sentence, Niakliaieu received four years, opposition headquarters were raided, and several media outlets shut down. The KGB obtained warrants to enter people's apartments and make arrests, and a period of acute repressions followed. Ramanchuk appeared on state television to condemn the decision to move to Independence Square. Mikhalevich was released on February 11, 2011, and left Belarus permanently.

The aftermath of the elections left many Western leaders disillusioned with the Belarusian leadership and the prospects of any changes. For the opposition, a period of relative inertia followed as well as uncertainty about the best tactics to adopt in the future. The EU, which had reduced sanctions that followed the previous elections, banned Lukashenka and 156 others from entering its countries, and EU ambassadors in Belarus declined to attend his inauguration ceremony. Four days after the election, the foreign ministers of Poland, Sweden, Germany, and the Czech Republic issued a statement declaring that it was a "waste of time and money" to continue engagement with Lukashenka. Sannikau received a pardon in April 2012, left Belarus, and was granted political asylum in the United Kingdom. Mikhalevich also left the country permanently.

Overall, the emergence of so many political parties in Belarus hindered their effectiveness. Lukashenka claimed they were competing for foreign (mainly EU and US) funding and trying to subvert the government. During elections, the most open period, the opposition parties often tried to compete despite the restraints placed upon them by the regime: difficulties in gathering signatures, lack of presence on the election commissions, investigations of the candidates' backgrounds by the KGB, and restrictions on gathering supporters. Inevitably, the various party leaders found themselves bickering among themselves rather than focusing on removal of the president. Many served prison sentences, both short and long. This traditional opposition had intended to take part in the 2020 elections, but a combination of apathy and the effects of COVID-19 ended their campaign. In August 2020, however they joined the election belatedly as fellow travelers rather than candidates but nonetheless received lengthy prison sentences.

When was the Russia-Belarus Union State founded and how did it evolve?

The idea of forming a Union State between Russia and Belarus originated in the last year of the Soviet Union. In March 1991, on the initiative of General Secretary of the CC CPSU Mikhail Gorbachev, a nationwide referendum approved the idea of transforming the state into a Union of Soviet Sovereign Republics. The results were positive throughout, with 77.5% in favor, and in Belarus the vote was higher at 83.72%. The Gorbachev version failed to materialize after a revolt of Communist hardliners, which ended with the victory of Boris Yeltsin, the first Russian president, who promoted the authority of the Russian Federation over that of the Soviet Union. Lukashenka had begun to advocate a policy of closer ties with Russia, and what he termed a "rapprochement" of the two states during his campaign for president in the spring of 1994. Once he became president, he tried to work with Yeltsin, despite his earlier support for the Russian president's rivals in the parliament.

On January 5, 1995, the two states signed an agreement on forming a Customs Union, though efforts to form a common currency that would have brought the Russian ruble into Belarus failed. A month later, Russia and Belarus signed a Treaty of Friendship, Good Neighborhood, and Cooperation, with a timeline of ten years. These led directly to the April 2, 1996, Treaty on the Creation of a Community of Belarus and

Russia, and the title became more formal on its first anniversary and became the Treaty on the Union of Belarus and Russia. The Treaty on the Creation of a Union State was finalized on December 8, 1999, and the Russian Duma voted in its favor by 371 votes to 2, as the new Russian prime minister Vladimir Putin supported a common economic space, customs territory, and budget. The treaty then came into effect officially on January 26, 2000.

The Union remained very much a paper treaty in these earlier years. The treaty coincided with a difficult period both in Lukashenka's presidency, which legally ended in the summer of 1999, as the president sought to extend his period in power based on the 1996 referendum. There followed an uncertain period as the two countries began to argue over the price of gas, with the Belarusian side expressing anger that it had to pay the same prices as EU states, rather than the earlier subsidized price. Formally, in the period 2008–2012, Putin served as head of the Council of the Union State in his role as Russian prime minister. In 2010, the gas dispute overshadowed the question of further integration through the Union agreement. Russia seemed to take a distant attitude to the Belarusian government's draft agreement, which was issued under the slogan "two countries, one market" in September 2019. The two countries developed thirty-one road maps in this same period.

The deepened integration caused much concern among the Belarusian public, not least since it followed a period characterized by soft nationalism, the promotion of the state of Belarus through slogans, wall posters, and TV programs. Street protests were prominent in December 2019 before Belarus entered the critical election year of 2020. The mass uprising that followed the August 9, 2020, election pushed the embattled Lukashenka toward Moscow, an about-face from the early days of the campaign when he feared that Russia sought to remove him from office. On September 10, 2021, the respective Prime Ministers Mikhail Mishustin and Raman Halauchanka approved twenty-eight of the thirty-one road maps for the period 2021–2023. The document was ratified by both leaders on November 5, 2021.

The Union Agreement extends to military affairs as well. Russia and Belarus have conducted a series of exercises under the mantle of Zapad (West), anticipating a conflict with NATO and on one occasion following up a rebuke to an intrusion by that alliance with a swift annexation of Latvia. Zapad-2021 involved 200,000 troops using over 760 different types of weapons. It followed earlier joint exercises in 2009, 2013, and 2017. In early 2024, the two armies carried out another exercise under the heading Operation Allied Resolve, following which the Russian side invaded Ukraine from Belarusian territory. The Belarusian army did not join in the invasion and has remained out of the war in Ukraine, despite Russian pressure. The two countries now have a common media company, based on an agreement signed on January 29, 2004, although in practice, the Belarusian media has been following Russia's instruction since late 2020. Russian media workers have taken over several positions vacated by their Belarusian counterparts since the 2020 protests.

In terms of structure, the Union State is made up of a Parliament, Supreme State Council, Court, Accounts Chamber, and Standing Committees. The key organ is the Supreme State Council, which includes the heads of state, the parliamentary leaders, and the chairmen of the two parliaments. The parliament is divided between a Chamber of Union (36 deputies from each state) and a House of Representatives (ratio 75–28 in Russia's favor). The budget is also divided, with Russia contributing 65% and Belarus 35%. Thus, integration threatens the sovereignty of Belarus and its independent decision-making. On the other hand, the Union State is far from a finished entity, and many of its positions have remained unfulfilled. Russia has been fighting a war since February 2024, which has limited the time available for meetings of the dual entity.

What was Belarus's "economic miracle"?

The term "economic miracle" has been applied generally both to the period from the 1950s when industrial development accelerated in Belarus and the early Lukashenka period from 1994 to about 2006. The former period represented a dramatic change during which a mainly rural republic, badly damaged by the war, recovered and became an important economic region of the Soviet Union in several areas: machine building, oil refining, chemicals, thermal power stations, the production of agricultural fertilizers, and dairy products. The symbolic addendum to the industrial development was the impressive Minsk metro, fast and efficient, and the chief means of transport in the city, as it remains today. Belarus became the "assembly room" of the Soviet Union. As industry developed, there was also a demographic change as the rural population, consisting mainly of ethnic Belarusians, moved to the cities and became industrial workers.

During the Soviet period, the growing cities also became a factor in political propaganda, Sovietization, and the advancement of Russian culture and language. The Chernobyl disaster, occurring toward the end of the Soviet period, acted as a severe brake on these developments and brought such progress to a halt. The republican government relied heavily on the central ministries in Moscow to come to its aid. In turn, by 1990–1991, the Soviet Union's economic decline had caused repercussions in the national republics. The early years of independence were perhaps the most difficult for Belarus, before it developed its own banks and local currency, and with the loss of connections with other Soviet republics that facilitated its industries, particularly neighboring Russia and Ukraine.

The Lukashenka regime came to power in part because it promised to renew the connections with Russia. Lukashenka recognized that for many residents, the loss of the link to Moscow had profound consequences. He actively encouraged the perception that the Republic of Belarus could not survive without Russia. In 1992, the Beltransgaz pipeline came into operation to carry Russian gas to buyers in the European Union, with two lines, Yamal-Europe and Northern Lights. Lacking domestic energy resources, Belarus also relied on imports of about 18,000 billion cubic meters of gas annually from Russia. Thus, its future economic stability was dependent on good relations with Russia, particularly with its first president Boris Yeltsin and the state-run company Gazprom. But the relationship was two-way in that Russia depended on pipelines that ran through Ukraine and Belarus to transport its gas to Europe.

By 1993, the struggling Belarusian economy had run up a debt of $100 million to Russia for the supply of gas. The Minsk government could not pay such debt without more foreign borrowing and was obliged to apply for a loan from the International Monetary Fund (IMF), and later from China. The situation was difficult, but it was also becoming a political dilemma. In 1991, Belarus had helped to form the Commonwealth of Independent States (CIS), which replaced the Soviet Union. While the CIS never operated efficiently and was in some ways a device used by Yeltsin to remove the Gorbachev Soviet Union, it marked the beginning of a series of Russian-led moves to integrate the former republics. Russian foreign policy began to move from one oriented toward the West—the main ally in 1991—to one of increased control over the former republics using economic means. The Russia-Belarus Union was another device, although in terms of its economic impact it became more significant in the Putin period.

The link between cheap gas and oil supplied to Belarus and political integration soon became evident. Russia intended to continue maintaining two military installations on Belarusian territory with the possible expansion to an air force base. Gazprom alternated its prices, partly in response to world prices for oil and gas but partly based on relations with the receiving states. Thus, as relations worsened with Ukraine and Georgia in the early twenty-first century, those states began to pay far more for Russian oil and gas than Belarus. But for the latter, prices were never stable. While they lasted, with Belarus paying between \$120–\$130 per cubic meter of gas, the Minsk government was able to siphon off gas, and with oil imports, to refine the oil and sell it at a higher price to various buyers, boosting the economy and enabling a constant rise in GDP for about a decade. Belarus also became a conduit for Russian arms sales, which in turn led to further profits. These added to the sales of potash through Belaruskali company, soon the largest and financially stable enterprise in the republic.

In February 1996, Russia and Belarus signed an agreement that removed Belarusian debts for oil and gas imports, but allowed Russia to deploy its army on Belarusian territory without charge, and end any demands the Minsk government had for its efforts to eliminate the consequences of the Chernobyl disaster. With this and later agreements involving the Russian government and Gazprom, the Russian side tried to assert some control over its smaller neighbor through prices, the Russia-Belarus Union, or control over the transit company Beltransgaz. Belarus was invariably in the weaker position as the debtor nation, its small size, and its need for resources. But even Lukashenka began to look for alternative arrangements to avoid complete subjugation to Moscow.

The relative prosperity of Belarus in the first twelve to thirteen years of Lukashenka's presidency contrasted with that of other former Soviet republics. Ukraine, a better-endowed state in terms of natural resources, struggled with corruption and the stagnancy of formerly profitable industries such as coal and iron and steel. But the retirement of President Yeltsin in 1999, and his replacement by Vladimir Putin, changed the relationship with Moscow. Putin's emergence saw an immediate cooling of links and a personal animosity between the two presidents. The new Russian leader refused to accept that there could be a union between two such unequal partners and suggested that Belarus could become a western region of the Russian Federation. Nevertheless, the disputes that followed did not negate the continuing relative success of the Belarusian economy, which Lukashenka used as part of a so-called social contract with the population, supplying their needs while increasing his own authority as the Father (Batka) of the nation.

The world recession of 2008 ended the economic miracle. Prior to that year, the GDP grew by an average of 8% each year from 2000. Until 2006, Belarus had been able to purchase Russian oil at Russian domestic prices and resell it at world prices, which could be four to five times higher. In turn, it could also buy and re-export Russian gas. In 2008, oil prices collapsed, and Belarus's foreign reserves dwindled to a dangerously low level. In the period 2008–2011, Lukashenka's government resorted to requests for loans from the IMF and China as the relationship with Russia worsened because of uncertain oil and gas prices. Another factor was Belarus's failure to recognize two pro-Russian regions of Georgia—Abkhazia and South Ossetia—as independent states following a brief war between Georgia and Russia. Russia also began to exploit the deteriorating Belarusian economy to take over several significant Belarusian companies. Gazprom gradually took over the Druzhba pipeline company Beltransgaz. Initially, ownership was shared and each side had 50% ownership. By 2011, however, Gazprom acquired complete control.

Russia tried to make further inroads by proposing a merger between the Minsk Wheel Tractor Plant (MAZ) and Russia's KamAZ. An evaluation by an external company at Russia's request valued the MAZ company at $800 million, but Belarus rejected that price as too low. Eventually a joint company was established, with Russia's investment at $2 billion and Belarus's $1.6 billion. Russia also achieved significant control over the Belarusian banking system. By the end of the global recession in 2012, six of the major ten banks in Belarus had Russian owners, with another under CIS Regional Holding GmbH of Austria. The three remaining ones were state-owned.

However, not all dealings went smoothly. The Russian Ministry of Energy was concerned about the program of exporting duty-free oil to Belarus that would then be returned in the form of petroleum products. But Belarus was reselling it as solvents and thinners, and the total amount of petroleum arriving in Russia in 2012 was only about 2% of the expected total. But such subterfuge did not work for long since Russia then demanded a sum of $1.5 billion with the possibility of repayment in the form of shares in the MAZ company. Russia also began to pressure Belarus to sell its main source of revenue, the potash company Belaruskali, but the Belarusians again valued it much higher than Russia's assessment. Further, Lukashenka realized that while some state assets could be made available for sale, Belaruskali was not among them. One survey conducted at the time suggested that 58.7% of respondents were against the sale of the company under any circumstances and only 8% supported the idea.

If the social contract was tied to the "economic miracle," then all illusions dissipated in 2017, when Lukashenka tried to impose a tax amounting to more than two monthly salaries on those who had been unemployed for more than six months in a year. Known as the "parasite" tax, it prompted mass protests across Belarus and eventually was suspended and later withdrawn. The impasse between president and workers was compounded in 2020 with the onset of the COVID-19 pandemic, when Lukashenka assured his population that there were easy remedies available, such as going to the countryside, or a sauna, drinking vodka, and others. The state excused itself from a direct response at a time when the death rates were increasing. Belarusians began to realize that self-help and grassroots initiatives were the only ways to resolve their dilemma. The economy likewise never again achieved the growth rates of the late twentieth and early twenty-first centuries.

What was the relationship between Belarus and the European Union in the period 1991–2025?

Relations between Belarus and the European Union began in late 1991, following the collapse of the Soviet Union. In 1995, the two sides signed a Partnership and Cooperation Agreement, but it was not ratified by the EU, which was concerned about what it perceived as anti-democratic trends in Belarus. By 1997, after the two referendums (described above), the agreement was formally ended. In particular, the EU objected to the changes made by the Lukashenka leadership to the 1994 Constitution and suspended direct contacts. As a result, Belarus was no longer considered part of the EU Neighborhood policy, despite its geographical proximity to EU countries Poland, Lithuania, and Latvia.

In the early 2000s, the EU allocated funds to assist the growth of "civil society" in Belarus. It involved supporting independent television and radio stations broadcasting into Belarus, suspending and freezing the assets abroad of Lukashenka and other leaders, and placing travel bans on them to prevent their entry into EU countries. A grant was also awarded to the Russian station RT, which allowed it to make a daily thirty-minute broadcast to Belarus.

The situation began to change in 2008 as a result of both internal and external initiatives. It arose after the release of a number of political prisoners, many of whom had been arrested in the protests that followed the 2006 presidential elections. State media also began to stop their denunciations of the EU and, as a result of the initiative of the Swedish and Polish ambassadors, Belarus was invited to join the Eastern Partnership project, beginning in 2008 and formally signed the following year. In the same period, the Europeans ended sanctions against the Belarusian state, and the IMF loaned $2.5 billion to the Minsk government.

The following two years were perhaps the most successful in the relationship between Belarus and the EU. With Belarus a member of the partnership, its internal stability was seen positively in contrast to the situation in Georgia (which was still grappling with the aftermath of the Russia's attack on it in 2008), and the tense relationship between Ukraine and Russia during the presidency of Viktor Yushchenko. The Parliamentary Assembly of the Council of Europe was prepared to return Belarus's special guest status conditional upon a moratorium on the death penalty. The Lukashenka leadership, however, never abolished the death penalty. Still, the 2010 election campaign took place quite peacefully, with candidates permitted to campaign freely until the day of the election. After the campaign ended, however, the brutal dispersal of a rally that had moved to Independence Square abruptly ended closer association.

Sanctions were restored thereafter, and the EU has constantly demanded the release of those arrested at the demonstration on December 19, 2010, and to waive any criminal records assigned to them. Sanctions were expanded to a wider group of prominent people linked to the regime: police, lawyers, judges, and businesspeople. Matters reached an apex in 2012, when Belarus called home its ambassadors in the EU countries and the United States and demanded that those European and US ambassadors in Minsk return home to explain that Belarus did not accept the imposed sanctions. As a result, the twenty-seven ambassadors of EU countries and the US ambassador left Minsk for three years.

Nevertheless, the Delegation of the European Commission to Belarus in Minsk, which opened its doors on March 7, 2008, continued to work on about thirty small-scale projects, including one to prevent illegal migration over the border; cooperate with the authorities and civil society, universities, and the media; and explain the position of the European Union on various issues. As of July 2023, the Delegation was led by Danish diplomat Steen Noerlov, who has served formerly in the UN, OSCE, and Council of Europe. The office also provides consular protection for EU citizens in Belarus.

Prior to the contentious August 2020 elections, matters improved. In April of that year, an agreement was signed on visa facilitation, which came into effect in June. The agreement cut the costs of an EU visa for Belarusian citizens from $60 to $35, and allowed visits to Belarus of up to 180 days rather than the earlier 90 days, with the prospect of similar easing of laws for Belarusians visiting the EU (cut short because of the protests that followed later in the year). The aftermath of the election campaign, however, saw a renewal of sanctions that were gradually expanded. Most EU countries refused to recognize Lukashenka as the winner of the 2020 campaign and supported the mass protests taking place in Minsk. On May 21, 2021, the diversion of the RyanAir flight carrying opposition activist Raman Pratasevich led to heightened sanctions and the freezing of an investment aid package from the EU worth 3 billion euros. Lukashenka retaliated by fomenting a border crisis, sending migrants to the Polish border and encouraging them to cross illegally.

The heightened tension also had an impact on the Readmission Agreement between the EU and Belarus that had accompanied the visa facilitation and came into force in July 2020. It permitted the return of citizens illegally residing in EU countries or Belarus. In early June 2021, the Belarusian foreign minister Uladzimir Makei remarked that as the funding for projects related to the Readmission Agreement had been suspended by the EU, Belarus would end its participation and would no longer allocate any funds to the question of monitoring its borders to protect the EU from illegal migrants. The EU also suspended its export of technological equipment or software that could intercept telephone or Internet communications and cut back sharply on trade in other products. Once the border agreement came into effect, the migrant crisis sharply increased, putting pressure on the borders of Poland and Lithuania and leading to a number of deaths among migrants unable to cross the border.

The EU has given support to the 2020 opposition leader Sviatlana Tsikhanouskaya, whose group has campaigned officially for Belarusian membership of the EU. The European Commission donated 25 million euros to a campaign to support democracy in Belarus in late 2022. The EU also declined to recognize the electoral victory of Lukashenka in February 2025, following the rejection of the request for monitoring by the OSCE supporting states. In a joint statement on January 9, 2025, the OSCE Office for Democratic Institutions and Human Rights and the Parliamentary Assembly of the Council of Europe declared that the decision was "deeply regrettable and prevents an impartial and independent assessment of the election process."

The EU has consistently supported the rights of Belarusian prisoners and those displaced by violence and repressions. Tsikhanouskaya has campaigned for a democratic Belarus while stressing its European ties and a "vision of a European future." Though her influence may wane with time—and by 2024–2025 there were already signs that her movement had several rivals—the aspirations remain.

How does the Belarusian state commemorate the past?

Since 2020, the Lukashenka regime has made a concerted effort to use history as a form of legitimization. Since it failed to win popular support in the presidential elections, and much of the democratic world refused to recognize Lukashenka as the legitimate president, there has been renewed focus on the past, and particularly the Second World War. The commemoration of the period 1941–1945—known as the Great Patriotic War—began in the mid-1960s, and most of the monuments and memorials in the republic derive from the 1960s and 1970s. Thus, there was a base from which to construct a more elaborate historical narrative that has become enshrined into law and is used to educate children in schools and in textbooks for all levels of education. There are several key components to this version of the war years, both old and new.

First, as we have seen, the partisans remain a focal point. A new monument to the partisans appeared near the Partyzanskaja subway station in Minsk in 2005, adding to the plethora of monuments and memorial parks in the city center, which include Victory Park, Victory Square with a small museum in the subway below, the Mound of Glory on the city outskirts en route to the Minsk National Airport, the stella outside the spacious Museum of the Great Patriotic War, and others. Every city contains an official war monument, though the main memorial site is at the destroyed village of Chatyń near Lahojsk, with a large statue of the sole remaining resident carrying a child at the entrance and a bell tolling dolefully every few seconds. After Chatyń, the most notable memorial park is the Brest Hero Fortress, and the more recent Liniya Stalina (Stalin's Line), created with the support of the Afghan veterans' association.

The Yama (The Pit) is a monument dedicated to the victims of the Holocaust in Minsk. The memorial is located at the site where, on March 2, 1942, Nazi forces shot roughly 5,000 Jewish residents of the Minsk Ghetto. The memorial features an obelisk erected in 1947, and a bronze sculpture called *The Last Way*, added in the year 2000, which depicts the Jewish victims descending into the pit before their execution. The inscription on the obelisk is written in Yiddish and Russian.

The other main Holocaust site is in the village of Maly Traścianiec, east of the city along the road from Minsk to Mahilioŭ. During Germany's occupation of the area during the Second World War, the village became the location of a Nazi extermination site, where Belarusians, but mostly Belarusian and German Jews, were killed. Belarus's largest death camp, although the area is vast and also includes the killing grounds of the Blahaŭščyna forest about 2 miles away. Many victims were transported there from the Minsk ghetto, and many of the deaths occurred in the Blahaŭščyna Forest just prior to the Nazis' retreat from Minsk in the summer of 1944.

The first part of the memorial complex was completed in 2015 and was devoted to the remaining parts of the Lenin collective farm, converted into a camp for prisoners. The Maly Traścianiec memorial expanded in 2018, with the addition of the "Road of Memory," a path that leads to a former execution site and is lined with large stone blocks bearing plaques that list the sites where Nazi crimes were committed in Belarus. The wagons used to transport Jews from various European sites to Minsk for extermination are also depicted. The Blahaŭščyna Memorial Graveyard and several other monuments were added, as was a memorial to more than 10,000 Austrian Jewish victims in 2019. It is a harrowing experience to walk around the site, on a similar scale to Birkenau in occupied Poland. The site was funded by a number of European organizations from Germany, Austria, Poland, the Netherlands, and the Czech Republic. At its opening, Lukashenka appeared alongside the presidents of Germany and Austria, Frank-Walter Steinmeier and Alexander Van der Bellen. An address by Polish president Andrzej Duda was read publicly (he was not present).

Official reports maintain that 206,500 people died at Maly Traścianiec, making it the fourth largest Nazi death camp in Europe. But the figures have never been clearly verified, and Yad Vashem reports the deaths of 65,000 Jews. Other historians have put the figure over 100,000, mostly executions by shootings and gas vans. Initially, at the first memorial site on the foundations of the Lenin collective farm, the posted signs make no mention of Jews at all, with the victims subsumed under the all-embracing adjective "Soviet." Between 2014 and 2018, there were hints that Belarus was at last prepared to acknowledge the Holocaust and the murder of Jewish people as a distinct phenomenon; yet, after August 2020, it seems the focus has shifted again to the "genocide of the Belarusians" narrative.

The demographic change caused by the elimination of the BSSR's Jewish population transformed society and particularly the towns, which became Belarusian-Jewish as opposed to the earlier Jewish-Polish prewar population in the western regions, or Jewish-Belarusian in the east. But in Lukashenka's Belarus very little weakens constant propaganda about the Belarusian victory in the Second World War and the suffering of its people.

Evidence of the Soviet period remains, particularly through extant statues of Lenin in Independence Square and of Mikhail Kalinin on a major eastern road. There is a bust of the first leader of the secret police, Feliks Dzerzhinsky, a native of the territory that eventually became the BSSR and Belarus, opposite the ornate Lubyanka building in Minsk, formerly the national headquarters of the KGB. Soviet hammers and sickles can still be seen on the building's facade. Stalin's bust can be found at the entrance to the Liniya Stalina historic site.

Commemorative days and statutory holidays are also linked mostly to the Soviet period: Armed Forces Day on February 23; International Women's Day on March 8; Constitution Day on March 15; May Day on May 1; Victory Day on May 9; Day to remember the national flag and coat of arms, and the Belarusian national anthem on the second Sunday of May; Radunitsa, an Orthodox Church memorial to the departed (the date varies according to the Orthodox Church Calendar); Independence Day of the Republic of Belarus, July 3 (the date of the liberation of Minsk from Nazi rule); and October Revolution Day, November 7. More recently, the Belarusian government added September 17 as a national holiday, the date when western and eastern territories of Belarus were reunified under the Nazi-Soviet Pact.

Lukashenka has occasionally recognized the March 25 Independence Day of 1918, which is celebrated by the opposition, and April 26, the day of remembrance for the 1986 nuclear disaster at Chernobyl. The opposition also remembers the 1514 Battle of Orša between the Grand Duchy of Lithuania and Kingdom of Poland against the Grand Duchy of Moscow; the uprising of Tadeusz Kościuszko (Belarusian: Kaściuška) in Poland against the Russian Empire in 1794; and the Kastus

Kalinouski uprising. It also annually commemorates the night of the dead poets on October 29, 1937, when the Soviet government executed over 140 Belarusian cultural leaders, including 22 poets and writers (see above). At times, Lukashenka has made attempts to monopolize such memorial dates and memories. He has also denied the Belarusian connections of past heroes such as Kastsiushka (Kościuszko in Polish) and Kalinouski, arguing that they represent Poland rather than Belarus. But anomalies persist, and Lukashenka has allowed recognition of the Lithuanian period of Belarusian history. In 2006, when the new National Library of Belarus opened in its new location along the main highway to the east, its exterior featured a large bronze sculpture of Francysk Skaryna, the sixteenth-century printer and translator, and at the entrance a quote from the Skaryna Bible. Both the library and sculpture were designed in part by Viktar Kramarenka, a native of Hrodna.

Why were relations tense with Putin's Russia after 2000?

Following the deepened Union Agreement signed with his Belarusian counterpart, Russian president Boris Yeltsin resigned on December 31, 1999, designating Prime Minister Vladimir Putin as his preferred successor. In March, Putin won a new election in the first round, beginning his lengthy tenure as head of state. He was dissatisfied with the existing terms of the Union Agreement, arguing that the two partners could not be regarded as equal, and suggesting as one alternative that Belarus should join the Russian Federation as a western region. Lukashenka, who may have held out hopes that he would succeed the Russian president as the head of the Russia-Belarus Union, strongly rejected this notion.

The impasse led to several clauses of the agreement being put in abeyance, including the idea—suggested earlier—that the Russian ruble should become the common currency of both states by January 1, 2005. At this stage also, the two leaders failed to agree on a deal that would have seen Belarus pay $28 per 1,000 cubic meters of gas in return for conceding to Russia 50% of the company controlling the transit of Russian gas to Europe (Beltransgaz). The Belarusian side's estimate of the value of the company was ten times higher than the official estimate of Moscow. The Russian company Gazprom, which headed negotiations, was mostly state-owned and had close links with government officials. It promptly began to raise the gas price to over $50.

Lukashenka's reaction was to refuse payment and accuse the Russians of betraying a close partnership. The wrangling over gas prices continued for some time and spilled over into other areas of the two economies. As the weaker partner, and one that relied heavily on Russian imports, Lukashenka's position was vulnerable, particularly with the threat of power cuts looming. Russia cut off supplies for lack of payment several times, but the Belarusian side simply siphoned off gas intended for export elsewhere as it traveled through the pipeline. At the time, about 30% of Russian gas was exported through Belarus and about 70% through Ukraine. Neither was to prove a particularly reliable partner for Russia.

Belarus's position was weakened further by external events. These years saw several "color revolutions" taking place in the region, with unpopular leaders removed after public protests in Serbia, Ukraine, Kyrgyzstan, and Georgia. Lukashenka saw these changes as Western-engineered and -funded. One option was to increase trade with the European Union, but relations with Brussels deteriorated after official Belarus held another referendum in 2004 that extended indefinitely the time the president could remain in office. On the other hand, the antipathy between the West—particularly the United States—and Belarus that led to US sanctions being imposed in 2004 provided Lukashenka with a loophole. Russia strongly objected to the sanctions and was prepared to make some concessions on the price of gas in response.

Over the next years, the two leaderships quarreled constantly without threatening to sever relations. Periodically, Russia issued bans on imports of Belarusian dairy products, particularly milk, on sanitary grounds. Gas and oil prices fluctuated wildly and there were periodic stoppages of passage, but none that really endangered the livelihood of Belarusian customers since the authorities could always "steal" supplies meant for other destinations. One culmination point concerned Russian foreign policy and the war with Georgia, which broke out in 2008 while Mikeil Saakashvili was the Georgian president and tried to end the separatist movements in South Ossetia and Abkhazia. Although the Russians quickly intervened and defeated the Georgian army, Belarus declined to follow Russia's recognition of the independence of the two breakaway republics.

The economic dilemma also expanded into direct Russian attacks on Lukashenka. In early July 2010, the Russian channel NTV aired the first of a four-part series on the Belarusian president entitled *The Godfather* on the Russian program *Emergency Investigation*. The programs provided a no-holds-barred exposé of the crimes of Lukashenka, starting by belittling his alleged economic successes and declaring that they were only the result of Russian largesse. The first program showed him praising Hitler and accused him of being responsible for the murders of Zakharenka, Krasouski, Hanchar, and Zavadski, as well as Henadz Karpenka. It also alleged that Mikalai, the president's third son, had been taken away from his mistress, Iryna Abelskaya, Lukashenka's personal doctor.

The following programs, which ran until June 2011, provided accusations of money laundering through his family, cooperating with the enemies of Russia such as Saakashvili and former Kyrgyzstan president Kurmanbek Bakiyev, who had been offered asylum in Belarus, as well as Vladimir Putin's arch-enemy Boris Berezovsky, then living in London. The program maintained that Berezovsky was backing the Lukashenka regime financially. It also suggested that when

Lukashenka became a people's deputy, he evaded prosecution for the beating of a state-farm machinist. The series ran freely in Russia but was censored in Belarus, although some opposition media happily printed excerpts from the script. The bigger question is whether NTV acted independently or whether it had the approval of the Russian authorities to run it. Most sources concur that the timing of the series—amid the disputes between Minsk and Moscow over energy and trade—was not accidental. Yet its beginning coincided with the announcement of a new Customs Union between Russia, Belarus, and Kazakhstan, suggesting the ambivalent nature of the relationship between the two governments.

The disputes in the economic and even political spheres did not have a significant impact on military cooperation. At independence, Russia had two military installations on Belarusian territory: a missile warning system near Baranavičy to track ICBM launches; and a communication center with the Russian navy operating in the Indian, Atlantic, and Pacific Oceans near Viliejka. In 1995, Russia obtained a twenty-five-year lease on the former that was renewed in 2021 for both sites. Russia and Belarus have also carried out the Zapad (West in English) series of military exercises that simulate responses to an attack from NATO. Four Zapad exercises have been held to date between the Russian and Belarusian armies: 2009, 2013, 2017, and 2021, with another scheduled for September 2025. In 2022, Russia and Belarus conducted an unrelated exercise on Belarusian territory that preceded the Russian attack on Ukraine. Russia also supplies virtually all the military equipment used by the Belarusian army.

Personalities of leaders inevitably play an important role in the relations between neighboring states. Lukashenka benefited from the foibles and health problems of Boris Yeltsin, particularly after the Russian president's re-election in 1996 through 1999. Putin, however, represented a different personality: serious, ruthless, and dedicated to restoring Russian power, particularly in the vicinity. Putin never regarded

Belarus (or Ukraine) as equal partners, and there is plenty of evidence that he never recognized either as bona fide independent states. Moreover, although Putin did not enter politics as a very recognizable figure—he was Yeltsin's fifth prime minister and the others had not lasted long—his KGB background rendered him difficult to deal with, particularly during negotiations over prices or Belarus's role in Russian-led organizations. His training negated any idea of concessions as part of deal-making, adding to Putin's natural inflexibility on key issues.

On the other hand, the two leaders had some common interests: both feared NATO and Westernization, both were innately suspicious of Western influences and culture, and both were lovers and participants of sports, especially ice hockey. The burly Lukashenka and diminutive Putin played hockey frequently, sometimes against each other. In 2014, Lukashenka hosted the World Hockey Championship in Minsk, the same year in which Putin attended the Winter Olympic Games in Sochi. Both presidents propagated the image of a masculine leader who could achieve impressive physical feats, sometimes to levels that invited ridicule, but distancing themselves from the image of bloated Soviet leaders or the frequently drunk Yeltsin. In this respect, they adopted a sort of kinship that became more pronounced after the events of 2020–2022.

And they both established political dictatorships, extending their terms in office well beyond constitutional terms. The violent methods employed by Lukashenka in repressing public demonstrations and protests after elections eventually were replicated by Putin in Moscow. One should add one significant caveat to this picture, which is that while Putin was prepared to use the Russian army beyond the borders of the Federation, Lukashenka, recognizing the negative views of his public on this question, was careful to emphasize the peaceful nature of Belarus, and the fact that the Belarusian army would not be dispatched to wars in Chechnya, Georgia, or Ukraine. That is not to suggest that Belarus independently could have launched a war on one of its neighbors, but rather that the state would not join Russia in any foreign aggression. Moscow's resentment toward this was offset partly by Lukashenka's offers to mediate in Russian conflicts, including Ukraine and the Donbas in 2014 and 2015, and between the Russian government and its maverick oligarch Evgeny Prigozhin in 2023.

Which strata of society most strongly oppose the current regime?

Opposition to Lukashenka has varied over the three decades he has been in power. For the most part he has retained popularity among rural communities, blue-collar workers, and the military. The widespread disaffection for his continuing presidency dates from 2017 to 2020, culminating in the mass protests of the latter year. But the difficulty in answering this question is a result of the impediments to and inaccessibility of accurate polling. Internet polls, for example, have consistently placed the president's popular standing lower than have more traditional methods. The repressions in place at the time of writing mean that potential respondents are reluctant to answer or prefer not to express their views openly. As a result, the true standing of Lukashenka is partly based on speculation.

In 2020, an Internet poll announced that the popularity of Lukashenka, during the election campaign, had dropped to 3%. Slogans and T-shirts with the words "Sasha 3%" were in wide circulation. As Andrei Vardamatski, Oleg Manaev, and other sociologists have pointed out, Lukashenka's popularity never fell that low in the country. Some analysts maintain that his popularity did fall sharply in 2020, but not under 20%. In the post-election period, various factors may have stabilized his support: relative economic recovery in part of the economy, the decision not to join Russia in its invasion of Ukraine, apathy, and distance between the electorate and the leaders of the opposition, now in jail or in exile.

Nevertheless, one can discern certain strata that remain deeply opposed to his continuing leadership. After 2020, students, intellectuals, diplomats, and security officers were foremost among those expressing anger and disillusionment with the existing system. To a certain extent, university faculty members, IT workers—many of whom left the country—and, more recently, workers with less than full employment or wages that do not keep pace with inflation and the falling ruble can be added. Again, one cannot witness many open expressions of dissension within the country, but it is highly doubtful these sentiments have simply disappeared. Several athletes, including former world champion swimmer Aliaksandra Herasimenia and other signatories of the list of the athletes from 2020, have expressed revulsion for the regime.

Over the three decades of Lukashenka in power, the opposition has always been able to command around 25% support among the electorate. The most accurate recent poll of voters' preferred presidential candidate indicated that the imprisoned Viktar Babaryka is a more attractive choice than Lukashenka, although the current leader had a slight lead over former culture minister Pavel Latushka and former presidential candidate Sviatlana Tsikhanouskaya. Babaryka is serving an eighteen-year prison sentence, and the others are living abroad, so there is little chance of an election in which all could run.

That Lukashenka retains some popularity is a result of longevity, media coverage, and the popular need for economic and political security rather than genuine affection or support. Since people do not see the possibility of change, they tend to accept the existing leadership as long as they retain some security, wages, pensions, and so forth. But 2020 was about generational change, and the young well-informed, well-educated, and well-traveled stratum rejected Lukashenka. For a time, workers at the Minsk Tractor Works also held him in contempt, jeering during one of his public talks to them and taking advantage of a rare opportunity to express themselves.

On the other hand, the public's view reflects in part its exposure to local, national, and Russian news services that project a negative image of the West, the United States, and NATO. Views inside Belarus are the antithesis of those one might encounter in Warsaw, Vilnius, or Riga. Thus, rejection of Lukashenka in some sectors of society does not translate into abhorrence for authoritarianism, state-run industries, Vladimir Putin, or the Russian army. There are Belarusians who accept that there is an existential or spiritual threat from the West, and there is deep distrust of NATO among them. Yet the attitudes to the European Union have generally been positive, and the Eastern Partnership project was quite popular.

6

BELARUS AND RUSSIA'S WAR IN UKRAINE

What have been the main aspects of relations with the EU under the Lukashenka regime?

The three decades of Lukashenka's rule have inevitably seen many fluctuations and changes in foreign policy. But one can discern certain trends. Notably, Lukashenka was elected in 1994 on a policy of reviving relations with Russia and restoring the economic links that became severed after the dissolution of the Soviet Union. Belarus was a founding member of the Commonwealth of Independent States (CIS) and a partner in the Russia-Belarus Union. During some of the more tempestuous periods in his leadership, Lukashenka relied on the guidance and mediation of the Russian Federation. But in the 1990s, Russia, led by Boris Yeltsin, was rarely able to pay much attention to Belarus and was preoccupied with a war in Chechnya and the division of the Black Sea Fleet with Ukraine.

The countries of the European Union represent the biggest trading partner other than Russia, and relations between them have been mixed, with periods of cooperation and periods of freeze and sanctions. In 1995, Belarus and the EU signed a Partnership and Cooperation Agreement (PCS), but it preceded the 1996 referendum in Belarus at which Lukashenka greatly expanded his powers. The changes to the Constitution were not well received in Brussels, and the Europeans opted not to ratify the PCA. The EU ended its technical assistance programs to Belarus as well the inclusion of that country in the European Neighborhood Policy. After a third referendum in 2004, which permitted Lukashenka to remain in power indefinitely, ending the policy of a two-term presidency, the EU turned its attention to civil groups in Belarus to promote regime change.

Aid from the EU to such groups was small but effective. But Lukashenka often changed direction, particularly when relations with Russia ran into difficulties, and a new dialogue began in 2008. On March 7, the EU office in Minsk was approved, and it opened its doors on January 1, 2009, with the status of a diplomatic mission. The president released those political prisoners who had been arrested after the 2006 post-election protests, and the EU ended the imposed sanctions. On the initiative of Poland and Sweden, Belarus became a member of the Eastern Partnership Project whereby Belarus would receive benefits with a tacit agreement to allow freedom of assembly, more open elections, and recognize human rights. Belarus was also asked by the Council of Europe to end the death penalty, but without result. The government also managed to solicit an IMF loan of $2.5 billion, which ended the immediate fears of economic collapse as the world recession reached its height.

The rapprochement continued into the 2010 presidential election campaign, which allowed opposition candidates to appear in public and on television but ended abruptly on election day, December 19, after the violence in Independence Square. The EU then increased the list of people facing travel bans to include judges, businesspeople, and lawmakers. Lukashenka responded in a typically idiosyncratic manner by putting pressure on the diplomatic community living in the Drazdy area, near the president's own home. Ambassadors reported sudden cuts in electricity and requests to vacate their homes. He then demanded that the EU and US ambassadors return to their countries to discuss with their governments the folly of their sanctions policy against Belarus.

In response and in protest, the ambassadors staged a mass exit from Belarus. Sanctions were increased. Most of the ambassadors eventually returned to Minsk but were rehoused in a different area. A further period of conciliation began in 2015, following peaceful presidential elections that Lukashenka won comfortably, as most opposition parties opted to boycott them. The EU had numerous projects in Belarus, including the Bombel-4 project, which enabled advanced communications at both the Belarus-Poland borders in 2001 and the Belarus-Lithuania border in 2009–2011, as well as the training of Belarusian border guards. By February 2016, EU sanctions against Belarus were ended and a further four years of amicable relations followed.

In 2017, the Belarusians began a visa-free regime on their western border, permitting those with passports from forty countries (including the EU, UK, and North America) to enter Belarus via the Minsk-2 airport for five days. The entry was expanded to thirty days a year later. The goal, ostensibly, was to encourage more business, and perhaps occupy the plush hotels opened in 2014 for the World Hockey Championships in Minsk. In April 2020, a further agreement on easing visa rules was signed between Belarus and the EU. The presidential election in August and its aftermath ended the period of a warmer relationship, although Belarus did not immediately end the visa-free regime. Sanctions were reapplied by the end of 2020 in three stanches targeting Lukashenka and his ministers, security force leaders, members of the election commissions, and the managers of the major state enterprises.

Relations worsened further with both the EU and the democratic world generally when Lukashenka and his security forces mounted a crude attack on a public airline. The object was to arrest Raman Pratasevich, the former editor in chief of the NEXTA and Belarus of the Brain Telegram channels. Pratasevich was prominent during the protests of 2020, channeling information to protesters from Warsaw. He was traveling with his Russian girlfriend Sofia Sapega on RyanAir

Flight 4978 between Athens and Vilnius on May 23, 2021. The flight route took the plane into Belarusian airspace shortly before the plane was due to land in Vilnius, at which point, controllers at Minsk-2 airport demanded that the pilot divert the plane to their location, claiming there was a bomb aboard. The claim was soon elaborated to specify that the Hamas group had planted the bomb. Minsk also sent a fighter jet to accompany the plane.

Pratasevich recognized immediately that he was the target and began to divest his luggage to Sapega. Once the plane landed, both he and his girlfriend were arrested, and the aircraft remained on the ground for several hours before departing for Vilnius. Hamas denied responsibility, and the forged message allegedly authored by one of its members arrived well after the plane was diverted. The Vilnius airport received no warning and unsurprisingly no bomb was found. On July 19, 2022, the International Civil Aviation Organization condemned the plane's diversion. Pratasevich confessed to organizing protests while in custody, almost certainly having suffered torture, and his nose appeared to be broken. On June 25, he was moved from the high-security SIZO-1 prison in Minsk to house arrest at his home. He had agreed to a plea deal whereby he would incriminate his "co-conspirators." On February 16, 2023, he was put on trial, with new charges added for a second trial in April that included the accusation of "inciting social hatred." He received an eight-year sentence but was pardoned by Lukashenka three weeks later. Sapega was also eventually released by Russia.

In October 2024, Pratasevich gave an interview to the Russian socialite, journalist, and former presidential candidate Ksenia Sobchak, whose father was Vladimir Putin's boss during the 1990s in Saint Petersburg. Pratasevich spoke about his new life, new job, and new wife, praising Lukashenka and life in Belarus and criticizing Belarusian opposition. He also changed his mind and argued that he was not the target of the plane diversion; it was directed against Tsikhanouskaya, who was taking the same route a week before his trip. Many people in the comment on YouTube pitied him, acknowledging his status as a hostage in Belarus and placed little credibility on his explanation of the motives behind the hijacking of the plane. In spring 2025, Pratasevich publicly announced he was looking for a job and his mood was rather low as he had been rejected in many places he wanted to work.

The Pratasevich episode had serious consequences for relations between Belarus and the EU. Belavia, the national airline, saw its flights to Europe and the UK suspended indefinitely. The EU suspended a $3 billion package of investment support to Belarus and sanctions were widened considerably. Exports of potash and other products through EU ports in Lithuania were also targeted. The hijacking of a plane did more damage to the Lukashenka regime than the repressions conducted after the 2020 mass protests. The EU also banned the export of software and equipment dealing with telecommunications and goods that could be diverted for military use. The blacklist of Belarusians banned from travel to the EU was widened. Lukashenka's response to the loss of the telecommunications systems was to renounce Belarus's responsibility for monitoring or detaining the passage of illegal migration to the EU through Belarusian territory.

In August 2021, the Belarusian authorities began inviting migrants from the Middle East and North Africa to enter Belarus on seven-day visas, after which they were transported to the border with Poland and encouraged to cross. The scheme, a form of hybrid warfare, took the Poles by surprise, but as anticipated, they began to fortify the border and to prevent the migrants from crossing. Matters were complicated by the fact that the western border is the massive forest area of Biełaviežskaja pušča, and the would-be migrants could find few food supplies to sustain them after failing to cross. As expected by the Minsk authorities, the Poles' attitude was criticized in some circles, particularly after some twenty migrants died during the winter months. Poland meanwhile erected a large iron fence at the border. The crisis reached a peak in late 2021 to early 2022 and eased somewhat afterward, although it did not end. In the summer of 2024, it again resurfaced.

In the relationship with the EU, and to some extent the UK, the Lukashenka regime calculated reactions to his policies, alternating between rigid obstructionism and periods of cooperation. On July 19, 2024, Lukashenka announced the broadening of the visa-free regime with thirty-five countries, much curtailed after the RyanAir incident as the Western airlines no longer ran flights into Minsk, to include entry by rail and road. The new rules were to remain in effect until December 31, 2024 (they were subsequently renewed). The proposal specified that "This will give foreigners more options to visit Belarus in the wake of artificial obstacles and restrictions imposed by neighboring Western countries." The phrasing thus laid blame on Western countries for the sanctions against Belarus and implied that the Minsk government was seeking ways to evade them. Another interpretation was that Belarus was devising ways to differentiate itself from Moscow in a period of deepening integration.

What have been the main aspects of relations with the Russian Federation under the Lukashenka regime?

In addition to the Russia-Belarus Union, relations with Russia are conducted through several different organizations as well as the usual diplomatic channels. Russia and Belarus are stated to be in a "special relationship." We have also noted that Russia maintains two major military facilities on Belarusian territory. The main entities are the Customs Union, the Eurasian Economic Union, the Collective Security Treaty Organization, and the Shanghai Cooperation Agreement, which Belarus joined officially in 2024. In March 2021, the two countries signed a strategic partnership program and Lukashenka agreed that Russian planes could be based on Belarus for use by both countries. They agree to a common foreign policy with a program that is renewed every two years and a common defense and security policy. The two countries regularly carry out military exercises and align both their media and official textbooks for schools. The 2020 protests in Belarus and the full Russian invasion of Ukraine in 2022 have brought the two countries into an even closer partnership, one that sometimes conceals underlying issues that still emerge occasionally.

The 1990s began with a Free Trade Agreement between the two states, followed by the Customs Union on February 21, 1995, although the anticipated monetary union never materialized. In February 1995, Russia and Belarus signed a Treaty of Friendship and Cooperation. As the Russia-Belarus Union developed, it became evident that Lukashenka had broader ambitions, anticipating that his own potential leadership of the Union might provide him with broader powers over Russia as well. Accordingly, he became a familiar and popular figure in several Russian regions after visits there. But the two states approached economic issues in different ways. Having introduced economic shock therapy early in 1992, Russia expected Belarus, likewise, to privatize its industries. Lukashenka preferred state control, which included subsidies to keep afloat struggling enterprises. For some time, opposition leaders also looked to Russia for support in moving toward a democratic structure, but there were limits to how far Moscow would abandon Lukashenka.

Once Putin came to power in 2000, the relationship between the leaders became more complex. Lukashenka rejected the idea of a single currency, while Putin rejected his counterpart's wish to take turns ruling the Union state. As noted, there were lengthy and acrimonious disputes over the export and price of Russian gas and the slow takeover of the Belarusian transit company by Russia. At the same time, Lukashenka's relationship with Ukraine was much warmer, and once Viktor Yushchenko became president of Ukraine, the Belarusian leader always had another outlet to counter Putin. By 2008, relations between Ukraine and Russia became strained as the former declared its interest in NATO's Membership Action Plan and in 2010 when Yushchenko declared Ukrainian nationalist Stepan Bandera to be a Hero of Ukraine.

Russia and Belarus also drew closer after a series of "color revolutions" brought leadership changes in former Soviet republics, including in Ukraine, Kyrgyzstan, Georgia, Moldova, and Armenia. Neither Putin nor Lukashenka felt particularly secure and believed the uprisings were all sponsored and organized by Western powers, particularly the United States. Still, the long-awaited Constitutional Act of the Union State was never resolved and a proposed referendum on its terms was constantly delayed by the Belarusian side. The relationship turned sour, exacerbated by Russia's introduction of customs duties on exported oil to various countries, including Belarus. The duties meant that some refineries in Mazyr and Navapolack could no longer make profits from refining and reselling Russian oil, as before.

Nevertheless, the two sides continued to deal with each other, partly because both were acquiring the status of rogue states. In 2011, two new books on Belarus that appeared in English, one by Andrew Wilson, the other by former British ambassador to Belarus Brian Bennett, contained the words "last dictatorship of Europe" in their titles. The phrase, according to Wilson, was coined by US secretary of state Condoleezza Rice. Putin's reputation, despite the brutal subjugation of Chechnya, was somewhat better and for a time he cooperated with US president George W. Bush in the war on terrorism, which for the Russian leader included Chechens.

The Customs Union between Russia, Belarus, and Kazakhstan began to operate from July 2010. Russia was Belarus's chief trading partner, accounting for almost half its imports by this period, though trade with the EU states, particularly the Netherlands and Austria, had increased exponentially. The other Russian-led integrationist projects could be regarded as more protective. The Collective Security-Treaty Organization was initiated in 2002 and consisted of six states of the former

Soviet Union: Russia, Belarus, Kazakhstan, Kyrgyzstan, Armenia, and Tajikistan. Initially it was called the Unified Armed Forces and a counterpoint to NATO, stipulating that if a member country should be attacked, the others would come to its aid. It has held military exercises, most notably in southern Russia and Central Asia in 2010, and has sent peacekeeping forces to conflict zones. It was deployed in Kazakhstan in January 2022 to quell major disturbances against the ruling regime. However, Armenia failed to receive any assistance when attacked by Azeri forces in 2021, and it lost control of its enclave of Nagorno-Karabakh.

Russia was also a founding member of the Shanghai Cooperation Organization (SCO), formed with China in 2001 and a successor to an earlier unit called the Shanghai Five in 1996 between China, Russia, Kazakhstan, Kyrgyzstan, and Tajikistan. Later it was joined by India, Pakistan, and Iran, and Belarus became a member in July 2024. The countries combined make up 40% of the world's population; the SCO is concerned primarily with security issues, such as drug trafficking and terrorist activities, but also to some extent with what is considered to be hostile propaganda against member states. It is not considered to be a military alliance, and its war games ironically are termed "peace missions." Though there were discussions of unifying with the CSTO, Russia's invasion of Ukraine in 2022 discouraged some members from military cooperation with Russia. Further, the effectiveness of the CSTO in a military is undermined by the long-term enmity between two of its members, India and Pakistan.

These organizations, with the possible exception of the SCO, can be considered efforts by Russia to maintain the dominant role it possessed within the Soviet Union. For Belarus, there are obvious dangers in becoming too close to Russia, particularly involvement in its military operations outside its borders in Ukraine, Syria, Georgia, and other states. The relationship often appeared as one in which the larger and more powerful state attempted to deepen integration, only to be rejected by the leadership in Minsk, including, most forcefully, by Lukashenka. But after the events of 2020, Lukashenka's choices were more limited, and on many occasions he could be found boarding his plane to travel to Moscow to secure a loan or gain support. In Western media, the two were often depicted together as the source of the sustained conflict in Ukraine, and after 2020, most Western states did not recognize Lukashenka as the legitimate president.

Lukashenka has remained ambivalent about Russia's annexation of Crimea—he supported it in the UN—and while he backed and helped organize the attack on Ukraine, he has refrained from sending the Belarusian army over the border. Yet he is concerned that several hundred Belarusians are fighting for Ukraine in the Kalinouski Regiment, with the specific object of following a Ukrainian victory with his (Lukashenka's) removal. Conversely, all opinion polls show that at least 70% of the population opposes Belarus's entry into the war. He has also resisted Russian attempts to create pro-Moscow political parties in Belarus, and although he has accepted tactical nuclear weapons, his rhetoric always suggests that they are to protect Belarus from a NATO invasion from the west.

How did Belarus react to the Euromaidan protests (Revolution of Dignity) in Ukraine in 2013–2014?

The events in Ukraine from late November 2013 to the summer of 2014 caused consternation in Belarus because of the rise in violence and eventual bloodshed in the central square of Kyiv, and later in the war in the east Ukrainian Donbas. In addition, Belarusians witnessed the Russian annexation of Crimea in March 2014 and the deaths of fifty-five pro-Russians in the trade union building in Odesa. The former event was an international incident but took place without violence as Ukraine surrendered their control over the peninsula, which had been transferred from Russia to Ukraine as a friendly gesture in 1954. The reactions in Belarus at the official level were neither consistent nor always clear and reflect the importance of both neighbors in terms of trade, historical and cultural ties, and the lengthy borders with each state.

In late March 2014, Belarus joined Russia, North Korea, Venezuela, Zimbabwe, and six other states in voting no to a motion in the United Nations refusing to recognize the Crimean referendum that sanctioned the annexation of the peninsula by Moscow. But the vote did not signify that Belarus intended to sever relations with the new Ukrainian leadership, and Foreign Minister Uladzimir Makei insisted that between Belarus and Ukraine it would be business as usual. The first notable response of the opposition was recorded on the Day of Freedom, March 25, when those in the march chanted "Glory to Ukraine!" along with "Long live Belarus!" For the opposition, the removal of the corrupt pro-Russian leader was a sign of hope that something similar could happen in Belarus.

Such sentiments were not shared widely among the population of Belarus. An independent polling association operating in Minsk at that time conducted a survey that it published in April 2014, which showed that 54% of respondents considered the Maidan uprising to be "a seizure of power" by the protesters, and 78% thought the costs of the change of leadership, the spilling of blood and deaths, were much too high. Support for the uprising was not widespread, but it was higher in the 18–29 age group; the more elderly population were more inclined to support the former president Viktor Yanukovych. The events in Ukraine bolstered the popularity of Lukashenka's presidency largely from a sense of relief that such violence had not occurred in Belarus and that the republic had remained both stable and peaceful. The prevailing rhetoric was that such events could not happen in the republic where law and order presided, in contrast to the Ukrainians who preferred to live in a state of anarchy.

Lukashenka's reaction was ambivalent. He dismissed the notion of Ukraine as a federal state, which some Russian leaders had advocated, but nonetheless feared the possibility of the southern neighbor joining the NATO alliance. He expressed a fear of NATO on the border of Belarus, ignoring the fact that Poland, to the west, had joined the alliance in 1999. He was scathing about the flight of Yanukovych, pondering why he had not deployed the Ukrainian army to dispel the demonstrators. Yet he had been much more sympathetic toward Kurmanbek Bakiyev, ousted in 2010, who had received sanctuary in Belarus together with his family.

In turn, Lukashenka expressed support for Ukraine's new acting president Oleksandr Turchynov, whom he considered to be "a good man and a friend." He maintained that trade between the two states should continue. Concerning the fear of some in Ukraine that the Belarusian army might take part alongside Russia in a wider invasion, Lukashenka responded that if he came to Ukraine, it would be on a tractor with a plow, to assist with harvesting. Although Belarus had stood with Russia in the United Nations, it would never join in any coalition against Ukraine. The position was important since it signified that as long as Lukashenka remained president, he would follow the baffling line that both countries were allies and friendship would be maintained with both Kyiv and Moscow. That was not a position that could be maintained for long if war continued.

On the other hand, the Belarusian leader recognized the limitations of his position. Belarus was not a free agent and could not perform as an independent actor. Russia was its protector, the main source of resources that fueled the Belarusian economy, and the principal source of loans to keep it afloat. Thus, if it came to a crunch decision, Belarus would always stand alongside Russia. Lukashenka's position changed somewhat on May 2, 2014, when a clash of pro-Maidan supporters carried out a rally in Odesa and about 2,000 people clashed with some 300 pro-Russians, with the two sides exchanging petrol bombs and both suffering mortalities. The outnumbered pro-Russians took refuge in the Trades Union Building, which caught fire, causing the deaths of forty-eight people.

Lukashenka compared the losses to those at Chatyń in March 1943, and expressed regret that no one had come to the aid of those trapped in the building.

Thus, overall, while official Belarus tried hard to remain neutral on the results of Maidan and Russia's intervention, it was only partially successful. Both existing alliances and economic needs obligated the Minsk regime to stand firmly with Russia. There is also evidence that the Belarusian government considered Ukraine to be a puppet in a much wider confrontation between Russia and the West in the form of the NATO alliance and the European Union. Lukashenka insisted that no one in the EU was anxious that Ukraine should join, and just as he had opposed color revolutions earlier in the century, so the Maidan or, as Ukrainians termed it, the "Revolution of Dignity," could never receive a positive reception in a twenty-year-old dictatorship on its northern border.

How has Lukashenka served as a mediator in the Russian war with Ukraine?

Although official Belarus has remained a firm ally of Russia during its protracted invasion of Ukraine, which began in the spring of 2014, Lukashenka has used his position as leader to intervene as a mediator on three occasions: in September 2014 and March 2015; and in June 2023. The former resulted in the two Minsk Accords that brought a temporary halt to major fighting in the Donbas, while the latter followed the rebellion by Wagner Group leader Evgeny Prigozhin against the Russian military leadership. Both brought partial but temporary success and represented an effort by the Belarusian leader to move beyond his role as a junior partner to Vladimir Putin into the role of peacemaker. However, in none of these discussions did he play a decisive role.

The Minsk Accords have long been controversial, particularly from Ukraine's perspective, since both followed Ukrainian military defeats: Minsk I followed the battle of

Ilovaisk, at which Ukraine lost about 1,000 troops after the Russian side violated an agreement to allow the Ukrainian side to surrender; and Minsk II followed the battle of Debaltseve, after which Russia occupied the important communications center between the two major Donbas cities of Donetsk and Luhansk. Minsk I was signed by Ukraine, Russia, the two separatist states (called the Donetsk People's Republic and Luhansk People's Republic), and the Organization for Security and Cooperation in Europe (OSCE). A twelve-point ceasefire agreement stipulated that the two sides should stop fighting and remove heavy weapons from the conflict area. It proved only a temporary halt as fighting soon broke out again and continued until February 2015, when another attempt was made to call a halt, with Minsk again being the center for discussions.

The second Minsk Accord was quite similar in content to the first, with the added weight of French and German participation. Russia insisted that it was also participating as an outsider, arguing that it was not taking part in the Donbas war. Ukraine's president Petro Poroshenko was not in a position to argue, since the Ukrainian army badly needed breathing space. Its defeats came precisely after the intervention of the regular Russian troops, backing up the separatist regimes with inferior armies. One point of the agreement stipulated that all armed foreign forces should be removed from the Donbas conflict region, but the point could hardly be fulfilled while the Russian side was denying its involvement.

The other points that proved impossible to fulfill demanded that Ukraine provide some autonomy to the Donetsk and Luhansk regions and move toward a federal system, and that after the withdrawal of armies, the Ukrainian government should resecure its control over its eastern border. Neither the Poroshenko nor subsequent Zelensky presidency saw much movement on the first point, and Ukraine never secured control over its eastern border. Still, the Minsk II Accord served as a sign that the two sides could come to the table. Both accords built on a June 2014 meeting known thereafter as the Normandy format (France, Germany, Russia, and Ukraine), followed by a Trilateral Contact Group (Russia, Ukraine, and the OSCE) to try to find a solution to the Donbas conflict. Belarus's role was never more than that of a host to the Minsk meetings. Moreover, Minsk II never worked fully and ended abruptly with the widened Russian invasion of Ukraine in February 2022.

Lukashenka's intervention in 2023 followed a rebellion by Prigozhin and the Wagner Group, which had carried the brunt of the Russian advance in the Donbas earlier in the year, with frontal assaults on towns and the brutal battle of Bakhmut, which the invaders eventually occupied. Prigozhin argued that the regular army was sabotaging the efforts of his group, even to the extent of the regular army firing rounds at its members. He also complained that the mercenaries had been deliberately deprived of ammunition. On June 24, Prigozhin and Wagner mercenaries crossed without opposition from the Luhansk region into Russia and occupied the city of Rostov before starting to march toward Moscow. Putin denounced his erstwhile friend as committing treason, although Prigozhin insisted that his rebellion was directed only against the Ministry of Defense. Evidently at the request of Putin, Lukashenka spoke with Prigozhin and brokered a deal whereby the Wagner Group would move to Belarus.

Only three years earlier at the beginning of the presidential election campaign, Lukashenka had ordered the arrest of over thirty Wagner mercenaries who were billeted temporarily in Minsk, fearing that they had been sent to overthrow him. Now he was offering a base to the entire group at an abandoned military camp at Asipovičy, about 53 miles southeast of Minsk and about 120 miles north of Ukraine. Though Vladimir Putin had demanded that the members of the Wagner Division should join the regular Russian army, and Lukashenka's intervention appeared to have prevented mass retributions, only a portion of the mercenaries arrived in Minsk. Prigozhin began to travel frequently between Moscow and St. Petersburg. On August 23, a plane on that same route carrying Prigozhin and other leaders exploded, killing all aboard. The rebel leader had lasted less than eight weeks after giving up his march on Moscow.

Although there were reports that the Wagner troops might be involved in training the regular Belarusian army, the Asipovičy camp gradually dispersed, particularly after the violent deaths of their leaders. Once again, Lukashenka's mediation achieved only temporary success.

Why did Lukashenka decide to support Putin in Russia's broader attack on Ukraine in 2022?

Lukashenka's unequivocal support for the broader Russian invasion of Ukraine in February 2022 was a result of two factors. First, the enhanced sanctions placed on Belarus after the hijacking of the Ryanair flight in 2021 essentially cut off links with the European Union and left the country isolated. It brought an end to a multi-vector foreign policy that had allowed Lukashenka to pursue simultaneously good relations with both Russia and the EU. Though he developed other contacts in the Middle East, Africa, China, and Latin America, trade with these states was relatively limited. Despite the difficulties of the past, Russia and official Belarus were drawn together by the election campaign of 2020 and Russian demands for closer integration in return for loans essential to the Belarusian economy.

The second reason was a result of Vladimir Putin's misreading of the likely Ukrainian response to Russian troops crossing the border from Belarus and advancing toward Kyiv. He anticipated a swift victory, catalyzed by strong local support, and the takeover of the Ukrainian government. Similar views prevailed in Washington, DC, and other Western capitals, following the experience of Russian military successes in 2014. Lukashenka himself talked of meeting with Putin in

Kyiv a few days after the invasion. But the Ukrainians not only fought, they became unified under the leadership of President Volodymyr Zelensky and his commander in chief, Valerii Zaluzhny, and the invasion failed in its initial goals.

Arguably, Lukashenka has lost any claim to legitimacy after the events of 2020, and thus he had no means to resist Russian demands and the long-term continuation of the war. By allowing Russia to base troops on Belarusian territory, to treat the wounded in hospitals, and to use railways to transport supplies to the Russian army in the field, he accepted that much of the world would regard Belarus as Russia's loyal partner, if not puppet state. It is likely that Putin's perception of Belarus was precisely that he was working with a client state that was historically linked to the former Russian Empire.

On January 7, 2025, the I-Sans Bulletin issued in Warsaw cited comments by Ukrainian president Zelensky that a few days after Russia launched its full-scale invasion from the north, Lukashenka phoned him to apologize for the attack. According to Zelensky, Lukashenka claimed he played no role in the invasion, that he had asked Vladimir Putin not to launch it, but "I'm not in charge." He even reportedly suggested that Ukraine bomb the Mazyr factory in retaliation, "You know how much I care about it." His press secretary, Natallia Eysmant, denied that Lukashenka had made such comments, although she acknowledged that the phone call did take place. She added that it was made because Mikalai Lukashenka, the third son of the Belarusian leader, had been upset about the invasion.

Official Belarus's predicament changed the nature of the relationship between the two leaders. After the 2020 presidential election, Lukashenka was weakened, and Putin was quick to take advantage. Even the language used by Lukashenka toward Putin changed to one of deference. Though each leader had visited the other's capital quite frequently, now Putin generally remained in Moscow, and Lukashenka was obliged to fly to visit him like a vassal rather than a leader of equal standing.

It was an unusual situation for the outspoken Lukashenka, but he adapted because he had no choice if he was to remain in power. The opposition of 2020 was dangerous but could not compete with the potential threat of Russian power backing up the security forces.

On May 9, 2023, Victory Day, Lukashenka was ill. Nevertheless, he flew to Moscow for the official ceremony but was unable to walk about 500 feet alongside Putin. During the short ceremony, Lukashenka sat close to Putin and his generals with his left hand bandaged. It was later reported he had spent some time in a Moscow hospital, and once he returned to Minsk he was taken to a special clinic for examination. There was speculation that he had died. When he did reappear in public, he could barely talk. Yet he recovered and by the summer of 2024 was acting much more confidently.

In short, Lukashenka supported Putin's new move into Ukraine because he had no choice. Russia was more powerful, with a much larger army, and he lacked allies elsewhere. All the same, such unlimited support was not natural for the sort of statecraft Lukashenka pursued. His instinct is not to close off pathways to the West, as with the 2017 visa-free entry system into Belarus mentioned above. In the summer of 2024, the system was expanded to include entry by railways and buses, likely because sanctions and the ban on Belavia in the EU countries and the UK had sharply reduced the number of international flights arriving at the Minsk International Airport. Once again, Lukashenka was seeking alternatives to the role of a supplicant to Moscow.

What was the reaction of the Belarusian opposition and the society to the full-scale war in Ukraine?

The Belarusian opposition unanimously condemned the full-scale war, initiated by Russia in Ukraine on February 24, 2022. As the attack happened three days before the main election day of the referendum of the Belarusian constitution, the opposition, mostly located abroad, had to quickly develop a strategy for dealing with changes in legislation in light of the presence of Russian troops on the Belarusian territories, bordering Ukraine.

The approach agreed upon by Tsikhanouskaya and most of the opposition, with the exception of Zianon Pazniak and his followers, was to vote and then spoil the ballots. People were asked to send the photographs of the ballots via the Voice system to enable representatives of the platform and IT experts working on the collected data to assess them. Most people coming to vote would put anti-war slogans on ballots. Several hundred protesters went out to the streets on February 27 and 28, 2022, to express their discontent with the involvement of the Belarusians in the war and the referendum taking place with the presence of the Russian troops on Belarusian territory.

People were also actively reposting on social media and expressing their disagreement with the war, openly condemning Russia and supporting Ukraine. Consequently, most of them were identified and arrested, and many of those detained became political prisoners. Those who protested in person were also rounded up and charged.

It is important to note the widely held perception of war or any type of violence in Belarus and Russia, as Belarusians are often accused inaccurately of supporting Russia's aggression against Ukraine. Belarusian society remains extremely traumatized by the collective memory of the Second World War, which is still called the Great Patriotic War in state historiography. Even today, the vast majority of Belarusians keep alive memories of their grandparents and great-grandparents who either fought in the war, were killed, wounded, or witnessed terrible atrocities which they revealed to their families decades later, mainly in the 1980s and 1990s, when they felt freer to talk about both the Nazi and the Soviet armies, and the Polish army (Armia Krajowa) and the crimes of Soviet partisans.

The scale of atrocities, committed also on the Jewish and Roma population during the war; the image of a "partisan" republic; and widespread presence of the Great Patriotic War in national literature and art, as well as school textbooks, have made the fear of war a permanent element of Belarus's collective memory. Family stories of Stalinist repressions permeated the postwar years, such as of those who allegedly "aided" Nazi soldiers by offering a piece of bread, for example, who then were banished to GULAG camps or suffered from severe poverty, evident in villages well into the 1960s.

This fact also helps the authorities to manipulate the collective fears of Belarusians. Thus, after the start of Russia's aggression in Ukraine in 2014, Lukashenka not only initiated the Minsk Accord talks, he also used state propaganda to persuade Belarusians they should vote for him in the 2015 elections to save Belarus from becoming a military battlefield. This propaganda worked to a certain extent, enabling Lukashenka to secure some electorate support, especially in Belarusian rural regions.

The fear of war and violence was behind the largely peaceful protests in 2020 in Belarus. Many neighboring countries were criticizing Belarusians for the lack of violent acts and were laughing at the photographs showing how Belarusians would take off their shoes before standing on benches during the big Sunday marches that took place every week from August 16, 2020, until the end of the year.

Belarusian social media channels became hubs of activity as the war in Ukraine progressed. NEXTA, Belarus of the Brain, and other channels gained a massive international audience, and gained especial popularity among Ukrainians, who distrusted both Russian propaganda and Ukrainian official sources. Anton Matolka, a Belarusian photographer, blogger, and activist, founded Belaruski Hajun, an OSINT project which aimed to monitor the activities of the Belarusian and Russian troops on Belarusian territory. Sadly in February 2025 it ceased its operations as their Telegram bots were hacked by the Belarusian secret service, which led to numerous arrests and charges of those who had been informing the Hajun about the movements of the troops.

ByPol and Cyberpartisans also emerged as vital online information hubs. On February 26, 2023, an A-50 Russian military plane, stationed in Mačuliščy military base, was blown up remotely; ByPol quickly admitted its responsibility for organizing its destruction. Several people, including Belarusian IT experts, were detained in Belarus, but ByPol and Cyberpartisans only claimed they would continue their underground activities.

From February 2022, ordinary Belarusians citizens organized themselves into "railway partisans," who damaged or derailed trains carrying Russian military equipment through Belarusian territory to the Ukrainian front. Dozens of people involved in these activities were later arrested: many were tortured and sentenced to lengthy prison terms on charges of terrorism.

In Ukraine, many Belarusians joined the Ukrainian forces under a separate, volunteer battalion named after the Belarusian and Polish national hero Kastus Kalinouski, who was a leader of the January Uprising in 1863 against the Russian Empire in Belarus and Lithuania. Recruitment to the Kastus Kalinouski Regiment was arranged mostly in Warsaw by Belarusian organizations, which preferred not to do it very publicly for security reasons. In December 2022, Cyberpartisans began to cooperate with the Kastus Kalinouski Regiment by providing cybersecurity and intelligence to the Ukrainian army. Many fighting on the ground lost their lives: one, Aleksei Skoblya, was a Belarusian soldier who was deputy commander of the Kastus Kalinouski Regiment under the Armed Forces of Ukraine. Skoblya died defending Kyiv from advancing Russian troops during the Battle of Kyiv. He was posthumously conferred the title of Hero of Ukraine by President Zelensky in April 2022. (It should be noted that some Belarusians served in the Russian army, but their known numbers are notably lower than those who have fought for Ukraine.)

The Belarusian diaspora in Poland and Lithuania, mainly comprising those who fled after the violent crackdown on the 2020 protests, has helped house and assist Ukrainian refugees fleeing war. Belarusian feminist initiatives operating in Poland assisted Ukrainian women who were victims of sexual assault and rape by Russian soldiers. These initiatives, often operating as part of larger solidarity networks, have provided vital support to Ukrainian women. Some groups have covertly distributed "rape pills" (abortion pills) to women impregnated through rape. Abortion is prohibited in Poland, unless a pregnancy is proved to be the result of rape or if the mother's life is at risk. As many women cannot provide legal proof of rape during ongoing war, such assistance has been vital. Belarusians of the diaspora have also organized cultural events, inviting children and adults from Belarus and Ukraine to work on theatrical and music performances, and participate in dance classes and film festivals.

What changes has Lukashenka made to the Belarusian Constitution?

The Constitution was adopted by the Minsk regime in February 2022 after a national referendum. It went into effect the following month. It bore no resemblance to the original document of 1994, and very little to the versions that included Lukashenka's amendments after the referendums of 1995, 1996, and 2004. In fact, much of the 2022 version appears to be modeled on the Russian Constitution. It was introduced after the 2020 uprising as an attempt to strengthen the position of the presidential system in Belarus and the personal ascendancy of Lukashenka. Though the public was consulted and invited to submit comments, conditions for the actual vote were far from democratic. Voters had to deal with the removal of curtains in voting booths, with the excuse that it was a measure to prevent the spread of COVID-19.

The early voting for the referendum itself began on February 22, 2022, continued for four days, and was based on one question: Do you accept the amendments and additions to the Constitution of the Republic of Belarus? The date overlapped with the Russian full invasion of Ukraine, which began two days after the polls opened and completely overshadowed the events in Belarus. According to official figures, the turnout for the vote was 78.63%, and 86.4% voted yes (4.4 million people) and almost 685,000 no (13.36%). The process was controlled by the Central Election Commission, and prior to the vote, Lukashenka dismissed his longtime chair and close ally, Lidziya Yarmoshyna, replacing her with Ihar Karpenka, the former minister of education and leader of the pro-government Communist Party. A Constitutional Commission was headed by Piotr Miklashevich, the chair of the Constitutional Court, with Uladzimir Andreichanka and Natallia Kachanava, loyal Lukashenka's high-level *apparatchiki*, as vice chairs.

The changes reflected the political situation and recent events. Candidates for president henceforth are required to have been resident in Belarus as citizens for at least twenty years (rather than ten), and those with two citizenships or residency in foreign countries are excluded. The new law immediately removed the possible candidacy of the opposition leader Sviatlana Tsikhanouskaya and the former minister of culture Pavel Latushka. A second major measure was the elevation of the All-Belarusian People's Assembly (ABPA) as the country's highest representative body of "people's power" in Belarus. Included in the ABPA automatically are the president (Lukashenka was already "elected" to this position), former presidents—a category that does not apply to the country at present—government ministers, judges and lawyers, members of regional government, and representatives of civil society.

The regular parliament's term was expanded to five years but clearly it is now subservient to the ABPA, which in the past has been a body gathered by Lukashenka to endorse his election victories and economic programs. However, the new version indicates that Lukashenka himself can serve as the head of the ABPA, either along with being president or at some future time, presumably when it is time to designate a successor. Former presidents also become lifetime members of the Council of the Republic, the upper house of the parliament. Thus, Lukashenka now has a foothold in all the power-wielding bodies in the country, along with his extended presidency.

As with the changes introduced by earlier referendums, the president's term in office, while restricted to two terms, can begin again with the first election after the 2022 referendum, that is, in 2025. It means in theory that Lukashenka could serve for two more terms, until 2035, when he will turn eighty-one. It is modeled, it seems, on Putin's constitutional changes in Russia that extended his presidency until 2036. In fact, Lukashenka called another election in January 2025, prevented anyone living outside the country from voting, and appeared to be ready to continue ruling as before, despite the supposed empowerment of the ABPA.

A second body that was consolidated by the referendum is the Security Council. If the president should die through violence or other means, the Security Council will be his immediate successor. In turn, a president who steps down becomes immune from prosecution for his actions during his time in office. Also, a president is a permanent member of the Security Council for his or her lifetime. In this way, Lukashenka, almost unseated in 2020, has taken steps to ensure that such a situation could not arise again.

The 2022 Constitution followed the Russian version in declaring that marriage can only be between a man and a woman, a clause that appears directed to more tolerant laws in Western countries. It also speaks of the development of nuclear energy and allowing Russian troops and nuclear weapons to be based on the territory of Belarus, a volte face from the 1994 version, which declared Belarus to be a non-nuclear and non-aligned country.

As well as protecting Lukashenka, the Constitution is also intended to make it much more difficult for the 2020 opposition to make a second bid for power. First, its members are non-residents, and second, there are no obvious means to arrest or detain Lukashenka legally, based on the changes. Second, there is little evidence that the 2022 version strengthens the state as an independent entity. Rather, it seems geared to closer integration with Russia. Already, Russia has reportedly transported tactical nuclear weapons to Belarus. Civil society, while receiving some theoretical recognition in the ABPA, in reality is further curbed because only certain groups will be allowed to take part: pro-Lukashenka trade unions, the Belarus Republican Union of Youth, official sporting organizations, and political parties that support the authorities such as Belaya Rus and the Liberal-Democratic Party.

How is the Belarusian regime using the "Great Patriotic War" as an identity marker in schools and society in the context of Russia's invasion of Ukraine?

As noted above, Belarus has long used the Second World War, usually confined to the period 1941–1945 as the "Great Patriotic War," as the defining symbol of national identity. The process began in 1965 on the twentieth anniversary of the end of the war in Europe and continued until the end of the Soviet period. In official narratives, museums, monuments, school textbooks, and other sources, the focus was on the partisans, the brutality of the occupation regime with the Chatyń memorial as the symbolic memorial, and the 1944–1945 advance through Belarusian territory into Poland and Germany. After 2020, with the Lukashenka leadership drawn ever closer to Russia, and with its legitimacy in question, it returned to the war years to modify and deepen some themes, but also to create a single narrative with the Russian Federation, and a new textbook together with Moscow.

The changes that occurred after the 2020 uprising made a concerted effort to link the war with modernity. To some extent the changes reflected the need to coordinate new narratives with Russia. The Putin leadership has never referred to a "war" with Ukraine but has described its invasion as a "special military operation." Its argument is that Western powers, through the expansion of NATO to the former Soviet bloc countries and to the three Baltic States, had placed Russia in an untenable situation. In its view, with the direct assistance of NATO, neo-Nazis had taken over the Ukrainian government in a coup d'état in 2014 and removed the democratically elected president Viktor Yanukovych. Putin maintained that in doing so, the Western powers and their "puppet" Ukraine had crossed a red line to which Russia was obligated to respond.

For the Belarusians, Russian support had become crucial, and Lukashenka opted to accept the Russian narrative, but also to exploit it for his own survival. Thus, along with the far-fetched equation of the Western powers with Nazism, those involved in the 2020 uprising would also be linked to the Nazi occupation regime. The line was not new, since the Belarusian Popular Front had also been accused of pro-Nazi extremism, but it was particularly inappropriate to describe young protesters seeking a change from the authoritarian regime that had shown itself to be so inadequate during the pandemic. Several new laws were adopted in Minsk, including a May 2021 Law against the rehabilitation of Nazism. The law was broad enough to be applied to any civil protest as well as the display of the white-red-white national flag.

The year 2022 was designated the Year of Historical Memory, and the government, Minsk Council, and Office of the State Prosecutor assigned the task of preparing the country for the coming changes. On January 4, another law was introduced that was also modeled on a similar Russian law and entitled "Law on the Genocide of the Belarusian People." It maintained that the Nazi invaders singled out Belarusians for extermination from the moment of the invasion. The new line signified a complete rewriting of the war period to change the focus from one of general suffering to genocide. The introduction simultaneously of new laws soon made it a criminal offense to deny the theory that "Genocide of Belarusians" was the key goal from the outset of the invasion. In turn, this change of direction also brought other consequences.

First, it undermined the uniqueness of the Jewish Holocaust in Europe, of which Belarus was a key location, with about 600,000 Jews living there before the war, and about 200,000 more brought to the occupied territory during the war for extermination. Ironically, just a few years earlier, Lukashenka had appeared at ceremonies with the leaders of Germany, Austria, and other central European countries for the opening of newly designed memorial complexes at the Maly Traścianiec death camp, one of the largest in Europe. The new complexes reversed a long period in which Belarus had neglected to focus on the Jewish Holocaust. There were some memorials, some of which were quite dated, including the Yama (The Pit in English) memorial near the center of Minsk. But these were relatively isolated. Most of the former camps had signs concerning the massacres of the "Soviet people" rather than Jews specifically. Thus, the new memorials had appeared to signal a period of change.

Second, the new slogan prevented further research on NKVD massacres in the republic that had been under way, with breaks, since the late 1980s. These investigations had been conducted mainly by opposition groups and hindered at times by the government. In late 2018, a memorial had been erected at the main burial site at Kurapaty, but thereafter, the authorities refused to follow up discoveries of other sites near the major cities of the pre-1941 Soviet era: Viciebsk, Orša, and Homiel. Commemorative signs at these sites were vandalized, and those conducting research were often forced to leave the country or were subject to arrest.

Third, the "Belarusian genocide" concept required the amendment and even fundamental changes of the narrative of the war. In the 1970s, party leader Masherau claimed that one in four Belarusians had died in the Second World War. There was no scientific basis for such a claim, but the number held firm for several historians and writers. Lukashenka took this one stage further after he became president, and the official figure rose to one in three, with the number of mortalities rising from 1.8 to 2.2 million. Presumably included in this number—but almost never stated openly—are the 600,000–800,000 Jews, making up about one-third of the total deaths. It is also very difficult to estimate losses for Belarus because the BSSR was divided between various sections of German command.

Today, the number of reported deaths has risen to 3 million. Under the supervision of Andrei Shved, the prosecutor general, the authorities have embarked on a quest to find more gravesites to raise the number of victims, as well as compiling new lists of perpetrators. In October 2021, Shved announced that he was in possession of the names of 400 living people responsible for mass deaths in Belarus during the war that had been uncovered in cooperation with his Russian counterpart, Igor Krasnov. They were all former members of the SS currently living in seventeen different countries. Some were in Latvia and Lithuania, but these states had refused to cooperate. The goal was to demand extradition to Belarus to be tried for the "genocide of Belarusians."

Several trials have already taken place. In April 2024, Belarusian the prosecutor general charged posthumously Volodymyr Katriuk, who had allegedly been involved in the Chatyń massacre and died in 2015 in Canada, where he moved after the Second World War. Andrei Savitski became the first real victim of the new law in November 2024, when he received three years of imprisonment for the "denial of the genocide of Belarusians." In his online discussion, Savitski argued that Chatyń might have been burned down by the partisans, not the Nazis; and he also criticized Lukashenka.

Fourth, the ruling regime in Minsk is now attempting to railroad this expansion of the war narrative into the school and higher educational system through what is described as a "patriotic education." In February 2024, Tatsiana Shchyttsova, advisor on education and science for the shadow government of Sviatlana Tsikhanouskaya, reported the following: in June 2023, a Forum of Russian and Belarusian Historians was held in Moscow as a prequel to the introduction of common history texts, followed by a Memorandum of Understanding that resulted in a joint commission on writing new history textbooks.

It is too early to assess the effectiveness of this program, but one can make several remarks. With the passage of time, the possibility of conducting new versions of the war is somewhat limited. Historians are in general agreement over some events and no longer have access to reliable eyewitness accounts. Further, the program politicizes the discipline of history and links it to state propaganda. Thus, authentic research on the war years in Belarus (and likely Russia) has ended, and it is not possible to write an objective account without the fear of arrest and imprisonment. Also, if such measures are intended to create a distinctive Belarusian narrative, they are tied too closely to the framework created in Russia, as part of the "Russian World" concept deployed in the invasion of Ukraine.

Is Belarus today a functioning sovereign state? Does it have a future?

Belarus is widely regarded as a puppet state of Russia because it is perceived through the lens of the invasion of Ukraine. In some ways, Lukashenka appears in the media as a supplicant of Russia, requesting support, loans, and potential backing against further uprisings. He destroyed the facade of a popular leader in 2020 and inaugurated himself illegally. Thus, he is not widely recognized as the legitimate president. In fact, since we cannot determine the precise results of the 2020 presidential election, Belarus is in a legally ambiguous situation. And it was not resolved by the ritualistic 2025 elections since the state has punished any form of dissension from the official ruling group headed by Lukashenka. What is in place is a de facto government rather than a de jure one. But Belarus is creating new rules to abide by a quasi-democratic process of municipal, parliamentary, and presidential elections.

In terms of sovereignty, the key question is how it is measured. Belarus has well-defined borders, its own army and police, its Security Council, and other institutions. Though it was a member of significant integrationist organizations, such as the Russia-Belarus Union, the Collective Security Treaty Organization, and the Eurasian Economic Union, these were offset by its participation in the Eastern Partnership Program, and its willingness to allow prominent US officials to visit Belarus for talks with the Minsk leaders such as former secretary of state Mike Pompeo (February 2020) and former national security adviser John Bolton (August 2019). Pompeo stressed that the United States supported the independence of Belarus. Neither visit had a long-lasting impact, however. Bolton was fired by President Trump a month afterward, and Pompeo left office in early 2021 after Trump's defeat in the 2020 presidential elections.

Lukashenka has frequently taken steps to differentiate himself from Russia, and particularly from his counterpart Putin. Aside from the energy and dairy disputes, he refrained from recognizing the Russian annexation of Crimea or the independence of South Ossetia and Abkhazia from Georgia. And as noted, he has tried to adopt the role of a peacemaker on several occasions during the wars in Ukraine. Still, though Belarus has tried to maintain ownership of its fundamental institutions and industries, Russia has gradually encroached in areas like banking, machine building, and transit companies, buying out successful companies. Lukashenka has indirectly promoted Russian influence by closing Belarusian schools and limiting memory of the past to the Soviet period and Russian triumphalism.

Western sanctions have only catalyzed Russian-Belarusian integration at the leadership level. By 2021, after the West responded to the RyanAir incident with deeper sanctions against Belarus, the regime had little alternative but to seek the protection of Russia. The loss of some prominent managers, IT experts, security personnel, and media workers weakened the position of Lukashenka, who resorted to some desperate measures to deflect the various threats. He invented an assassination threat, replete with arrests; introduced a new Constitution through referendum; empowered the All-Belarusian People's Assembly; and replaced some leading officials. The Kremlin's support and transfer of nuclear weapons to Belarus prevented further divisions within the Belarusian elite. Mass terror remained in place, adding to the tens of thousands arrested after 2020, even for the most minor offences.

At the same time, the deterioration of Lukashenka's position mirrored his physical decline. Even with manipulation of the media, observers have noted that he has difficulty walking, has become obese, and has noticeably aged in appearance. Lukashenka will not be leading Belarus for long. But it is an error to identify Belarus with the man in the presidential palace. The country has survived despite Lukashenka, and the enthusiasm that was expressed in the 2020 protests has not gone away. It remains beneath the surface. But there are several prerequisites for any fundamental change to take place in the country.

First, the outcome of the Russia-Ukraine war is pivotal. A Russian victory would bolster the status quo and the respective leaderships in Moscow and Minsk. There would be little prospect of change in Belarus were this to happen. The potential collapse of Ukraine and loss of 20% or more of its territory would serve as a boost to the Putin leadership's expansionism and may lead to further annexations. In turn, the power of the European Union would be undermined as a major player.

Second, a negotiated peace would likely have the same impact as a Russian victory, given that one of the incentives for Putin to come to the table would be the retention of four Ukrainian provinces in addition to Crimea. There would be no guarantee of Ukrainian security, as the settlement would acknowledge that Russian aggression has brought its rewards. Conversely, and third, a Ukrainian victory would alter the current balance of power in the region, likely topple Putin and his Security Council, and open the way for new challenges to Lukashenka in Belarus. A Ukrainian victory is the raison d'être of the Kalinouski Regiment as well as the Belarusian opposition in exile.

At the time of writing, there appears to be little prospect of an immediate result to the conflict. American president Donald J. Trump initiated a peace plan in 2025, but it failed to gain traction on the Russian side. Neither side in the war appears to be close to victory. Russia has failed in its attempts to capture Kyiv in 2022 and Kharkiv in 2024, Ukraine's two largest cities. It has made painstaking gains in the Donbas at huge cost to its army. Ukraine's 2023 offensive stalled and it has been unable to mount a new one because of the lack of weapons and troops. Highly rated weapons, such as the F16 aircraft, are reaching the Ukrainian military only after lengthy delays, and the United States, one of the main donors, was enmeshed in a bitter election campaign that could also have an impact on the course of the war.

Thus, Belarusians who seek change must be patient. They also need to remain united. Groups in exile tend to splinter with the passage of time, and the same applies to the Tsikhanouskaya Shadow Cabinet and Coordination Council. The Kalinouski Regiment fighting in Ukraine changed its leadership in the summer of 2024 and appeared to lose some of its autonomy through decision-making being subordinated to an International Brigade. For some time, different individual actors have opted to pursue their own political ambitions rather than unify under Tsikhanouskaya. Together, these diverse groups represent the ambitions and hopes of the 2020 uprising.

In official Belarus in 2024, a personality cult of Lukashenka was launched publicly, with cries for his designation as a

"Hero of Belarus." The movement—if it can be called such—reflects both the separation of the ruling elite and security forces from the rest of the population, but it also seems to be another move to legitimize the Belarusian leader and solidify his place as head of state. In this same period, the elite tried to reopen relations with some European states such as Poland, but the results have been limited. Latvia and Lithuania closed their borders to cars with Belarusian license plates, a move that frustrated Tsikhanouskaya, who claimed that it was hurting the public rather than the government.

Yet despite the current predicaments, Belarus survives. The population supports an independent state and its independent stance on the war in Ukraine. The authorities cannot resist Russian intrusions, but there is little interest in or support for becoming part of the Russian Federation. Ultimately, it must take its place in Europe as a state that is part of neither the Russian World nor the NATO alliance, but as earlier experience suggests, it could logically become part of the European Union. The dictatorship will soon end, and the question then will be whether the elite can make common ground with the exiles, declare an amnesty of political prisoners, and begin discussions as to the nature of a state without the vise-like grip of a Lukashenka. It is more plausible than it might seem from the vantage point of the first quarter of the twenty-first century.

REFERENCES

Applebaum, Anne (2021). *GULAG: A History.* Penguin Books.

Arlou, Uladzimir (2016). *Ajčyna: ad Rahniedy da Kaściuški.* Minsk: Technalohija.

Arlou, Uladzimir (2023). *Ajčyna: ad Ahinskaha da Bahuševiča.* Bielastok: Fond Kamunikat.org.

Artiukh, Volodymyr (2021). "The Anatomy of Impatience: Exploring Factors behind 2020 Labor Unrest in Belarus." *Slavic Review* 80 (1): 52–60.

Astapova, Anastasiya, et al. (2022). "Authoritarian Cooptation of Civil Society: The Case of Belarus." *Europe-Asia Studies* 74 (1): 1–30.

Astrouskaya, Tatsiana, Andrej Kotljarczuk, and Franziska Exeler (2022). *Ghosts of War: Nazi Occupation and Its Aftermath in Soviet Belarus.* Ithaca, NY: Cornell University Press.

Beichelt, Timm (2004). "Autocracy and Democracy in Belarus, Russia and Ukraine." *Democratization* 11 (5): 113–32. https://doi.org/10.1080/1351034041233130461 5.

Bekus, Nelly (2010). *Struggle over Identity: The Official and the Alternative "Belarusianness."* Budapest: Central European University Press.

Bekus, Nelly (2014). "Ethnic Identity in Post-Soviet Belarus: Ethnolinguistic Survival as an Argument in the Political Struggle." *Journal of Multilingual and Multicultural Development* 35 (1): 43–58. https://doi.org/10.1080/01434632.2013.845197.

Bekus, Nelly (2021). "Echo of 1989? Protest Imaginaries and Identity Dilemmas in Belarus." *Slavic Review* 80 (1): 4–14. https://doi.org/10.1017/slr.2021.25.

"Belarus i Rossiya – Soyuznoye Gosudarstvo" (2023). "Belarus i Rossiya podpisali memorandum o sozdanii sovmestnoy komissii po istorii," January 26. https://soyuz.by/novosti-soyuznogo-gosudarstva/belarus-i-rossiya-podpisali-memorandum-o-sozdanii-sovmestnoy-komissii-po-istorii.

Bennett, Brian (2011). *The Last Dictatorship in Europe: Belarus under Lukashenko*. London: Hurst.

Beorn, Waitman Wade (2014). *Marching into Darkness: The Wehrmacht and the Holocaust in Belarus*. Cambridge, MA: Harvard University Press.

Bikanau, Philip (2022). "Belarusian Identity in 2022: A Quantitative Study." Kyiv: Friedrich Ebert Stiftung. https://library.fes.de/pdf-files/bueros/belarus/19777.pdf.

Bosse, Giselle (2011). "From 'Villains' to the New Guardians of Security in Europe? Paradigm Shifts in EU Foreign Policy towards Libya and Belarus." *Perspectives on European Politics and Society* 12 (4): 440–61. https://doi.org/10.1080/15705854.2011.622960.

Buhr, Renee L., Victor Shadurski, and Steven Hoffman. "Belarus: An Emerging Civic Nation?" *Nationalities Papers* 39 (3): 425–40. https://doi.org/10.1080/00905992.2011.565319.

Bulgakov, Valeriy (2021). "Coming to Terms with the Past." *Deutsche Welle*, March 23. https://akademie.dw.com/en/coming-to-terms-with-the-past/a-56958099.

CSTO (Collective Security Treaty Organization) (2020). *The Contribution of the Belarusian People to the Achievement of the Great Victory Is Invaluable*. https://en.odkb-csto.org/75-letie-pobedy/pobeda-na-vsekh-odna/neotsenim-vklad-belorusskogo-naroda-v-dostizhenie-velikoy-pobedy/#loaded.

Dorman, Michael (2017). "Khatyn and the Myth of Genocide in Lukashenko's Belarus." MA thesis, University of Texas at Austin.

Exeler, Franziska (2022). *Ghosts of War: Nazi Occupation and Its Aftermath in Soviet Belarus*. Ithaca, NY: Cornell University Press.

Ganzer, Christian (2011). "Remembering and Forgetting: Hero Veneration in the Brest Fortress." In *Returning to Europe: Belarus. Past and Future*, edited by Sioban Doucette, Andrej Dynko, and Ales Pashkevich, 138–45. Warsaw: Lazarski University.

Gerlach, Christian (2016). *The Extermination of the European Jews*. Cambridge: Cambridge University Press.

Glantz, David, and Mary Elizabeth Glantz (2016). *Battle for Belorussia: The Red Army's Forgotten Campaign of October 1943–April 1944*. Lawrence: University Press of Kansas.

Goujon, Alexandra (2010). "Memorial Narratives of WWII Partisans and Genocide in Belarus." *East European Politics and Society, and Cultures* 24 (1). https://doi.org/10.1177/0888325409355818.

Hansbury, Paul (2023). *Belarus in Crisis: From Domestic Unrest to the Russia-Ukraine War*. London: C. Hurst & Co.

Ioffe, Grigory (2008). *Understanding Belarus and How Western Foreign Policy Misses the Mark*. Lanham, MD: Rowman & Littlefield.

Ioffe, Grigory (2014). *Reassessing Lukashenka: Belarus in Cultural and Geopolitical Context*. Lanham, MD: Rowman & Littlefield.

Kasmach, Lizaveta (2023). *Belarusian Nation-Building in Times of War and Revolution*. Budapest: Central European University Press.

Korostoleva, Elena, ed. (2025). *The Unbroken Generation: Youth Voices of Belarus 2020*. London: Skaryna Press.

Korostoleva, Elena, Irina Petrova, and Anastasiia Kudlenko (2023). *Belarus in the Twenty-First Century: Between Dictatorship and Democracy*. London: Routledge.

Laputska, Veranika (2023). "2020 Women's Emancipation in Belarus: From Housewives to Symbols of Freedom." In *Freedom Taking Place: War, Women and Culture at the Intersection of Ukraine, Poland, and Belarus*. Vernon Press.

Laputska, Veranika (2020). Die belarusische »Evalution« hat ein weibliches Gesicht, Belarus-Analysen, NR. 52. https://www.laender-analysen.de/belarus-analysen/52/die-belarusische-evalution-hat-ein-weibliches-gesicht/

Laputska, Veranika (2020). *Digital Media Has Fueled an Unprecedented Challenge to the Regime in Belarus*. GMF. https://www.gmfus.org/news/digital-media-has-fueled-unprecedented-challenge-regime-belarus

Laputska, Veranika (2018). Frauen in Staat und Politik, Belarus-Analysen, NR. 36. http://www.laender-analysen.de/belarus/pdf/BelarusAnalysen36.pdf

Laputska, Veranika (2021). The power of internet as a game changer for Belarusian protests. New Eastern Europe, Issue 5/2021, https://neweasterneurope.eu/2021/09/12/the-power-of-internet-as-a-game-changer-for-belarusian-protests/

Lewis, Simon (2017). "The 'Partisan Republic': Colonial Myths and Memory Wars in Belarus." In *War and Memory in Russia, Ukraine, and Belarus*, edited by J. Fedor et al. Basingstoke: Palgrave Macmillan.

Lewis, Simon (2020). *Belarus—Alternative Visions: Nation, Memory, and Cosmopolitanism*. London: Routledge, 2020.

Marples, David R. (2014). *"Our Glorious Past": Lukashenka's Belarus and the Great Patriotic War*. Stuttgart: Ibidem.

Marples, David R., and Veranika Laputska (2020). "Kurapaty: Belarus' Continuing Debates." *Slavic Review* 79 (3): 521–43.

Marples, David R., and Veranika Laputska (2021). "Maly Traścianiec in the Context of Current Narratives on the Holocaust in the Republic of Belarus." *Europe-Asia Studies* 74: 1–19.

Marples, David R., and Veranika Laputska (2023). "The 'Genocide of Belarusians' and the Survival of Lukashenka's Regime." In *Belarus in the XXI century: between dictatorship and democracy*, edited by Korosteleva, E. Petrova, I., Kudlenko, A. Routledge.

Marples, David R., and Per Anders Rudling (2009). "War and Memory: The Annexation of the Western Borderlands and the Myth of the Brest Fortress, 1939–41." *Białoruskie zeszyty historyczne* (Bialystok) 32: 225–44.

Navumčyk, Siarhej (2015). *Dzievianosta čacviorty*. Radio Free Europe/Radio Liberty. https://docs.rferl.org/be-BY/2015/03/23/f356ac68-562d-485f-a64c-f716d1d769a4.pdf

Navumčyk, Siarhej (2015). *Dzievianosta piaty*. Radio Free Europe/Radio Liberty. https://docs.rferl.org/be-BY/2015/08/24/34b28591-5dfd-48bd-bc0c-30860f75cf2d.pdf

Navumčyk, Siarhej (2021). *Dzievianosta šosty*. Radio Free Europe/Radio Liberty. https://docs.rferl.org/be-by/2022/11/21/05820000-0aff-0242-c97d-08dacbadaab1.pdf

Navumčyk, Siarhej and Zianon Pazniak (2010). *Deputaty Adradžžennia*. New York, Vilnius, Warsaw. Tavarystva Bielaruskaj Kultury u Lietuvie. https://files.knihi.com/Knihi/uploaded01/Siarhiej_Navumcyk_Zianon_Pazniak.Deputaty_niezaleznasci.pdf

Pazniak, Zianon, Mikola Kryvalcevič, Aleh Iou (1994). Kurapaty. Miensk, NVK Technalohija. https://knihi.com/Zianon_Pazniak/Kurapaty.html

President of the Republic of Belarus (2022). "The Law on the Genocide of the Belarusian People during the Great Patriotic War was Signed." January 5. https://president.gov.by/ru/events/aleksandr-lukashenko-podpisal-zakon-o-genocide-belorusskogo-naroda.

Press Service of the President (2015). "Aleksandr Lukashenko Signed the Law 'On the Genocide of the Belarusian People.'" *SB News/The Minsk Times*, January 12. https://www.sb.by/en/aleksandr-luk

ashenko-signed-the-law-on-the-genocide-of-the-belarusian-people.html.

Rudling, Per Anders (2008). "'For a Heroic Belarus': The Great Patriotic War as Identity Marker in the Lukashenka and Soviet Belarusian Discourses." *Nationalities Papers* 32: 43–62.

Rudling, Per Anders (2015). *The Rise and Fall of Belarusian Nationalism, 1906–1931*. Pittsburgh: University of Pittsburgh Press.

Schwartz, Matthew, and Nina Weller, eds. *Appropriating History: The Soviet Past in Belarusian, Russian and Ukrainian Popular Culture*. Bielefeld: Transcript.

Smilovitsky, Leonid (2000). *Holocaust in Belorussia, 1941–1944*. Translated by Clayton Simon. Tel Aviv. https://www.jewishgen.org/yizkor/belarus/belarus.html.

Snyder, Timothy, and Ray Brandon, eds. (2014). *Stalin and Europe: Imitation and Domination*. Oxford: Oxford University Press.

Snyder, Timothy (2011). *Bloodlands*. Vintage Publishing.

Snyder, Timothy (2004). *The Reconstruction of Nations: Poland, Ukraine, Lithuania, Belarus, 1569–1999*. Yale University Press.

Solly, Meilan (2021). "Remembering the Khatyn Massacre." *Smithsonian Magazine*, March 22. https://www.smithsonianmag.com/history/how-1943-Khatyn-massacre-became-symbol-nazi-atrocities-eastern-front-180977280/.

Shushkevich, Stanislav (2012). *Moya zhizn, krusheniye i vosstaniye SSSR*. Moskva: ROSPEN.

Walke, Anika (2015). *Pioneers and Partisans: An Oral History of Nazi Genocide in Belorussia*. Oxford: Oxford University Press.

Wilson, Andrew (2011). *Belarus: The Last European Dictatorship*. 2nd ed. New Haven, CT: Yale University Press.

Zaprudnik, Jan (1993). *Belarus: At a Crossroads in History*. New York: Basic Books.

Zaprudnik, Jan, and Vitali Silitski (2010). *The A to Z of Belarus*. Lanham, MD: Scarecrow Press.

Zaprudnik, Janka (2002). *Dvanaccatka*. New York, Bielaruski Instytut Litaratury i Mastactva. https://knihi-online.com/dvanaccatka-janka-zaprudnik.html

INDEX

For the benefit of digital users, indexed terms that span two pages (e.g., 52–53) may, on occasion, appear on only one of those pages.